Inequality in Economics and Sociology

Inequality remains one of the most intensely discussed topics on a global level. As well as figuring prominently in economics, it is possibly the most central topic of sociology. Despite this, there has been no book until now that unites approaches from economics and sociology.

Organized thematically, this volume brings international scholars together to offer students and researchers a cutting-edge overview of the core topics of inequality research. Chapters cover: the theoretical traditions in economics and sociology; the global and national structures of inequality in the contemporary world; the main dimensions of inequality (including gender, race, caste, migration, education and poverty); and research methodology. In presenting this overview, *Inequality in Economics and Sociology* seeks to build a bridge between the disciplines and the approaches.

This book offers an encompassing understanding of an increasingly fragmented and highly specialized field of research. It will be invaluable for students and researchers seeking a single repository on the current state of knowledge, current debates and relevant literature in this key area.

Gilberto Antonelli is Full Professor of Economics at the Department of Economics of the University of Bologna, Italy, and Chairman of the School of Development, Innovation and Change (SDIC).

Boike Rehbein is Professor of the Sociology of Asia and Africa at Humboldt University Berlin, Germany.

Routledge Studies in Development Economics

Inequality in Economics and Sociology

New Perspectives

Edited by Gilberto Antonelli and Boike Rehbein

Routledge
Taylor & Francis Group

LONDON AND NEW YORK

First published 2018 by Routledge

2 Park Square, Milton Park, Abingdon, Oxfordshire OX14 4RN
52 Vanderbilt Avenue, New York, NY 10017

Routledge is an imprint of the Taylor & Francis Group, an informa business

First issued in paperback 2019

British Library Cataloguing-in-Publication Data
A catalogue record for this book is available from the British Library

Library of Congress Cataloging-in-Publication Data
A catalog record for this book has been requested

ISBN: 978-1-138-67847-7 (hbk)
ISBN: 978-0-367-87848-1 (pbk)

Typeset in Bembo
by Apex CoVantage, LLC

Contents

Illustrations

Contributors

Gilberto Antonelli is Full Professor of Economics at the Department of Economics of the University of Bologna and Chairman of the School of Development, Innovation and Change (SDIC). His main research fields are: economic theory, economic analysis of "broad production factors", innovation, structural change and economic growth theories, employment and unemployment theories, economics of education and human capital, local economic development and international cooperation and multi-dimensional inequality.

Pinuccia Calia is Assistant Professor of Economic Statistics at the University of Bologna. She specializes in micro-econometric modelling with applications to businesses and policy evaluation, inequality measurement and decomposition methods.

Giovanni Guidetti is Lecturer in Economics in the Department of Economics at the University of Bologna. His research interests include inequality in income distribution, skills mismatch in the labour market, human capital formation and training in firms and institutional economics.

Michael Hartmann is retired Professor of Sociology at the Technical University of Darmstadt. His main research areas are elites, globalization and national management cultures and the international comparison of systems of higher education.

Surinder S. Jodhka is Professor of Sociology at the Jawaharlal Nehru University and Senior Affiliate Fellow at the Centre for Social Science and Humanities (both in New Delhi). His research interests include the study of rural society and dynamics of agrarian change; social inequalities – old and new – and their reproduction; the dynamics of caste and the varied modes of its articulation with the nature of social and economic change in contemporary India; and the political sociology community identities.

Michael Kinville completed his PhD in Sociology at Humboldt University Berlin in 2016 and is now a writer and consultant in the field of international education. His areas of specialization are education, inequality and historical sociology.

Anirudh Krishna is the Edgar T. Thompson Professor of Public Policy and Professor of Political Science at Duke University, in Durham, North Carolina, USA. His research investigates how poor communities and individuals in developing countries cope with the structural and personal constraints that result in poverty and powerlessness.

Riccardo Leoncini is Full Professor of Economics at the University of Bologna and Research Associate at IRCrES-CNR of the Italian National Research Council. He specializes in the economics of innovation and technological change and the theory of the firm.

Gerhard Maré is Professor Emeritus of Sociology at the University of KwaZulu-Natal, Durban, South Africa. He specializes in the sociology of labor, race and contemporary South Africa.

Giulio Pedrini, PhD in Law and Economics, is a Research Fellow of the Interuniversity Research Centre on Public Utilities (CRISP) – University of Milan-Bicocca and an Adjunct Professor of Economics of Innovation at the University of Bologna. His primary areas of research are labour economics, economics of education and local development.

Boike Rehbein is Professor of the Sociology of Asia and Africa at Humboldt University Berlin. He specializes in globalization, inequality, social theory and Southeast Asia.

Christian Schneickert is a Postdoctoral Researcher in Sociology at Otto-von-Guericke-University Magdeburg, Institute for Social Sciences, Department of Macrosociology. He specializes in inequality, globalization, elites, education and culture.

Emanuelle Silva obtained her PhD in Sociology at Humboldt University Berlin in 2017 and is now Lecturer at various institutions in São Paulo, Brazil. She specializes on gender and inequality.

Jessé Souza is Professor of Political Sciences at UFF, Niterói, Rio de Janeiro, Brazil. He specializes in inequality and social theory.

Florian Stoll is a Visiting Postdoctoral Scholar at the Center of Cultural Sociology, Yale and Postdoctoral Scholar at the Bayreuth Academy of Advanced African Studies. His research foci are global sociology (mainly Kenya and Brazil), milieus/stratification/middle-classes, urban sociology and cultural sociology.

Anja Weiß is Professor of Sociology with a focus on macro-sociology and transnational processes at the University of Duisburg-Essen. Her research interests include sociology of globalization, theory of social inequality, high skilled migration and professional knowledge, racism and ethnic conflict.

Introduction

Gilberto Antonelli and Boike Rehbein

Inequality has been one of the key topics during the past years, not only in academia but also in public discourse. The discourse is dominated by economists, even though inequality has formed the core of sociology ever since its emergence in the nineteenth century. The classics of sociology, from Marx and Durkheim to Weber and Bourdieu, wrote their most famous works on inequality. Up to this day, inequality is the most important sub-discipline of sociology in most countries of the world.

Economic thought has chosen a detour to arrive at the topic of inequality. First, the effort by the classics of economics has been devoted chiefly to develop paradigmatic models emphasizing the impact of distribution on crucial economic outcomes, such as growth and efficiency. Second, since income and wealth distribution have been considered among the main determinants of potential inequality in the economic realm, a deeper analysis of their impact on inequality has been left to the specialized interest and feelings of a few scholars in the application of their favored paradigmatic model. The majority of economists have remained disinterested in the topic of inequality.

However, in the past decade or two, inequality has become a key topic for economists as well. Economics is presenting us a broad and impressive account of inequality today. For instance, this is true not only for the Thomas Piketty book, *Capital in the Twenty-first Century* (2014), but also for the White Paper of David Autor and Lawrence Katz, *Grand Challenges in the Study of Employment and Technological Change* (2010), focusing on polarization, another way of tackling inequality. Piketty begins his book with the clarification that it can only shed light on some aspects of inequality, since other aspects have to be covered by sociology. However, according to him, the sociological literature that would be needed is missing.

How is this assessment possible, since inequality is the core topic of sociology? There are two main answers to this question. First, research on inequality is dominated by international organizations, such as the World Bank or UNDP, and these employ mainly economists and not sociologists. Furthermore, the economists do not read sociology. If Piketty had looked more closely, he would have found literature addressing exactly the points he brings up in his book. However, this lack of communication is not only due to individual shortcomings of some economists. It is a general phenomenon. And it is not only a flaw on the part of the economists. Sociologists have created their own jargon and seem to try very little to cross the boundaries of their discipline.

The esoteric character of contemporary sociology is connected to two other reasons for the domination of economics in visible inequality discourses. The first reason consists in the lack of the big picture in contemporary sociology. Very few sociologists give us an overview of global inequality. A book like Piketty's is unlikely to be written by a sociologist of our times. While economists write books about capital in the twenty-first century or *Worlds Apart* (Milanovic 2005) or *The Price of Inequality* (Stiglitz 2012), sociologists write about unequal educational opportunities in the suburbs of Minneapolis. Studies like these are important but they do not appeal to a broad public that wishes to know more about inequality.

Refusing to address a broad audience also connects with a lacking will to exert a political influence. Debates on inequality always have a political and normative dimension. In its quest to become accepted as a science, sociology has attempted to stay clear of politicized issues. The void has been filled by economics as far as inequality is concerned. Economists, however, have addressed the issue head-on – with the self-confidence of an acknowledged science and without much reflection of the normative and epistemological presuppositions implied by their interventions.

At the present time, the sociology of inequality can teach economics a humbler empirical approach as well as more reflexivity. Economics, in turn, can teach sociology the aim of drawing a broader picture and the recognition of the inevitably political character of a topic like inequality. On the other hand, economists may exaggerate their self-confidence and disregard the multi-dimensional nature of inequality by reducing the issue to merely quantitative indicators.

In our opinion, at least all of these lessons have to be learnt in order to develop an appropriate understanding of inequality. They are best learnt in a communicative process between economists and sociologists. We wish to suggest two more lessons to both disciplines. The first is the study of the role of social classes in contemporary societies. And the second is to compare varied economic and social settings in a rigorous way.

This volume addresses the lack of communication between economics and sociology with regard to inequality. All chapters, except two, the first one and number twelve, have been written either by economists or by sociologists. However, they were written in an attempt to be understood by proponents of the other discipline. The authors aim at a comprehensive perspective on inequality that includes the other discipline as well as the public at large. The aim of the first chapter is to trace the theories of inequality developed by each discipline in order to clarify their possible contributions to the other discipline. Half of the chapters will be somewhat trivial to the student of the respective discipline, while much of the other half will be new and surprising.

In his influential book, Piketty (2014) shows that inequality is reproduced because capital is passed on from one generation to the next. It becomes more concentrated in the hands of few if capital returns exceed the rate of economic growth. However, he does not study the process of capital inheritance. Neither does he show who inherits capital and why. These are topics for sociology. They are addressed in the chapter by Rehbein and Souza in this volume. It explains how economic capital is passed on from one generation to the next and how this is related to a structure of social classes.

Rehbein and Souza argue that a similar structure of social classes emerges in all capitalist societies but that it differs according to a nation state's history and culture. Each state has a unique social structure, even though the emerging classes are similar. The chapters on lower, middle and upper classes in the world aim at clarifying this relationship. They reveal similarities between the nation states but also a wide range of local and national variations, which are addressed in some detail.

This variation is visible not only from the perspective of sociology in the social fabric but also from the perspective of economics in the capitalist economy and its institutions. The chapter by Antonelli deals with inequality in income and wealth distribution, globalization and models of capitalism and seeks to underline important characteristics of capitalism in general and their national variations. In combination, not only a wide variation but also a limited number of types of capitalist institutional set-ups emerges from the analysis.

The third part of the book is largely sociological in its orientation. It studies important topics in inequality research, mainly those that receive less attention from the mainstream in both disciplines, since they do not deal with stratification or class. Studies have shown that class does not explain everything and that other forms of inequality persist in a stratified society. This has been agued under the heading of "intersectionality" (Crenshaw 1989). A white man in the lowest class may still be privileged over a white woman or a black man, let alone a black woman. These dimensions of inequality and their interplay have to be understood in order to gain a comprehensive view of inequality.

An example for the cross-fertilization between sociology and economics in practice is chapter twelve of the book. By looking at the broader relationship between skill density, human capital and income inequality, the authors cross-fertilize the reflection on the relationship between skill-biased technical change, human capital and inequality. They argue that a sociological analysis alone will not appropriately understand the constantly changing requirements to the education system, while a merely economic study will fail to understand the social reproduction of inequality through the system of education.

The final part of the book introduces important methodological tools developed by quantitative and qualitative approaches to inequality. The chapter on quantitative methodology has been written by a statistician, the one on qualitative methodology by a sociologist. Even though much of contemporary inequality research in sociology follows a quantitative approach, qualitative approaches are entirely absent from economics. This means that a sociologist had to write the corresponding chapter.

References

Autor, David H. and Lawrence F. Katz (2010) 'Grand Challenges in the Study of Employment and Technological Change', A white paper prepared for the National Science Foundation, Harvard University and NBER, September.

Crenshaw, Kimberlé (1989) 'Demarginalizing the Intersection of Race and Sex', *University of Chicago Legal Forum*, No. 1: 139–67.

Milanovic, Branko (2005) *Worlds Apart: Measuring International and Global Inequality*, Princeton, NJ: Princeton University Press.

Piketty, Thomas (2014) *Capital in the Twenty-First Century*, Cambridge, MA: Harvard University Press.

Stiglitz, Joseph E. (2012) *The Price of Inequality*, London: Allen Lane (Penguin).

Part I
Theoretical background

1   Theoretical approaches to inequality in economics and sociology

Giovanni Guidetti and Boike Rehbein

This chapter discusses approaches to inequality that have been advanced in the disciplines of economics and sociology.[1] It argues that a communication between both disciplines is necessary to make sense of the drastic increase in socioeconomic inequality that we are observing at present. The aim of the chapter is neither to trace the history of research in the field nor to give an overview of all available data. It rather seeks to assess the most relevant contributions in view of a research agenda that encompasses the virtues of existing approaches while avoiding their shortcomings and pitfalls. The main goal, however, is to build a bridge between economics and sociology. Both disciplines have advanced research on inequality, partly in a parallel fashion. It is time to establish a transdisciplinary research agenda.

The first part of the chapter distinguishes between three traditions of research on inequality, each of which has been elaborated in both economics and sociology. The second part discusses the main issues of contemporary inequality that have been acknowledged by the three traditions and that need to be taken into account. In the final part, we draw conclusions of the discussion by critically assessing the explanatory power of existing approaches and by pointing to desiderata in theory building.

Theoretical traditions

Sociological research on inequality can be divided into three main traditions, which could be called quantitative, structural and intermediate. While the quantitative tradition grew out of economics and was developed in sociology by the school of Talcott Parsons, the structural tradition certainly draws on Karl Marx. While the quantitative tradition is more descriptive, the core of the structural tradition is theoretical. A third strand, trying to link theory with empirical research, can be traced back to Max Weber but it does not form a homogeneous school.

The quantitative tradition is linked to the development of economics as a discipline but has deeply influenced the discipline of sociology as it evolved in the twentieth century. Economic theories of inequality have been largely quantitative and focused on the relation between inequality and growth. Adam

Smith has taken inequality for granted. In his *Wealth of Nations* (2007; originally 1776), he develops the idea of a free market for goods and labour that leads to an increasing division of labour and thereby to economic growth. The overall product is distributed among the population so that everyone profits from this growth. However, the product is distributed not equally but proportionately. The "universal opulence . . . extends itself to the lowest ranks of the people" (2007: 7). Of course, Smith worked and thought in the framework of a feudal society, where rank largely determined profession and life-chances. Even though there is a tension between the idea of unfettered competition in the market and feudal ranks, Smith does not explicitly address the issue. Economic growth is the prime goal and its distribution is secondary as long as everyone gets a share. However, following Quesnay's approach, Smith shows that value added is distributed among three classes: the rentiers, the capitalists and the workers and, even though his interest was mainly focused on economic growth, he develops an embryonic theory of income distribution among wages, profits and rents. Interestingly, Smith is probably the first economist of the modern ages who refers explicitly to the conflict between capitalist and workers for the determination of wages. The Scottish economist was convinced that even though wages can temporarily peak over the subsistence level, eventually the greater bargaining power of capitalists with respect to workers prevails and pushes wages down to this subsistence level.

Smith also offered the first statement of what Lassalle called, a few years later, the iron law of wage: wages fluctuate around the subsistence level (2007). A couple of decades after Smith, Ricardo (1815) developed a framework of analysis based on the idea that the value of commodities depends on the amount of labour contained. In this approach, the distribution of income among the three classes, rentiers, capitalists and workers, Ricardo demonstrates that when the economic system reaches the steady state, the rate of profit tends to nil and the output will be distributed between rents and wages. In the mathematical outline of Ricardo's analysis, Pasinetti (1977) emphasises the distributive conflict between wages and profit, before the system reaches the steady state.

Marx made this conflict more explicit in economic analysis, introducing the notions of surplus value and exploitation (Marx 1953ff). According to Marx, profit depends on the surplus value that capitalists manage to extract from workers' productive activity. Roughly speaking, it can be defined as the difference between the value of the output produced by workers and their wages and as such it is a measure of worker's exploitation by the class of capitalists. In Marx's treatment one can also find the origins of the classes of capitalists and workers. The former are the owners of the means of production, the latter are the individuals exploited in the productive process. Conclusively, in classical economics one can find a deep analysis of functional income distribution, i.e. income distribution among different classes in society.

With the advent of the marginalist school around 1870 the approach to economic analysis changes drastically. The focus shifts from the analysis of production and the distribution of income to the analysis of exchanges among individuals with a given endowment of resources and the allocation of these resources. As a result, the level of wages depends on the interaction between labour demand and supply and the relative scarcity of supply with respect to demand. As far as income distribution is concerned, Wicksell (1954) demonstrates that, assuming a highly specific production function,[2] the remuneration of productive factors equals the factors' marginal productivity. This idea presupposes perfectly competitive markets and a correspondence of earnings of productive factors with their productivity. Income inequality is simply a result of the contribution of each productive factor to the production of income. The focus of analysis shifts from functional income distribution to personal income distribution. As the operation of markets entails that productive factors are paid on the basis of their contribution to production, income inequality is no longer a problem to be addressed through specific public policies. Inequality disappears from the agenda of mainstream economics.

In this tradition, Lucas (2004) in an often-quoted assertion has affirmed: "Of the tendencies that are harmful to sound economics, the most seductive, and in my opinion the most poisonous, is to focus on questions of distribution". Economic analysis should not focus on problems of either inequality or income distribution but rather on issues concerning growth and poverty because the "potential for improving the lives of poor people by finding different ways of distributing current production is nothing compared to the apparently limitless potential of increasing production" (Lucas 2004).

The seminal contribution in modern economic literature addressing explicitly the issue of economic inequality was developed by Kuznets (1955). Based on empirical evidence, Kuznets maintains that inequality tends to rise in the early stages of economic development, as a consequence of industrialization, then it declines in later stages, as capitalism matures. In this way income inequality presents the classical inverted-U shaped trend in time. In this stream of analysis, Kuznets' hypothesis has been questioned, especially in empirical economic literature, and the most relevant conclusion (Fields 2001) states that it is not growth per se, which gives rise to economic inequality but it is the nature of economic growth which determines the development of inequality. More precisely, Fields claims that the effect of growth on inequality depends on the factors which characterize the economic environment such as the structure of output, the degree of economic dualism, the structure of employment, the distribution of land, the operation of capital markets and the overall level of human capital.

In recent years, Kuznets' approach has been even more radically questioned, reversing the causation relation between growth and inequality underlying Kuznets' seminal contribution. Basically, the idea is that economic inequality affects the pace and the nature of economic growth and not the reverse as in Kuznets' analysis (Stiglitz 2012). This stream of the economic literature provides neither a direct causal link between inequality and rate of growth, nor a unique explanation. Actually, different theoretical frameworks point to different factors explaining the reason why inequality can affect economic growth

(Bourguignon 2004; Ehrhart 2009). There seems to be a wide consensus on the ideas that inequality can hinder economic growth and that country specificities matter in order to understand through which channels inequality slows down the pace of economic growth.

The quantitative tradition in economics focused on growth has not been able to explain inequality. Predictions about inequality trends extrapolated from the 1990s have been proven wrong – because they had focused on numbers and not on structures. This is particularly true for the influential World Bank publications (Jomo and Baudot 2007; cf. the Human Development Reports). These studies neglected the rise of the global South, as it was scarcely visible at the time. In the 2000s the discussion has mainly focused on the question of whether the world has become more or less unequal. Branko Milanovic (2005) has published the classic study of the topic, in which he compares different systems of measurement and earlier assessments of the question. In the end, he settles for a global comparison of weighted household consumption. Although Milanovic's predictions have not materialized either, his retrospective analyses are pertinent to any study of inequality. The absolute number of poor has remained almost unchanged over the past few decades, while the wealth accumulated by the richest individuals has risen to unprecedented levels, and multinational corporations report record profits virtually every year (Milanovic 2005: 108). There seems to be a consensus that these trends are alarming by most standards. Milanovic calculates the Gini index for the global population at 64, for the US at 80 and for the countries of the world taken as a whole at 53 (2005). And it is increasing in most countries, including most emerging societies.

The quantitative tradition in sociology did not contribute substantially to research on inequality in economics except for the attempt to look at the social structure behind the Gini index and other quantitative measures of inequality. Talcott Parsons (1939) developed the concept of social structure as the differentiation of society into social groups. He also established an explicit link between social structure and the division of labour without confounding the two. Following economics and Marxism, however, the distinction between social structure and division of labour was more or less forgotten. The quantitative and the structural traditions in sociology have basically identified social structure with the division of labour by presenting social structure as a hierarchy of professions.

This confusion is very evident in Goldthorpe's class model, which is the basis of the mainstream of quantitative research on inequality in many European countries. Goldthorpe (2007, vol. II: 104) groups the entire population of a nation state in seven to eleven classes. These classes are types of professions; the highest class comprising leading academic professionals, leading managers and entrepreneurs having more than 50 employees, the lowest class consisting of manual and routine labourers. Of course, the majority of the population is excluded from this analytical framework, as even in European countries less than half of the population is engaged in wage-labour. Furthermore, the criteria for distinguishing the classes are descriptive and somewhat arbitrary.

This is problematic because Goldthorpe's empirical research focuses on social mobility. If the criteria for distinguishing classes are arbitrary, the observation of mobility from one class to another is arbitrary as well. In fact, research by the Goldthorpe school exemplifies this (e.g. Breen 2004). Unfortunately, many governments and influential organizations rely on this research in their assessment of inequality and mobility. National statistics are rarely more than a combination of quantitative economic approaches with a descriptive notion of class as a professional group.

The notion of class also forms the basis of the structural tradition in sociology. However, here it is not a descriptive but a theoretical term. The main argument is that inequality exists and persists because different social groups have unequal access to socially relevant resources and power. This unequal distribution persists because each generation passes on its resources to the next, so that power and resources "remain in the family".

Karl Marx is probably the founder of the structural approach, which he developed out of a critical reading of Adam Smith. While Smith bases his theory on the idea of an unalterable individual, Marx claims that human nature is historical and social (MEW 40: 537). Through action, the human being creates him- or herself. Each historical condition constitutes the framework within which this creation takes place, each generation carries with it the entire history of the human species (MEW 8: 115). The human being embodies history as a tradition and applies it to contemporary reality. Thereby, reality and the human being are transformed. The individual, according to Marx, is not the original human being but its contemporary manifestation as the result of a long history (MEW 13: 615).

According to the young Marx, the self-creation of the human being through his or her interaction with the world changes in each social configuration. In unequal societies, only some segments of society perform interaction with the world as labour, while others reap the profits without having to perform labour. This is the basis of class divisions in society. Capitalism changes nothing in this unequal relation between the classes but transforms labour into a commodity. The essence of the human being, which is activity, is hereby transformed into an abstract, commodified and transferable entity (MEW 40: 514). Any commodity can be traded for money in capitalism, which includes labour.

The structure of a capitalist society, for the old Marx, consists in the opposition of the class that possesses enough money to buy labour and put it to work and the class that has to sell its labour force. Following Smith, Marx interprets society as economic reproduction and its capitalist manifestation as accumulation of capital through investment into means of production and labour. Against this background, inequality is merely the surface of the invisible structure, which consists in the unequal distribution of capital and labour. Other types of activity and being in capitalist society are irrelevant for the analysis that Marx presents in his seminal work, *Das Kapital* (MEW 23–25). Division of labour and social structure are identified, just as in the quantitative tradition. The owners of the means of production are also the class that holds the power within the nation state (MEW 13: 640). This also implies that the redistribution of economic capital would abolish inequality (see also Rehbein and Souza in this volume).

Between the structural and the quantitative tradition, a third strand of socio-logical research on inequality emerged. After Marx, Max Weber (1972; origi-nally 1921) argued that social structure was more complex. On the one hand, there are many groups that are neither capitalists nor workers; on the other, he proposed that factors apart from occupation and wealth should be considered. However, Weber also focussed his analyses on occupation and wealth. Theodor Geiger (1932) and his disciples came up with a complex model of stratification. These stratification theories follow Weber in his critique of Marx and set up elaborate and complex models of social structure. They are less theoretical than Marxism, and less focused on economic and historical factors.

Stratification theory has become especially sophisticated in Germany (cf. Hradil 1986; Schulze 1992). One of its leading representatives, Rainer Geißler (1996), has developed a model of social structure that might serve as an ideal type of the national social structure analysis. It is derived from Ralf Dahren-dorf's "house model". Each group in society inhabits a room in the house, although walls and individuals are mobile. The basic criterion for the distribu-tion of groups into "rooms" is their occupation (Geißler 1996: 85). In addition, ethnicity, mentality, life-chances and subcultures also play a role. Looking at Geißler's model, it immediately becomes evident that he cannot fit everyone into the house. Foreigners remain outside. Furthermore, as he explains, the walls have become extremely permeable, rooms overlap and intermingle and social agents themselves are hardly aware of their own distribution (1996: 87). On the theoretical level, these inconsistencies do not seem to be an issue for Geißler.

If an "explanatory" model is so imprecise that it fails to tell us very much about reality, there is surely a problem with it. The outsiders in Geißler's model remind one strangely of the "epicycles" devised to save Ptolemy's model of the universe. Migrants are from "another society". Yet they can no longer be ignored, as they make up around five percent of the world's population (and if their children are included, many European cities have an immigrant popula-tion of 30 percent). How should migrants fit into "our" society?

In France, Pierre Bourdieu's analysis of inequality can be situated between Marx and Weber. At the centre of Bourdieu's theory is the conceptual pair of habitus and field. These terms replace the traditional oppositions of sub-ject and object, action and structure, determination and freedom (Bourdieu 1984). Briefly and somewhat inaccurately, habitus is society embodied and field refers to society outside this embodied structure. More accurately, subject and object cannot be separated from each other. There is no subject without objec-tive structures, and subjectivity develops only within objectivity; but objec-tive structures only exist on the basis of subjective action. The subject emerges through the embodiment of courses of action, which precede the subject and are objectively prescribed (1984: 170–5). However, these courses of action are themselves modified and renewed through subjective action.

The habitus develops through – mostly unconscious – training. This is exemplified by learning to play a musical instrument or the acquisition of language. Many of these learned dispositions are necessary for a person to act in a society. Bourdieu shows that the dispositions can be interpreted as relevant for social structure in the same way as economic capital. Therefore, he comes up with a broader concept of capital, which includes dispositions, education and material cultural symbols as cultural capital and social relations that one can mobilize in one's favour as social capital (1984: 80–5). In his major work, *Distinction* (1984), Bourdieu focuses on economic and cultural capital. In other works, he focuses more on symbolic capital. Symbolic capital for Bourdieu is the prestige conferred by a title, a function or some other personal endowment (1984: 291). For example, economic capital does not only enable a person to buy something, it also gives him or her a certain prestige. In addition to these types of capital, Bourdieu introduces a host of other varieties in his writings without defining or explicating them. The various forms of capital can be converted into one another. According to Bourdieu, we need to take into account not only the total amount of capital a social group or an individual disposes of, but also the relative strengths of various types of capital and the history of their acquisition (1984: 109–12).

Bourdieu conceives of social structure as the distribution of capital. All social actions require some form of capital and whoever has the greatest amount of socially most valuable capital has a leading position in society. And as he claims that all fields have an identical (or more precisely, a "homologous") structure or attribute the same value to any type of capital, social structure can basically be reduced to one single field (1984: 113). In *Distinction* this field is aesthetic consumption, or taste. Social groups differ in capital, which offers them differing possibilities of action within the field. These differences are the basis of differential social positions, which are the basis for the existence of classes. However, Bourdieu distinguishes between the difference in social positions from an observer's perspective and active distinctions between classes (classifying and classified class) as well as a conscious class (mobilized class).

For Bourdieu, any social collective results from a process of classification and self-classification whose social recognition depends on the distance/proximity from the legitimate culture. Social class does not exist a priori as in Marx's framework of analysis, but it is the product of this classification clash (conflict), which is fought in order to impose a specific social representation. This process implies the exercise of symbolic violence.

In Bourdieu's approach the occupational division of labour plays a pivotal role. However, differently from Marx, the class structure does not depend solely on the ownership of the means of production, which rules out some specific occupations. His model of the class structure depends on three different dimensions. The first dimension is the distribution of the total volume of both economic and cultural capital. The second dimension takes into account the composition of the capital: i.e. the relative incidence of economic and cultural capital. The third dimension differentiates according to the trajectories, or according to the stability over time in the volume and the composition of the capital. The class structuring is an inherently dynamic process. All three of these dimensions are conceived as continuous variables, the identification of discrete class is just a heuristic convention. These three factors are the constitutive dimensions of the social space.

Even though Bourdieu's approach is a great step forward, there remain several problems with it. One would like to know where the unequal distribution of resources originates. Furthermore, it seems to be a highly descriptive framework of analysis. What are the determinants of the dynamics of capital distribution? Economists would state that in Bourdieu's approach, income and wealth distributions are exogenous and need integrating in this framework of analysis. Finally, Bourdieu focuses on the European nation state and professions and therefore excludes most social formations and groups, especially in the global South.

Michael Vester et al. (2001) has developed Bourdieu's approach further by including the historical dimension. The lack of this inclusion has been a major shortcoming both of sociological and economic approaches. Vester has interpreted Bourdieu's analysis of social structure as a historical development of habitus groups. In Vester's approach, capital is less relevant than habitus. Each generation trains the next generation in activities that are valuable for the particular social environment, e.g. physical characteristics in the working class and erudition in the intellectual elites. On this basis, each habitus group establishes a "tradition line", an idea that Vester derived from E.P. Thompson. Vester et al. (2001) offers an analysis of German society – amended by examples from other European nation states – that groups the population into "milieus". This approach solves some problems in Bourdieu's approach but still suffers from many of the same shortcomings.

An approach of economics that includes qualitative factors in the analysis of inequality and, like Bourdieu, focuses on the notion of capital has been the theory of human capital. This theory conceives the supply of skills as a consequence of the behaviour of income-maximising individuals with specific time preferences. The rate of return of their investment also depends on individual characteristics such as IQ (merits). As far as the demand side is concerned, training activities pursue the increase in individual productivity and the establishment of a wedge between individual productivity and the real wage.

However, human capital formation is not only a result of rational individual choices, but it also depends on both the class nature and the requirements of the production process. Here are two examples about the relationship between education and the requirements of the productive system. They show clearly how individual educational choices are actually affected by the industrial fabric, which means that the individual's calculation is not intelligible without looking at social institutions. The first example concerns the evolution of education in the Netherlands. It reflected the interest of capitalists in the skill formation of the masses. In particular, as early as the 1830s, industrial schools were established and funded by private organizations, representing industrialists and entrepreneurs. Ultimately, in the latter part of the nineteenth century, the state – urged by industrialists and entrepreneurs – started to support these schools (Wolthuis 1999).

The second example refers to training of blue-collar workers. In the late 1910s, technologically advanced industries demanded craft labourers who were trained in geometry, algebra, chemistry, mechanical drawing and related skills. The structure of education was transformed in response to industrial development and the increasing importance of human capital in the production process, and American high schools adapted to the needs of the modern workplace of the early twentieth century. Total enrolment in public secondary schools increased seventyfold from 1870 to 1950 (Kurian 1994). The relationship between schooling and the distribution of income cannot be understood with a model that lacks a theory of reproduction, for a central aspect of this relationship is the role played by the school system in legitimating economic inequality. Reproduction has not been studied very much by economics but is central to the non-quantitative traditions of sociology. Therefore, the inclusion of qualitative factors into the economics of inequality leads back to the sociological tradition of Bourdieu. While capital in the human capital approach remains a matter of individual strategies, in Bourdieu's approach it is a matter of social structure and its reproduction.

Inequality in contemporary capitalism

Sociological approaches

The quantitative tradition continues to be the most visible and influential approach in research on inequality. Methodology and measurement instruments have become very sophisticated, especially due to the development of IT. At the same time, social structure analysis increasingly discards simple models of stratification based on professions alone. Instead, the influence of discussions on intersectionality in the 1980s and 1990s (cf. Krizsán 2012) as well as Bourdieu's work have led to the adoption of multivariate analyses in the quantitative tradition. The term intersectionality indicates that different dimensions of inequality, such as profession, income, race and gender, cannot be reduced to one basic variable but tend to reinforce each other.

Against this background, quantitative research has adopted various strategies to assess and measure different dimensions of inequality. Apart from merely descriptive cluster analyses, two approaches of research seem to be particularly influential. One is the focus on life-styles or habitus as the variable, which combines different dimensions of inequality. This approach is adopted by scholars like Peter Berger (1990) or Gerhard Schulze (1996). The very influential German Sinus Institute has proposed a model of milieus for most European and some non-European societies that is based on similarities between individuals in their taste. Even though this model clearly draws on Bourdieu's Distinction, it has no theoretical ambitions and remains entirely descriptive. This distinguishes the milieu approach developed by Vester from the Sinus Institute.

The other approach of more quantitative research overlaps with the structural and the intermediate traditions. Instead of the synchronic perspective, it adopts a diachronic perspective by focusing on the life-course. An influential school has been established by Hans-Peter Blossfeld, who studies itineraries through social structure and especially the role of education. Blossfeld and his institute have conducted many large-scale studies in several Western countries on life-courses (e.g. Blossfeld et al. 2005). These are very important contributions to inequality research because they show the modes of generation and reproduction of inequality. However, Blossfeld lacks a general theory of inequality.

Exactly the opposite is the case with the two most influential systems theories developed in sociology. They offer a general theory of society but little empirical research. However, they are the first theories that explicitly refer to the global scale and propose to explain global inequality. Whereas almost all research on inequality until the 1990s has focused exclusively on the nation state, contemporary research aims at including the global and the transnational dimensions (Berger and Weiß 2008). To a significant degree, this is the achievement of the two systems theories developed in the 1970s.

While Niklas Luhmann based his theory of world society on Parsons and biology, Immanuel Wallerstein developed his world systems theory out of a critical reading of Marx. According to Luhmann, society can be interpreted as a functional integration of systems that follow an internally independent regulation, which has to accommodate the external requirements of the relation to other systems. Each system is defined by its medium of regulation. Society as a whole is defined by the medium of communication. Luhmann extended his theory to the global level in 1975 by postulating that communication has become globalized. This implies that society had to be analysed on a global level. Luhmann (1975) coined the term "world society" and called for redefining the unit of sociological analysis as the world. The issue of inequality had been absent from his theory until he visited Brazil and began to deal with the topic in the framework of his established theory. He defined inequality as exclusion from social systems, e.g. education or power. Luhmann's students have continued this line of research by studying forms of exclusion in the world society (cf. Wobbe 2000; Heintz, Münch and Tyrell 2005).

Immanuel Wallerstein published his global theory at the same time as Luhmann. He also claimed that any social phenomenon of the present had to be studied in the context of the world system (Wallerstein 1974). However, instead of a functional theory, Wallerstein proposed a structural theory of power. Its core consists of Marx's distinction between capital and labour, which Wallerstein merely amplified to the global level. The exploitation of labour by capital takes place within the nation state but also of poor by rich states (or former colonies by Euro-America). The only difference between Wallerstein and Marx consists in the absence of dialectical thought in Wallerstein's theory. While Marx develops the apparent form of contemporary society out of the mediation of the opposition between capital and labour (or, more precisely, the self-contradicting nature of labour in capitalism), Wallerstein poses a mediating class between capital and labour. On a global level, he distinguishes between centre, semi-periphery and periphery. The semi-periphery is supposed to mediate conflicts and to give the periphery hope for upward social mobility. Wallerstein's theory has been adapted to contemporary globalization (e.g. Therborn 2006) and is still as relevant as Luhmann's theory.

A new approach to inequality has been elaborated within a third type of systems theory, which is complexity theory. Sylvia Walby (2009) has constructed a theoretical framework that interprets the social world as a "global fitness landscape" shaped by disjunctive systems which adapt to this landscape according to "path dependencies" in a non-causal way. Walby proposes studying each system from the perspective of economy, polity, civil society and violence. On this basis, she presents a theoretical and empirical analysis of the world's structure. However, her empirical base is restricted to the familiar Western environment, analysed in a familiar way in terms of the opposition of social democracy and neoliberalism.

The general theories of systems have their charm and virtues but they remain too abstract to explain empirical phenomena, especially as far as the interaction between global, national and local dynamics is concerned. Recent attempts at the analysis of global and national inequality have been marked by their close interdependence as well as an escalation in complexity (Schuerkens 2010). Nevertheless, they have yet to develop an appropriate theoretical lens. One interesting attempt is Raphael Kaplinsky's book on inequality (2005), which explains global inequality as resulting from Western protectionism. He bases his argument on an analysis of global value chains, which concentrate the production of surplus value in the global North. Increasing productivity and the subsequent reduction of prices, already observed by Marx, fails to benefit the global poor because of overproduction, unemployment and lack of state control (Kaplinsky 2005: 208–25).

A good example of the state of sociological concepts offers a reader edited by Held and Kaya (2007). In the contributions of Gösta Esping-Andersen and Robert Wade the more Weberian tradition, which distinguishes an "Asian" capitalism from social democracy and neoliberalism, has a voice in the reader as well. What is utterly lacking in this collection, however, is a perspective on (and from) emerging societies – i.e. an acknowledgement of the post-Eurocentric structure of the world. This type of research is becoming increasingly important. While almost all research on inequality has been based on theories and concepts developed with regard to Western societies, they have been applied rather recklessly to other societies. On the one hand, empirical research on inequality in the entire global South forms a much smaller body of literature than that on either Germany or Great Britain. On the other hand, almost no concepts have been developed in the global South, apart from those referring to the specific situation of colonialism and postcolonialism. It still remains to be demonstrated what is common between inequalities in colonial, postcolonial and Western contexts. However, it has become evident at least that culture, national institutions and history matter for inequality. It is therefore very important to develop theories of inequality in the global South and comparisons between various regions.

A theory of inequality in the global South has been developed by Jessé Souza (2007). He argues that societies in the global South can only be understood against the background of colonialism and modernization programmes. They established a structure, which reminds of Wallerstein and dependency theory by creating an unequal relation between the centre and the rest. Souza deviates from Wallerstein, however, by his focus on the symbolic dimension. While economic and political dependency has largely disappeared, the unequal relation between centre and periphery has been embodied as a system of meaning. This system also informs national and local inequality by establishing a racism that declares characteristics of the modern centre (such as white skin, urban residence, Western education) as superior and characteristics of the underdeveloped periphery as inferior. Thereby, inequality in a postcolonial society is legitimized.

Souza's approach is developed further by Jodhka, Rehbein and Souza (2017). Based on case studies of Brazil, Germany, India and Laos, the authors develop a theory of inequality, which seeks to combine the national particularities or path dependencies with general structures of class. The book argues that all capitalist societies transform precapitalist hierarchies into class structures, while many aspects of precapitalist inequalities persist. The structure of inequality or domination is considered more fundamental than the organization of the capitalist economy, which is interpreted by the authors as merely one form of reproducing domination (see Rehbein and Souza in this volume).

Another sociological theory trying to understand inequality on a global level without assimilating all societies to a presupposed Western model has been advanced by Anja Weiß (2017). The author argues, following Bourdieu, that inequality is rooted in an unequal distribution of capital and habitus. She claims that capital and habitus have a different value in differing transnational contexts. The ability to employ capital and habitus in the best possible way is the core of Weiß' argument and subsumed under the concept "sociospatial autonomy". This concept bridges the gap between conditions and practice in Bourdieu's theory, operates on a global scale and includes the aspect of space. Sociospatial autonomy is equivalent to the ability to move anywhere without jeopardizing one's social position. The maximum sociospatial autonomy would be the access to all valuable functions and positions in society.

Sources of income inequality in the economic literature

Even scholars like Amartya Sen, who are very sensitive to the question of Eurocentrism, regularly invoke universal concepts of socioeconomic inequality without considering the local context or seeking out indigenous concepts of (in)equality. Nevertheless, Sen may have been the first (after Marx) to seriously address the question of why one should study inequality at all. He agreed with Marx that research on inequality should seek to discover the structures that prevent people from leading the kind of life they "have reason to value", and that the problem with inequality is that many people do not have this option (Sen 2006: 35). And both agree that the root of the problem is an unequal distribution of resources and the symbolic legitimation of this distribution. However, both propose a rather mechanistic genesis for these structures as well as the somewhat simplistic solution of redistribution.

Economics has not developed Sen's approach much further. It rather mostly sticks to approaches that cannot offer a general perspective on inequality. However, each approach has certain virtues that are still relevant for a research agenda today. In the economic literature eight different approaches can be outlined in the analysis of inequality. As inequality is a very complex and multidimensional phenomenon, each approach specifies a possible source of inequality, without ruling out the relevance of the other approaches; these approaches are not mutually exclusive.

Human capital

The human capital approach is the main theoretical framework used by neo-classical economists in order to explain the different individuals' earning profile in time (Becker 1964; Mincer 1974). For our purposes, it is important to mention that human capital theoretical apparatus analyses the process of skill formation from two different perspectives. On the one hand, this approach takes into account the individual educational choices, based on a constrained maximisation process. According to this approach, individuals invest in years of education for as many years so that the return to this investment is greater than the one of any alternative financial investment. The earning profile of a worker depends on the amount of this investment, whose level is substantially affected by two factors: the individual ability and the background characteristics such as gender, parental background and income. On the other hand, assuming a perfectly competitive labour market, Becker started the analysis of skill formation in firms through different typologies of training (on-the-job, off-the-job, etc.). He introduced the pivotal distinction between specific and general training[3] and showed that, while for employers it can be convenient to contribute to investment in specific training, the onus of general training weighs totally on the employees' shoulders, as the risk of free-riding by other employers can make investment in general training of little value. More recent developments in human capital theory (Acemoglu and Pischke 1998, 1999) have demonstrated that abandoning the assumption of perfect competition, in either the labour or the product market, can create the conditions for financing of investments in general training by employers. This makes training less quantifiable and less of an individualistic affair.

From both perspectives, inequality stems from a process of skill formation. In the analysis of individual educational choices, inequality depends on the level of investment in years of schooling, which in turn, depends on both background and individual characteristics; in the analysis of training activity in firms, inequality results from the decisions taken both by employers and employees.

From Bourdieu's perspective, education aims at favouring the reproduction of the existing social order, based on an unequal distribution of resources (capital). Of course, this approach to education is incompatible with the human capital approach, as the latter rules out class concepts.

This provides an interesting perspective for economists since it points to the social function played by the processes of formation/accumulation of human capital. As a matter of fact, one "must ask not only how variations in the level of investment affect the level of output and growth rates [and individual productivity], but also how the structure of human capital formation affects the social relations of production and the evolution of class relations" (Bowles and Gintis 1975: 80). Human capital formation is not only a result of rational individual choices, but it also depends on the class nature of the production process. In this "formulation, schooling may influence the rate of growth positively or negatively in ways which go considerably beyond the human capital theorist's notion of "labour quality": through its role in the extension and reproduction of the wage-labour system, through its capacity to attenuate class conflict and thereby to alter the rate of capital accumulation, and so on" (Bowles and Gintis 1975: 81). The analysis of the return to investment in education and human capital should be embedded within a framework including the societal class composition. Reduction in inequality is not only a mere result of the amount of investment in education or training.

> The relationship between schooling and the distribution of income cannot be understood with a model which lacks a theory of reproduction, for a central aspect of this relationship is the role played by the school system in legitimating economic inequality. Thus, it is illogical to suppose that the reduction in inequalities in the distribution of schooling might lead to changes in income inequality in any particular direction. Major changes in the distribution of human resources will predictably be associated with changes in the structural relationships (earnings functions) relating schooling to individual income. Indeed, an equalization of education might radically reduce economic inequality, not directly, but rather by undermining the legitimacy of inequality and thus enhancing the potential for a thoroughgoing reorganization of economic institutions.
>
> (Bowles and Gintis 1975)

The effect of skill-biased technical change

This approach emphasizes the role played by the introduction of new technologies, and the organisational restructuring encompassed by these new technologies, in the relative demand for highly-skilled workers with respect to middle-skilled employees. This occurs because new technologies are complements to the working activities of highly-skilled employees and can substitute for middle-skilled workers (Goldin and Katz 2007). Jobs related to routinised skills, both cognitive and non-cognitive, seem to be the most severely hit by this dynamic, giving rise to a remarkable downsizing of middle-income earners. The overall effect of this process has been the polarization of the distribution of jobs in the US and most European countries (Autor et al. 2006; Goos, Manning and Salomons 2009), with both an increase in jobs related to non-routinised cognitive skills, in the upper tail, and an increase in non-routinised non-cognitive job posts at the lower end. The number of middle-skilled jobs related to routinised cognitive and non-cognitive tasks has shrunk quite drastically, as a result of the techno-organisational change associated with the intensive introduction of computers in work process and organisation. This change in the intensity of relative demand for skills seems to be consistent with Braverman's (1974) approach who maintained that technological innovation was responsible for de-skilling of a component of the workforce. The same story, but from a different perspective, can be told as far as the analysis of the impact of the introduction of HPWP (High Performance Working Practice) is concerned, resulting in a flattening of the hierarchical structure in firms, due to a drastic downscaling of the middle-management.

Internationalisation of production

There is a wide range of literature on the effects of globalisation of markets on inequality (Mills 2009). The effects diverge according to the countries involved. The new international division of labour is deeply affected by the phenomena of outsourcing and offshoring, favoured both by the new institutional setting of international trade and the rapid spread of information and communications technology (ICT) in manufacturing activities. Roughly speaking, firms keep in advanced countries highly-skilled activities with few highly-paid employees, while cutting down jobs and wages for medium- and low-skilled office and factory workers, whose jobs are more likely to be transferred to low-wage developing countries. Basically, these events go in the same direction as the skill-biased technical change, giving rise to an increase in relative demand for highly-skilled workers with respect to medium-skilled ones. The outcome in these rich countries is a rise in wage inequality, and deeper polarisation of jobs and skills. Nevertheless, the effects of globalisation on developing economies can be quite different. As a matter of fact, globalisation can favour the process of industrialisation and job creation. New employment opportunities arise and the gap between the highly-skilled and the low-skilled wage earners narrows (Mills 2009). As a result, in developing countries outsourcing and off-shoring of economic activities, carried out by firms whose main site remains in advanced countries, favour a process of restraint and decrease of inequality.

Labour market institutions

Three different types of institutions have to be taken into account, as key determinants of income inequality and its dynamics. First, the range of labour contracts and the laws which regulate them affect the bargaining power of workers. The easier the activation of individual fixed-term labour contract, the weaker is the bargaining power of workers. Second, the degree of unionisation of the workforce matters. Third, the existence and the degree of coverage of collective bargaining has an effect. The role and the evolution of these three factors has deeply influenced the dynamics of income inequality, changing the balance of power in the process of wage bargaining. Without going into too much detail, the deregulation of the labour market of these last years has weakened collective bargaining, in favour of a vis-à-vis contracting between the employer and the employee. This has been probably one of the crucial explanatory factors in the increase in inequality experienced in most European countries in these last years (OECD 2011).

Role of the welfare state

Another effect of the deregulation process developed in these last years has been the downsizing of the role of the State as both economic actor and manager of the process of income distribution between profits and wages. The dismantling of the welfare state and the weakening of the redistributive role played by the government through progressive tax policy have favoured the soaring of inequality. The example of Sweden is clear and vivid. A clear-cut consequence of this process is the decrease in the provisions of public goods by governmental institutions due also the implementation of intensive programmes of privatisation (Freeman, Swedenborg and Topel 2010).

Inequality

The basic idea is that inequality can be conceived as an autoregressive process, where the degree of past inequality affects present inequality. This is related to recent analysis by Brunori, Ferreira and Peragine (2013) where the impact on inequality of exogenous factors such as birthplace, gender, race and family background is investigated. They have found that a remarkable percentage of income inequality can be explained by these exogenous factors. Of course, the relevance of these factors, which obviously individuals cannot influence, varies from country to country. The contribution of the three scholars highlights how inequality in opportunities deeply affects inequality in income distribution. Empirical evidence shows a negative correlation between inequality index and intergenerational mobility: the higher the level of inequality, the lower the possibility to improve the relative position in the social hierarchy. In addition to that, they have found a strong correlation between the educational level of parents and children. A relevant component of income inequality does not depend on the individual behaviour, but on the background traits: *qualis pater, talis filius.*

Models of capitalism and institutional complementarities

Starting from the 1990s, institutional economists have developed a theoretical framework based on the notion of institutional complementarity (Amable 2003; Aoki 2001). The basic idea of this approach is that institutions, defined by

North (1990) as "humanly devised constraints imposed on human interaction", interact among themselves, giving rise to institutional equilibria. Each of these equilibria affects the operation of markets and of all economic actors involved. Roughly speaking, the performance of markets also depends on these complementarity relationships and not only and simply on the interaction between demand and supply forces. Certainly, demand and supply matter, but their working cannot be abstracted from the institutional context and the network of interacting institutions which constitute it.

This approach has given rise to a large number of divergent classifications of types of capitalism and has been also widely adopted to discuss the relationship between the process of skill formation and labour market institutions. The idea is that the institutional architecture affects the individual choices at both firms' and employees' level. Particularly, this framework of analysis emphasises how individual propensity in human capital investment depends on some institutions operating in the labour market. Particularly, the approach by Estevez-Abe, Iversen and Soskice (1999) points to the degree of protection that the individual enjoys in the labour market. Protection in the labour market can have two different meanings. On the one hand, it can be intended as employment security. On the other hand, it refers to income protection in spells of unemployment. Employment protection favours employees' investment in firm-specific skills, as it positively affects job tenure. Differently, unemployment protection favours employees' investment in industry-specific skills, as the individual can withstand spells of unemployment, without dramatic decrease in the level of income. This literature allows the understanding of how models of capitalism affect the process of human capital formation, structuring the employment relations between employees and employers. Whereas the US combines low employment protection with low unemployment protection, Germany presents the opposite in both regards, Japan focuses on employment protection and Denmark focuses on unemployment protection. Each of the four ideal-types is linked to particular types of skills. Similar to the human capital approach, the literature on models of capitalism emphasises the process of skill development as potential source of inequality. The main difference between the two approaches lies in the role played by individual choices. The human capital approach conceives the process of skill formation as the solution to a problem of constrained maximisation of an individual objective function, as it is always the case in neoclassical economics; the institutionalist literature stresses the role played by institutions in orienting the path of this process. In conclusion, the difference lies in the factors promoting investment in human capital, not in the notion of human capital itself.

The governance of firms

The ways the governance of firms affects inequalities can be grouped into two different streams of the economic literature.[4] First of all, it is important to highlight the literature on internal labour markets and their evolution in time. Departing from the seminal contribution by Doeringer and Piore (1971) and their description of a typical Fordist manufacturing firm, Aoki (1988) and Marsden (1999) have both developed and enriched the descriptive framework. Aoki has analysed in detail the operation of the so-called J firm, whereas Marsden has successfully integrated the analysis of systems of production and training with the study of model of capitalism. Both of them have shown the rising of different remuneration systems within different institutional context of production. Aoki's analysis focuses on the Japanese organisation of work and production, whereas Marsden develops a more general framework of analysis discussing the intermingling between the organisation of production and the training system. Second, it is worth mentioning the vast literature on the remuneration of top management and the rise of top income, if only for the lasting and bitter controversy it has raised in main Western countries (Atkinson, Piketty and Saez 2011). This aspect of inequality is related to the microeconomic (mis-)management of markets accounting for the decrease in the degree of competition among firms and the consequent arising of oligopolistic positions (Stiglitz 2012).

Inequality in wealth distribution

In a recent and successful contribution, Piketty (2014) discusses the determinants of inequality in the distribution of wealth. His analysis focuses on the comparison between r, the rate of return on capital, and g, the rate of growth of the economy. The effects of shocks which can affect the distribution of wealth are magnified if r exceeds g. Piketty shows that the range of shocks that can affect the distribution of wealth is quite wide. He refers to a variety of shocks such as changes in labour market performance or in the demographic dynamics. Importantly, he maintains that the gap between r and g depends on the operation of institutions and the implementation of policies. This seems to imply that any change in the distribution of wealth due to exogenous shocks can be thwarted by the proper public interventions. Importantly, he maintains that the gap between r and g depends on the operation of institutions and the implementation of policies. This seems to imply that any change in the distribution of wealth due to exogenous shocks can be thwarted by the proper public interventions. Particularly, he focuses on the taxation of wealth as an effective tool to control the degree of inequality in wealth distribution.

Critical assessment

Those studies that have focused on structures instead of numbers have almost exclusively used theories modeled on the basis of research undertaken in Western Europe and North America. Research on inequality has been rather Eurocentric. This is regrettable, since alternative approaches to the analysis of social structure are already at hand. An excellent non-Eurocentric approach is found in Yoshio Sugimoto's *Introduction to Japanese Society* (2003). Rather than insisting on the peculiarities of Japanese culture, Sugimoto argues that Japan must be analysed just like any other society. At the same time, he demonstrates that the application of concepts derived from the analysis of Western societies fails in this task by pointing to the persistence of historical structures (or path dependency), which he exemplifies with reference to the symbolic sphere. He uses the conceptual tool of "subcultures" (which resembles the concept of "milieu" utilized by Vester et al. 2001) to make sense of intersecting inequalities and persisting hierarchies in Japan.

It is important to acknowledge that nation states have different histories and therefore rather different institutions and configurations of inequality. The introduction of capitalism and the standardization of the institutions of the nation state according to a Western model may lead to a convergence of some aspects of inequality but they do not erase history. Any research agenda on inequality has to abandon empty universalism in favour of a more localised empirical approach. This does not exclude generalisations but these have to be empirically grounded. Any theory has to make plausible that its propositions apply to different empirical cases around the globe.

Furthermore, the issue of transnationalism needs to be addressed. The exclusive focus on the Western nation state has tended to exclude the relevance of transborder, local and regional configurations of society and inequality in the global South. By now, the issue of migration to Western nation states has pushed transnational structures into the centre of research on inequality (cf. Berger and Weiß 2008; cf. Weiß in this volume).

The origin of research on inequality in the works of Adam Smith and Karl Marx has resulted in a strong bias towards the relation of economic capital and labour. Even from Pierre Bourdieu's model, house-workers, students, pensioners and informal workers are largely absent. This means to exclude more than half of Western populations and up to 90 percent of Southern populations from the discussion of social structure and inequality. It has become evident that inequality research has to combine a global framework with very precise local knowledge (Rehbein 2011). No phenomenon of inequality is intelligible without taking the impact of globalization into account but any phenomenon of inequality exists in a localized context (Jodhka, Rehbein and Souza 2017). Research on transnational structures of inequality, comparative research between inequality in different nation states and a better understanding of reproduction of inequality are absolutely necessary at this point.

This provides an interesting perspective for economists since it points to the social function played by the processes of formation/accumulation of human capital. As a matter of fact, one "must ask not only how variations in the level of investment affect the level of output and growth rates [and individual productivity], but also how the structure of human capital formation affects the social relations of production and the evolution of class relations" (Bowles and Gintis 1975). Human capital formation is not only a result of rational individual choices, but it also depends on the class nature of the production process.

Each of the economic approaches outlined in the previous paragraphs can catch a part of the story of inequality but it has to be framed within the approach of the models of capitalism (Aoki 2001; Amable 2003). Economic dynamics are regulated by the institutional framework in which they develop and, therefore, the approach of the models of capitalism provides the much needed analytical tools not only to understand and interpret these dynamics but also to complement the other theoretical attempts worked out to interpret the phenomenon of inequality. As argued above, the analysis of human capital formation through some form of training can be properly understood only if one takes into account the model of capitalism in which the firms operate, because the model itself affects the firm's propensity to privilege a specific form of training over another. As discussed, the propensity to emphasise a specific form of training depends strictly on the complementarity relationship established between different institutions. This interaction between institutions implicitly defines the level of inequality considered acceptable within a given economic system.

Consider the two polar cases, US and Germany. In the former case both employment and unemployment protection are totally missing, in the latter employees enjoy both kinds of protection. The lack of any buffer against any possible drop in the level of income of the American system compared to the articulated forms of assistance guaranteed by the German welfare system point to the different threshold of tolerated inequality which characterises each model of capitalism. The operation of institutions affecting the labour market contain an inherent level of inequality beyond which the public authority is bound to intervene. In the case of the US this threshold is substantially higher than in Germany or in the so-called Scandinavian model, because the operation of institutions in the US does not relieve from the risks inherent in the working of a flexible labour market. As a result it seems that the ultimate determinants of inequality are the factors themselves which bring about the prevailing of a specific model of capitalism in an economic system. For this reason the class composition of a socioeconomic system, which to a first approximation is a key determinant of the structuring of the institutional complementarities at the base of a specific model of capitalism, has to be taken into account, if one wants to understand with no prejudice the rise and the dynamics of inequality.

A relevant research agenda has to come up with a revised model of class (cf. Rehbein and Souza in this volume). It has to take the issues of models of capitalism and histories, of transnationalism and of non-labour activities into account. The unit of analysis should be global in the last instance. However, as research has to be empirically grounded and locally sensitive, a deductive and universalist approach is no longer feasible. The model of class needs to focus on reproduction of inequalities without falling back into simple reductions as the opposition between capital and labour or a ranking of professions. It also needs to make sense of the individualisation of lifestyles and tastes, which makes the class structure of society invisible.

Notes

1 This chapter is a slightly updated version of Giovanni Guidetti and Boike Rehbein (2014) 'Theoretical Approaches to Inequality in Economics and Sociology: A Preliminary Assessment', *Transcience*, Vol. 5, No. 2: 1–15. Reprinted by permission.
2 The production function must be homogeneous of degree 1.

3 Specific training augments employees' productivity only in the firm where training activity has been actually carried out; general training increases the workers' productivity in any firm.
4 A third stream of the literature on systems of governance of firms and production has been discussed in the section about internationalisation.

References

Acemoglu, Daron and Jorn-Steffen Pischke (1998) 'Why Do Firms Train? Theory and Evidence', *Quarterly Journal of Economics*, Vol. 113: 79–119.
Acemoglu, Daron and Jorn-Steffen Pischke (1999) 'Beyond Becker: Training in Imperfect Labour Markets', *The Economic Journal*, Vol. 109, No. 453: F112–42.
Amable Bruno (2003) *The Diversity of Modern Capitalism*, Oxford: Oxford University Press.
Aoki, Masahiko (1988) *Information, Incentives, and Bargaining in the Japanese Economy*, Cambridge: Cambridge University Press.
Aoki, Masahiko (2001) *Toward a Comparative Institutional Analysis*, Cambridge, MA and London: The MIT Press.
Atkinson, Anthony B., Thomas Piketty and Emmanuel Saez (2011) 'Top Incomes in the Long Run of History', *Journal of Economic Literature*, Vol. 49, No. 1: 3–71.
Autor, David, Laurence F. Katz and Melissa S. Kearney (2006) 'The Polarization of the U. S. Labor Market', *American Economic Review*, Vol. 96, No. 2: 189–94.
Becker, Gary S. (1964) *Human Capital*, New York: Columbia University Press.
Berger, Peter A. (ed.) (1990) *Lebenslagen, Lebensläufe, Lebensstile*, Göttingen: Schwartz.
Berger, Peter A. and Anja Weiß (eds.) (2008) *Die Transnationalisierung der Sozialstruktur*, Wiesbaden: VS.
Blossfeld, Hans-Peter, Erik Klijzing, Melinda Mills and Karin Kurz (2005) *Globalization, Uncertainty and Youth in Society*, London and New York: Routledge.
Braverman, Harry (1974) *Labor and Monopoly Capital*, New York: Monthly Review Press.
Bourdieu, Pierre (1984) *Distinction*, London: Routledge and Kegan Paul.
Bourguignon, François (2004) 'The Poverty-Growth-Inequality Triangle'. Paper prepared for the Indian Council for Research on International Economic Relations, New Delhi, February 4.
Bowles, Sam and Herb Gintis (1975) 'The Problem With Human Capital Theory: A Marxian Critique', *The American Economic Review*, Vol. 65, No. 2: 74–82.
Breen, Richard (ed.) (2004) *Social Mobility*, Oxford: Oxford University Press.
Brunori, Paolo, Francisco Ferreira and Vito Peragine (2013) 'Inequality of Opportunity, Income Inequality and Economic Mobility: Some International Comparisons', Washington, DC: World Bank Policy Research, Working Paper 6304.
Doeringer, Peter B. and Michael J. Piore (1971) *Internal Labor Market and Manpower Analysis*, New York: D.C. Heath and Company.
Ehrhart, Christophe (2009) 'The effects of inequality on growth, a survey of the theoretical and empirical literature', ECINEQ Working Paper series, n. 107.
Estevez-Abe, Margarita, Torben Iversen and David Soskice (1999) 'Social Protection and the Formation of Skills: A Reinterpretation of the Welfare State', in Peter A. Hall and David Soskice (eds.) *Varieties of Capitalism: The Institutional Foundations of Comparative Advantage*, Oxford and New York: Oxford University Press, 145–83.
Fields, Gary S. (2001) *Distribution and Development. A New Look at the Developing World*, New York, Cambridge, and London: Russel Sage Foundation and MIT Press.
Freeman, Richard B., Birgitta Swedenborg and Robert H. Topel (2010) *Reforming the Welfare State: Recovery and Beyond in Sweden*, Chicago: University of Chicago Press.

Geiger, Theodor (1932) *Die soziale Schichtung des deutschen Volkes*, Stuttgart: Enke.

Geißler, Rainer (1996; second edition) *Die Sozialstruktur Deutschlands*, Opladen: Westdeutscher Verlag.

Goldin, Claudia and Lawrence F. Katz (2007) 'Long-Run Changes in the Wage Structure: Narrowing, Widening, Polarizing', *Brookings Papers on Economic Activity*, Vol. 2007, No. 2: 135–65.

Goldthorpe, John H. (2007) *On Sociology*, Stanford, CA: Stanford University Press.

Goos, Maarten, Alan Manning, and Anna Salomons (2009) 'Job Polarization in Europe', *American Economic Review*, Vol. 99, No. 2: 58–63.

Heintz, Bettina, Richard Münch and Hartmann Tyrell (eds.) (2005) *Weltgesellschaft: Theoretische Zugänge und empirische Problemlagen*, Stuttgart: Lucius & Lucius.

Held, David and Ayse Kaya (eds.) (2007) *Global Inequality*, Cambridge: Polity Press.

Hradil, Stefan (1986) *Die Sozialstruktur Deutschlands im internationalen Vergleich*, Opladen: Westdeutscher Verlag.

Jodhka, Surinder S., Boike Rehbein and Jessé Souza (2017) *Inequality in Capitalist Societies*, Singapore and London: Routledge.

Jomo, Kwame S. and Jacques Baudot (eds.) (2007) *Flat World, Big Gaps*, London: Zed.

Kaplinsky, Raphael (2005) *Globalization, Poverty and Inequality*, Cambridge: Polity Press.

Krizsán, Andrea (2012) *Institutionalizing Intersectionality*, Basingstoke: Palgrave Macmillan.

Kurian, George T. (1994) *Datapedia of the United States, 1790–2000: America Year by Year*, Lanham, MD: Bernan Press.

Kuznets, Simon (1955) 'Economic Growth and Income Inequality', *The American Economic Review*, Vol. 45, No. 1: 1–28.

Lucas, Robert E. (2004) 'The Industrial Revolution: Past and Future', in *The Region*, Minneapolis, MN: Federal Reserve Bank of Minneapolis, 5–20.

Luhmann, Niklas (1975) 'Die Weltgesellschaft', in Niklas Luhmann (ed.) *Soziologische Aufklärung 2*, Opladen: Westdeutscher Verlag, 51–71.

Marsden, David (1999) *A Theory of Employment Systems: Micro-Foundations of Societal Diversity*, Oxford: Oxford University Press.

Marx, Karl (1953ff) *Marx-Engels-Werke* (MEW), Berlin: Dietz.

Milanovic, Branko (2005) *Worlds Apart: Measuring International and Global Inequality*, Princeton, NJ: Princeton University Press.

Mills, Melinda (2009): 'Globalization and Inequality', *European Sociological Review*, Vol. 25, No. 1: 1–8.

Mincer, Jacob (1974) *Schooling, Experience, and Earnings*, New York: Columbia University Press.

North, Douglass (1990) *Institutions, Institutional Change and Economic Performance*, Cambridge, MA: Cambridge University Press.

OECD (2011) *Divided We Stand: Why Inequality Keeps Rising*, Paris: OECD Publishing.

Parsons, Talcott (1939) 'The Professions and Social Structure', *Social Forces*, Vol. 17, No. 4: 457–67.

Pasinetti, Luigi L. (1977) *Lectures on the Theory of Production*, London: Macmillan.

Piketty, Thomas (2014) *Capital in the Twenty-First Century*, Cambridge, MA: Harvard University Press.

Rehbein, Boike (ed.) (2011) *Globalization and Inequality in Emerging Societies*, Basingstoke: Palgrave Macmillan.

Ricardo, David (1815) An Essay on the Influence of a Low Price of Corn on the Profits of Stocks, reprinted in Piero Sraffa (1951) (ed.) *The Works and Correspondence of David Ricardo*, Cambridge: Cambridge University Press.

Schuerkens, Ulrike (ed.) (2010) *Globalization and Transformations of Global Inequality*, London and New York: Routledge.

Schulze, Gerhard (1996) *Erlebnisgesellschaft*, Frankfurt and New York: Campus.

Sen, Amartya (2006) 'Conceptualizing and Measuring Poverty', in David B. Grusky and Ravi Kanbur (eds.) *Poverty and Inequality*, Stanford, CA: Stanford University Press, 30–46.

Smith, Adam (2007) *The Wealth of Nations*, Petersfield: Harriman House.

Souza, Jessé (2007) *Die Naturalisierung der Ungleichheit*, Wiesbaden: VS.

Stiglitz Joseph (2012) *The Price of Inequality*, New York and London: Norton.

Sugimoto, Yoshio (2003; second edition) *An Introduction to Japanese Society*, Cambridge: Cambridge University Press.

Therborn, Göran (2006) *Inequalities of the World*, London: Verso.

Vester, Michael, Peter von Oertzen, Heiko Geiling, Thomas Hermann and Dagmar Müller (2001) *Soziale Milieus im gesellschaftlichen Strukturwandel*, Frankfurt: Suhrkamp.

Walby, Sylvia (2009) *Globalization and Inequalities: Complexity and Contested Modernities*, London: Sage.

Wallerstein, Immanuel (1974) 'The Rise and Future Demise of the World Capitalist System: Concepts for Comparative Analysis', *Comparative Studies in Society and History*, Vol. 16: 387–415.

Weber, Max (1972; fifth edition) *Wirtschaft und Gesellschaft*, Tübingen: Mohr.

Weiß, Anja (2017) *Soziologie globaler Ungleichheiten*, Frankfurt: Suhrkamp.

Wicksell, Knut (1954) *Value, Capital and Rent*, London: G. Allen & Unwin.

Wobbe, Theresa (2000) *Weltgesellschaft*, Bielefeld: Transcript.

Wolthuis, Jan (1999) *Lower Technical Education in the Netherlands, 1798–1993: The Rise and Fall of a Subsystem*, Apeldoorn: Garant.

Part II

Inequality and globalization

Part II

Inequality and globalization

2 Inequality in income and wealth distribution, globalization and models of capitalism

Gilberto Antonelli

Introduction

Since its origin, economics as a science has granted a lot of attention to income and wealth distribution which are assumed to be the main economic determinants of inequality. But this simple sentence has to be qualified, taking into consideration the typical logic that economists traditionally are used to following.

First, their effort has been devoted chiefly to developing paradigmatic models[1] which have been mainly used to study the impact of distribution on crucial economic outcomes, such as growth and efficiency.

Second, since income and wealth distribution have been considered among the main determinants of potential inequality in the economic realm, a deeper analysis of their impact on inequality has been left to the specialized interest and feelings of a few scholars in the application of their favored paradigmatic model.

If we consider in retrospect the evolution that took place within this logic, we cannot be fully satisfied. Actually, this two-stage way of reasoning has encouraged the majority of economists to consider growth and efficiency neutral with respect to inequality.

Today, also due to the process of the global integration of markets, the influence of several layers of government on the operation of each model[2] and the importance attached to sustainable and inclusive development, it is much more difficult to deal with inequality as a second-step issue. A new vision emerges which has to be taken into serious consideration by economists. Therefore, in introducing the subject of how income and wealth distribution theories have influenced the study of inequality we need to move forward dealing with four main points, which will be analyzed in the next four sections of this chapter.

In the second section the traditional theories of income and wealth distribution will be briefly reviewed, in order to clarify their implications in terms of the interpretation of inequality.[3] This is not only relevant from a historical point of view, but can be rewarding also for contemporary studies on inequality.[4] We will also outline some of the major biases affecting mainstream economics. In the third section the main changes in the reference framework induced by globalization and global crisis will be outlined, suggesting the view that the new globalized nature of inequality should be examined. In the fourth section the multidimensional nature of inequality is explored and other elements useful to a deeper study of the new vision are collected. In the fifth section, we will explore some of the reasons why the models of capitalism theory can be relevant for better studying globalized and multidimensional inequality.

This chapter as a whole emphasizes that inequality is a global, multidimensional and cumulative phenomenon and it should not be conceived only as the result of the processes of personal and functional distribution of income and wealth, which, by the way, are intrinsically multidimensional on their own. The basic idea is that institutions, the cobweb of relations among them and their interaction with the economic structure define the model of capitalism which characterizes a specific country and this, in turn, affects the level and the dynamics of inequality. This approach is consistent with the sociological approach of Rehbein and Souza (2014), based on the analytical framework developed by Pierre Bourdieu.[5] The concluding comments will suggest an agenda for further studies.

Traditional framework

Since the origins of economic thought, income and wealth distribution theory and the notion of inequality have been interconnected, with the former mostly viewed as a main determinant of the latter. As Amartya Sen (1997: 77) points out, economic inequality "is sometimes viewed in relative terms, viz., as a departure from some notion of appropriate distribution. There are essentially two rival notions of the 'right' distribution of income, based respectively on needs and desert".[6]

In economic theory as a whole we can identify several major analytical approaches directly and indirectly relevant to the study of inequality. For the sake of simplicity, these can be grouped in ten research lines.

Microeconomic theory

When focusing on microeconomic theory we can distinguish five research lines mainly centred on the theory of production.[7] We first have to recall the theory of social income distribution which derives from the school of classical economists. The reference goes to such authors as Adam Smith (1723–1790), David Ricardo (1772–1823), John Stuart Mill (1806–1873) and Karl Marx (1818–1883). In this research line, land owners, physical and financial capital owners and workers form three distinct social classes, which participate in the distribution of the overall income respectively through rents, profits and wages. The composition of social classes is directly derived from the clear-cut roles played by their members in the production activity. While labor (wages) and capital (profits) share positive production roles, land owners (rents) play a parasitic one. Profits are conceived as a residual payoff after rents and wages have been deducted from the total product, and in the Marxian framework they imply exploitation. No overlapping is envisaged between social classes and the functioning of the production activity renders every needed account of the relevant class structure and the distribution shares. Inequality can be relevant, but mainly when comparing different social classes on the basis of both 'needs' and 'desert', while within each social class common economic conditions tend to prevail. Thus, inequality can bring about conflict between social classes over the distribution of income and wealth.

At the beginning of the 1960s this view influenced the development of the so called neo-Ricardian model, which proved the possibility of analyzing the distribution of income independently from the price system, in a different way from the pure labor theory of value. In this case the reference goes to the Piero Sraffa (1960) theory of income distribution in which the rate of profit can be interpreted as exogenous and linked to the rate of discount established by the central bank. In this case wages are conceived as a residual share and conflict between social classes is considered normal.

In deep disagreement with both variants of this model, the neoclassical (or marginalist) school proposed the second and fundamental (for mainstream economics) research line on income distribution theory, going back to scholars like William Stanley Jevons (1835–1882), Carl Menger (1840–1921) and Léon Walras (1834–1910). According to this theory, when we refer to a state of general equilibrium in the markets, the owners of the production factors take part in the distribution of income depending on the marginal productivity they are able to achieve. This means that only functional distribution of income matters for a good microeconomic performance. The assumption of constant returns to scale in the production function allows us to accept the Euler's, or product exhaustion, theorem, removing any dilemma about the distribution of the final residuum remaining after paying each production factor (including the workers) according to its marginal productivity. In other words, under these conditions, this residuum has a zero value. In this research line a good performance in the activity of production of each factor entails her/his full membership in the functional group to which she/he belongs, without any need to further care about the class structure. Inequality can be relevant, but, since it is fully explained by 'desert', it is quite acceptable from an economic and social point of view.

A different approach to the theory of income distribution linked to the study of market equilibria has been put forward by the Marshallian school, starting from the perspective of partial equilibrium analysis. The reference goes to Alfred Marshall (1842–1924). In this third research line the market forms differently from perfect competition, apart from leading to suboptimal results in terms of consumers' and producers' welfare, bringing about exploitation whenever the wages paid to the workers are lower than their marginal productivity. In this case, firms can benefit from a monopoly rent which adds to their normal profits. The case of monopsonistic exploitation in the labor market is a relevant instance in this respect.

This theory stresses the fact that exploitation can occur and this can leave room for disputes about the appropriation of the monopoly rent. This result, together with the so called Hicks–Marshall laws of derived demand,[8] helps to analyze the relative strength of workers with respect to entrepreneurs in wage bargaining. The aforementioned theory can be related to the study of inequality between functional classes and sectors of activity. Also, in this case, inequality is explained by 'desert', and no further investigation is made on the impact of these events on the social structure of economy.

In all the theories considered so far the distribution of income and wealth keeps a social or functional character. Even if, more or less directly, they also stem from the neoclassical school, the next two research lines focus on the personal character of distribution, which is viewed as a coherent and consequent feature of functional distribution.

In the fourth research line, we have to recall the Pareto distribution theory. This is a power law probability distribution that is used in the description and measurement of personal income distribution and inequality. The reference goes to Vilfredo Federico Damaso Pareto (1848–1923). The right tails of income and wealth distributions empirically observed often resemble the so called Pareto distributions or Pareto tails. The Pareto distribution emerges in many settings, both in economics (e.g., wealth and income distribution, firm size distribution, size of cities) and in other social sciences (e.g., language, family names, popularity, certain social network patterns, crime per convict), and even in various physical environments (e.g., size of large earthquakes, power outages). Pareto distributions might also provide some insights on the relationship between interest rates and growth rate and top inequality (Piketty 2014: 364). An important tool for measuring inequality has been developed by Corrado Gini (1884–1965). The Gini coefficient[9] can be used to compare income distributions across different population groups as well as countries. Within this framework of thought, inequality is taken as a fact of life and is described more than interpreted. Moreover, little investigation is made on its origins in the social structure of the economy (also because its nature is strictly personal and even social background is subjective).

For its relevance in theoretical and empirical literature a fifth research line is to be mentioned: the theory of long-run labor supply, which usually falls under the heading of human capital theory. Its foundations lie in the theory of personal income distribution first proposed by Jacob Mincer (1922–2006). Building on this, the human capital theory has been developed with essential contributions by Theodore William Schultz (1902–1998) and Gary Stanley Becker (1930–2014), regarding growth comparisons, labor market functioning in the long run and the economics of the family.

In this theoretical framework, assuming heterogeneity in the job and wage inter-temporal structure, the issue of optimal allocation of the market-time[10] by the individual is addressed between employments granting immediate earnings and employments yielding higher postponed ones through investment in human capital. Human capital is conceived of as the acquisition of cognitive skills which are able to increase individual productivity. The constraints under which the allocation of time takes place are given by the total time available, the social background of the individual, determining the opportunity costs of funding her/his investment and by the natural ability of the individual, influencing her/his capability to exploit the investment carried out. In the long run investment in human capital allows the individual to modify a constraint which is effective in the short run: the level of earnings she/he can achieve. This brings in earnings inequality because different endowments of human capital are differently rewarded even in perfect competition. This model is based on the compensating differentials theory put forward by Adam Smith,[11] which becomes a core linkage between the neoclassical theory of functional distribution of income and the human capital theory of personal income distribution.

This model has gained a very broad consensus in contemporary analyses all over the world, also due to its capacity of coupling sound paradigmatic extension of the neoclassical theory with robust empirical grounding.

Major bias

Currently, while a new reference framework is under formation, it is easier to detect some major bias in the way microeconomic theory addresses and studies inequality. While the classical and neo-Ricardian research lines have been caught off-guard by the deep transformation in class structure caused by structural economic change, the neoclassical research line and especially the two research lines focused on personal income distribution were able to endure in their respective roles of describing and interpreting inequality.

However, the adequacy of human capital theory to study inequality in present times is severely limited by at least three arguments. The first argument has been raised by James Heckman (2013; Cunha, Heckman and Schennach 2010) and concerns the disregard of human capital theory towards the effectiveness of early childhood education. This concentrates the analysis only on a limited span of the individual lifetime in which fundamental and irreversible choices concerning her/his knowledge accumulation have been already made. This limits the value of the theory in describing, interpreting and acting on inequality.

The second argument has been also raised by James Heckman, John Humphries and Tim Kautz (2014) and concerns the disregard of human capital theory towards the non-cognitive skills which, together with the cognitive skills, shape human capital and its economic effectiveness. This leads to restricting the analysis only to a subsection of human capital characteristics and to make impossible any interaction between human capital and social capital, while the notion of human development[12] could be a relevant linkage between the two previous concepts.

The third argument can be easily worked out by studies concerned, directly and indirectly, with the suitability of the human capital theory in post-Fordist economic environments[13] and/or in economies marked by the so called employment polarization[14] and the reduction of the middle class. Given the great attention paid to the middle class by the human capital theory, this could lead to limiting the analysis of inequality to a declining social group getting middle-wage jobs, leaving outside an increasing part of the population more and more concentrated, on the one side, in high-wage jobs, on the other, in low-wage jobs.

Very likely, the compartmentalization of human capital theory limits its value in describing and interpreting inequality and acting on it through policy measures capable of taking into account the various dimensions of human resources originating from their human capital components, but also from their human development and social capital components.[15]

Furthermore, we need to focus more on economic structure and embeddedness of human resources, because human capital can share the characteristics both of a private and a social good. In this respect, multidisciplinarity helps very much and this is why it is useful to also work in this line of thought in the present volume.

Macroeconomic theory

When focusing on macroeconomic theory we can distinguish five other main research lines, focused partly on aggregate production and partly on aggregate demand.

Main research lines

In a macroeconomic setting focused on aggregate production it is relevant to mention, first of all, a sixth research line designed by Simon Kuznets (1901–1985). Even if this theory mainly takes the form of an empirical law and concentrates its attention on inequality rather than income distribution, it has been highly influential in shaping the fundamental axioms concerning inequality on which the mainstream growth theory has been based. Kuznets (1955), using only US data for the period 1913–1948, suggested that in every country, over the course of industrialization and economic development, inequality follows a bell curve.[16] In this theory, inequality plays the role of an endogenous variable which decreases after a certain mean income threshold has been overtaken. Up until a few years ago, his optimistic prediction was able to persuade the majority of the economic profession.

A seventh and fundamental (for mainstream economics) research line on functional income distribution theory has been developed in a macroeconomic setting by Robert Solow (born 1924). He accepted and implemented in a macroeconomic model the theory of income distribution proposed by the neoclassical school (Solow 1956). In this framework, the shares of total income going to each production factor depend on its aggregate productivity. Therefore, only functional distribution of income matters for a good macroeconomic performance. Again, the assumption of constant returns to scale in the aggregate production function helps to remove, along the same lines seen before, any dilemma about the distribution of the final residuum remaining after paying each production factor according to its marginal aggregate productivity. In his model, technology is assumed to be the same across countries.

In a macroeconomic setting which is focused on aggregate demand, it is relevant to mention an eighth research line proposed by post-Keynesians economists such as Nicholas Kaldor (1908–1986), Joan Violet Robinson (1903–1983) and Luigi L. Pasinetti (born 1930). The main purpose of post-Keynesian distribution and growth theory has been to extend Keynes's principle of effective demand from the short run, taking the capital stock as constant and given, to the long run, in which the capital stock can vary. This means that aggregate demand is able to determine not only the level of output and employment in the short run, but also the growth of productive capacities and their utilization in the long run. Investment is the driving force of the process, and saving adjusts to investment, not only in the short run, but also in the long run. Whereas in the short run the focus is on the income effects of investment, abstracting from the effects of investment on the capital stock and on productive capacities, in the long run these effects have to be taken into account.

Kaldor (1956, 1957) found that income distribution matters because it affects the relationship between savings and economic growth. This comes in contrast, for instance, with the Solow (1956) growth model, where income distribution does not affect economic growth. More specifically, Kaldor showed that, assuming workers do not save, the natural rate of growth positively depends only on the rate of profit and the propensity of capitalists to save. Only investment and capitalists' saving propensity matter. This is the same result reached in the Kalecki and Keynes models. Kaldor's model was then adjusted by Pasinetti (1962), who identified a 'logical drift'. With his contribution, he achieved the result of re-stating Kaldor's original equations without relying on Kaldor's much criticized assumption. For that reason, we can speak of an integrated 'Kaldor-Pasinetti' model.

A very innovative feature is that this model deals with inequality on the consumption and saving side and not, as in the case of the previous typologies, on the production side. This feature is important because today, when dealing with income distribution, we can no longer confine our attention to only the production side, but we have to also consider how income and wealth are used in order to understand the channels through which the social structure of the economy can influence the sustainability of growth. Meanwhile, it becomes more difficult to distinguish between 'needs' and 'desert'.

The logic of the 'Keynesian theory of income distribution' has been extended by authors like Anthony Philip Thirlwall (2013) to the very controversial issue concerning the impact of trade liberalization on inequality. In the mainstream view, trade openness, monetary and fiscal policy, financial development and the rule of law are the more relevant determinants in explaining cross-country variation in growth rates.

Vicious circles fostered by austerity traps have been also studied under a ninth research line. They explain how ad hoc circumstances coupled with dominating consensus views can lead to failures which negatively impact on inequality.[17]

Adjustment patterns to the debt crisis of the 1980s have varied significantly among countries (Balassa 1989). Some developing countries, mostly in Latin America and Africa, adopted restrictive import regimes, deflationary government expenditure and macroeconomic policies and restraining wage policies, reduced subsidies, and liberalized their domestic markets to reduce their current account deficits, lower inflation and increase competitiveness. For the countries that followed this path, this was a lost development decade, with substantial increases in poverty, inequality and characterized by low-growth, from which these countries have started to emerge only in the 1990s.

(Adelman 2000: 8)

Studies on endogenous growth represent the tenth research line relevant for understanding the present attitude toward the analysis of income distribution in mainstream economics. The reference usually goes to economists like Paul Michael Romer (born in 1955) and Robert Emerson Lucas Jr. (born in 1937), even if the early contribution in this field can be attributed to Kaldor (1966).

In endogenous growth models (Romer 1986; Lucas 1988) technological change can give rise to increasing returns which affect long-term equilibrium growth prospects and can explain both low-level income trap and self-sustained per capita income growth. In particular, they assume that a 'social factor of production', not influenced by single agent's decisions, but influencing the productivity of all, can entail a positive externality. In this way, increasing returns to scale at the macro level are made compatible with constant returns to scale at the micro level, that is, with competition.

But, in considering the implications of these models on the theory of income distribution, we should acknowledge that with increasing returns to scale in the aggregate production function, we can no longer accept the Euler's or product exhaustion theorem. This leaves as unresolved the dilemma about the distribution of the final residuum remaining after paying each production factor according to its productivity, and conflict could emerge again.

Major bias

With respect to macro-economic theory we can detect four main biases. First, in contrast with the Kuznets' view, Adelman (2000: 14–18) stresses the fact that fifty years of development history show how inequality can play in several case studies the role of an exogenous variable which is negatively correlated with economic development. In these cases the relationship is reversed. Therefore a U-shaped course of inequality is not inevitable. More recently, Piketty (2014: 15) adds that:

The magical Kuznets curve theory was formulated in large part for the wrong reasons, and its empirical underpinnings were extremely fragile. The sharp reduction in income inequality that we observe in almost all the rich countries between 1914 and 1945 was due above all to the world wars and the violent economic and political shocks they entailed (especially for people with large fortunes). It had little to do with the tranquil process of intersectoral mobility described by Kuznets.

This dispute is of crucial importance for studying inequality, and, at least judging from the last evidence made available, the final outcome can be very influential in stressing that the multidisciplinary focus on the issue and its multidimensional character are essential ingredients of scientific research.

Second, since in the Solow model technology is the same across countries, the rates of growth in per capita income and in total factor productivity cannot diverge and give room to the study of preexisting baselines and social factors in the different regions of the world. The endogenous growth models introduced a correction in this respect, but with a serious consequence: the total irrelevance of a theory of distribution of income in current mainstream economics.

Third, under the assumption that growth is a process distribution neutral, the study of the impact of economic policies on within-country inequality can be split into two distinct phases: first, the main policies able to maximize the growth rate are identified; second, sign[18] and absolute value of the elasticity of inequality or poverty with respect to growth can be estimated (Berloffa and Segnana 2006: 374–5). The second phase is relevant not only for evaluating the impact of growth policies on inequality and poverty, but especially in order to assess the sustainability of growth in the long run. Moreover, the key role played in the growth process by the legal structure, and particularly by the security of property rights and by privatization, apart from allowing us to stress how composite is the nature of the determinants of growth and inequality even in the mainstream approach, is relevant also in order to assess the transferability of economic and institutional models in development, transition and reconstruction processes.

However, empirical evidence shows that the growth process can be "highly distributionally non-neutral", as it has been argued by Kanbur and Lustig (1999: 8). Furthermore, country specific conditions, which under appropriate circumstances may be ascribed to different models of capitalism, can make clear why the impact of the same policies is very different in terms of economic development and distribution of income and wealth or poverty.

> Trade and accumulation policies are important in determining the spread-effects of growth and how growth and inequality interact. . . . Export-oriented growth in labor-intensive, consumer goods industries is equalizing because it raises employment and returns to labor unless specific policies are instituted to foster low wages. Also, when export-oriented growth is accompanied by low tariffs and low exchange rates, it turns agricultural terms of trade in favor of farmers and lowers consumer goods prices, with favorable distributional consequences.
>
> (Adelman 2000: 16)

Fourth, Thirlwall (2013: 4) extends the investigation range to between-countries inequality and concludes that: "Trade liberalization almost certainly worsened the distribution of income between rich and poor countries, and between unskilled wage-earners and other workers within countries, contrary to the predictions of orthodox theory." If the global scenario is only approximately similar to the one drafted in the recent book by Piketty (2014), this causal factor of inequality has to be taken seriously into account.

Globalized nature of inequality

Main changes have occurred in the reference framework induced by globalization and global crisis.

Using stocks and flows of foreign direct investments (FDI) as indicators of globalization, we can observe that after a period of strong economic internationalization between 1870 and 1913, the stock of FDI fell by about one third relative to global GDP from 1930 to 1970. Afterwards, at the beginning of the 1990s, about 26 years ago, soon after the fall of the Berlin wall, the stock of FDI started to rise quickly, with the consequence that 85% of the global stock of FDI has been created after 1990. The sustained rise of the stock of FDI can be considered strong empirical evidence of the take-off of globalization.

The process is still continuing, even if with ups and downs after the year 2000, but the flow of FDI has been persistently slowing down since 2007. This has induced recent applied enquiries to distinguish two phases in the overall process of globalization, with the global crisis as an edge between the two. The first phase is supposed to go from about 1990 to 2007 and the second phase from 2007 to now.[19]

All these changes severely endanger some of the foundations of the economic models reviewed in section two and suggest that the very nature of inequality has changed.

In analyzing inequality within and between social classes, generations, regions and countries the conceptual framework has increasingly shifted towards the recognition that:

I   the overlapping of different levels of government contributes to mix up the institutional determinants of inequality, starting from taxation and incentives;
II   a leading role in driving general expectations on personal economic careers is carried out by the personnel strategies of global companies; and
III more information allowing for comparison of earnings opportunities and living standards in different regions of the world is spreading through social media and migration flows.

These are all reasons underlying a creeping inversion in the role played respectively by inequality analysis and distribution theory in economic thought. The vanishing of traditional social classes contributed to this shift and inequality seems to acquire a leading role relative to income and wealth distribution.

One of the essential reasons why this happens is to be found in a crucial feature of the globalization process. International companies, especially in the first phase of globalization, have become concerned with globalizing their customers, production and production factors. They strived for being run by global managers, owned by global shareholders, and for being able to sell global products to global customers. A crucial consequence is that traditional production factors (labor, capital and land) have been gradually transformed in 'broad production factors' (heterogeneous labor, human resources and management; physical and financial capital, innovation and technical change; natural and environmental resources).[20]

This concept helps to understand how firms become able to employ blends of more and more varied quantities and qualities of heterogeneous labor and human resources, physical and financial capital with technological change, natural and environmental resources. The increasing interaction, recombination, complementarity and mobility of production factors in international markets helped make them more flexible and operational in the innovative organization of networks and clusters.

The above transformation can also help to explain the decrease in the (actual and expected) share of national GDP going to employees both because of the increase of self-employment and the decline in quantity and quality of available jobs, due to other long run factors.[21] An analytical consequence of this is that the distribution of income and wealth and inequality cannot be completely ascribed to production activities and to the role individuals and social groups play in it.

What's more, the global crisis and its consequences still in action are showing us that even basic elements we used to regard as engines for equality in opportunities can be easily transformed over time into 'privileges' by adverse circumstances. This leads to blurring the boundaries, which are shaped by economic, social and institutional behaviors and constraints, between what we could define as a sustainable or unsustainable threshold of inequality. This can undermine the trade-off between the bad and the good side of inequality.

To the extent that this distinction in two phases of the globalization process is reliable and has to do also with the need of global companies to readjust their strategies, given that those pursued in the first phase have been put in danger by a strong decrease in profits in the second one, another analytical consequence is that variety in models of capitalism can persist, at least with respect to the more competitive of them.

While in the first phase, the apparent convergence of all countries towards the same model of democracy and capitalism seemed both a historical turning point and a huge opportunity, in the second phase a resurgence of different models of capitalism can be predictable. And this can have strong consequences on inequality.

Multidimensional inequality

It is rather common to distinguish between inequality in opportunities and inequality in outcomes. Much of the debate in development theory has been structured along these lines: the first is primarily concerned with factors that inhibit equitable outcomes, such as unequal access to employment or education; and the second deals with factors which influence the grade achieved in various material dimensions of human wellness, such as income or wealth. While the latter is regarded as a standard result of economic and social life, and particularly of a competitive game, the former begets disapproval as an infringement of democratic principles.

In any case, every judgment about inequality is extremely diverse for at least four indirect reasons: (a) Economies undergo deep transformations and are affected by outsourcing/unbundling and networks/value chains restructuring at a world scale. (b) Traditional economic and social classes are at the same time more and more fragmented, but less and less recognizable on account of specific roles performed in the economic systems (and in society in general). A range of income sources is available for the average worker, but these sources are not necessarily linked anymore to the factors of production the individual is endowed with. (c) Welfare perspectives vary according to the position held by the single agent in the household, in the society and in the networks in which she/he lives. (d) Different social and economic models of capitalism score rather different end results.

At the same time, different layers of inequality are becoming relevant: intra- and inter-generations; within and between genders; within and between countries (especially among developing countries, emerging powers, and less developed countries); within and between local economic systems; within and between employment categories (e.g., unions, professional associations); within and between social groups (e.g., economic, ethnic, religious groups).

Indeed, we must recognize, and the more so while we are still facing a global crisis, that: (a) income inequality represents only one of the several dimensions of economic inequality, (b) economic inequality may be determined by non-economic inequality and generate further economic and non-economic inequality and (c) non-economic inequality generates very important negative material and immaterial effects. All this makes it less simple to find easy compensations to the economic and non-economic costs of inequality.

Inequality, both at the macro-economic level, which refers to national and supra-national entities, at the meso-economic level, which refers to local communities, and at the micro-economic level, which refers to individuals and generations, is in its essence a multidimensional and cumulative phenomenon.

Even when we split income inequality, which depends on the personal and functional distribution of income and wealth, from other sorts of inequality this phenomenon remains multidimensional, meaning that it evokes different types of individual and social background leading to the final outcome. One of the most important reasons is that inequality depends on wealth and income distribution and that "in all societies, income inequality can be decomposed into three terms: inequality in income from labor; inequality in the ownership of capital and the income to which it gives rise; and the interaction between the two terms" (Piketty 2014: 238).

The relevance of ownership of capital and inheritance, which is strongly linked to the historical tradition, contributes to link economic inequality to the socio-institutional framework and the socio-cultural perspective. Talent and effort in this case are less important than inheritance and marriage in determining success and this in turns implies different tastes and behaviors. Just when we confine our research on inequality in income from labor, we have to be conscious that it can be derived from self-employment or wage labor, which imply totally different socio-economic conditions, in which also the provisional or permanent character of employment contributes to differentiate the socio-economic background.

Furthermore, economic inequality is critical, but the more we explore the extremes of the distribution the more we note an overlapping and a bumping up of different dimensions of inequality. Low per capita incomes are highly correlated with low quality of life, and therefore with variables like poor health, low education, higher uncertainty and insecurity of employment and low participation in civil society. Therefore, countries with a low human development index (HDI) suffer most because they tend to have greater inequality in more dimensions (UNDP 2013).

Besides, following Marmot (2013), we can distinguish between the material deprivation, which entails malnutrition, exposure to infected organisms, low resistance to their effects, exposure to hot and cold weather and to toxic elements and the processes conditioning adult mortality, which take place even when the poverty thresholds are overtaken. In this case, human capital and human development are affected by the living standard of the single person both in terms of their direct outcomes (life expectancy, productivity, income) and in terms of impact on their creation and destruction channels (education, healthcare). Another important implication is that a potential reduction in one dimension of inequality does not imply an even reduction in all its dimensions.

The multidimensionality issue becomes more and more important as the awareness of the constraints caused by the existence of a 'maximum sustainable inequality threshold' (MSIT) for the economy increases. We can define MSIT as the maximum level of inequality not inhibiting sustainable and inclusive growth in a given economic system (Antonelli 2013).

But, in order to pursue our argument in a more systematic way, it is convenient to investigate the different dimensions of inequality by singling out its basic characteristics, determinants and effects.

Nature

In the last quarter century, a deep rethinking on the notion of well-being led to a growing consensus that it results "from a combination of what a person has, what a person can do with what they have, and how they think about what they have and can do" (IDS 2009).

Along this line of reasoning, well-being embraces three basic components: (a) the material and economic one, stressing welfare conditions, standards of living and economic values; (b) the relational one, emphasizing personal and social relations; and (c) the subjective one, highlighting moral values and perceptions, side by side with option and existence values. The three components are merged together and their boundaries are highly fuzzy (McGregor 2007; Sumner and Mallett 2013).

This, in turn, has induced a multilayered revision of the notion of inequality, thanks to which nowadays experience and intuition also suggest that inequality is a multidimensional phenomenon.

It is important to specify that the multidimensional nature of inequality concerns each basic component per se as well as the connections between the three of them. We mean that, even separating the material and economic dimension from the others, and limiting the analysis of inequalities in each of the proxies for the standards of living, since this can concern variables such as income, wealth, education, health and nutrition, the multidimensional nature of inequality leaks out. Of course, the multidimensionality becomes broader if the three basic components are allowed to interact.

Among the non-economic components an essential role is played by ethnicity, gender and religion. In any case, beneath them, the access to many wants is often unevenly distributed and limited by economic constraints. Limiting ourselves only to very immediate examples, we could mention the option to use sophisticated drugs and cures, safe transports, qualified information and knowledge, natural and environmental resources of higher purity, and also a safe neighborhood in which to raise children. Direct and indirect linkages connect material and immaterial components of inequality. Income constraints can easily bring about fragilities and drive persons to suffer from non-economic dimensions of inequality.

The inequality in access to goods and resources and the limits to an inclusive growth process are often augmented by complementarities among goods and the increasing relevance of 'network products' which characterize the actual conditions of consumption. Moreover, the increasing diffusion of non-private goods, contrary to what could be envisaged, can contribute to increase inequality and decrease inclusiveness. It depends on the multiplicity of economic goods and the prevailing regulation structure for their provision. In both cases the quality of consumption is conditioned by the ease of use of related conditions and externalities.

Determinants

When we come to consider the determinants of inequality, we can easily realize how much the social and genetic components are able to influence the economic ones and conversely. Wealth, education and social privilege are strongly interrelated with psychological temper and genetic privilege.

At the personal and family level, a poor environment and lack of natural gifts tend to lower the probability of economic success and to increase income inequality over the life cycle. In fact, today, the majority of experts believe that behavior and development are influenced by both 'nature' and 'nurture', while a minority take the extreme nativist or extreme empiricist views. However, researchers and experts still debate the degree to which biology and environment influence behavior and performance. This suggests that the capability to take into account the interactions between the different dimensions of inequality is crucial.

At the nationwide and, especially, at the meso-economic level, the welfare infrastructure and public policies can be very important in supplying concrete and timely assistance to disadvantaged individuals and families in local communities. To the extent that micro-economic studies observe critical and sensitive periods in the life cycle of individuals, indicating, for instance, that some skills are more easily acquired during certain stages, for most configurations of disadvantage it is important to socially invest relatively more in the early stages of childhood than in later stages (Cunha, Heckman and Schennach 2010; Heckman 2013). Education, healthcare and social welfare services at the local level are therefore important drivers of the capability of a community to practice cohesion and civic virtues, with significant effects on the distribution of labor market performance and labor income opportunities.

In this respect, Adelman (2000: 18) adds another vital remark which is more appropriate in a meso-economic framework.

> Cultural factors play a significant role in shaping institutions and societal responses to new challenges and opportunities. . . . Both individualistic and communitarian cultures have advantages and disadvantages. . . . Individualistic responses foster innovation, dynamism, creative destruction and geographic and social inequality. . . . Communitarian responses foster social cohesion and the social ability to absorb change, and hence national resilience and malleability. They place a premium on social equity in growth outcomes and foster societal and governmental approaches to development. They also enable societies to more easily absorb short run decreases in personal welfare in the interest of the common long run good (Rodrik 1997, 1998).

Other determinants relevant at the macro-economic level have been discussed above.

Effects

Having so far stressed how much both basic characteristics and determinants of inequality are multidimensional, we cannot be surprised by the fact that the effects of inequality also share the same character. The relationship between inequality and growth or development has been examined, especially at the macro-economic level, by a number of authors proving that high initial levels of the former may be harmful to the second, in this way discarding the assumption that growth is a process distribution neutral.

Irma Adelman (2000) tried to single out eight main lessons about the process of economic development experienced in half a century by developing countries, which has been understood as both multidimensional and highly non-linear. In her view, "The distribution of income is established mainly through the primary distribution of income that is generated by the production-determined circular flow" (2000: 14) Moreover, "There is scope for choice in institutions, policies and in their sequencing, even at similar levels of development. The choices made, in turn, generate the initial conditions for subsequent development" (2000: 6). Therefore, stages of development matter and different case studies, mostly East Asian, suggest that equalitarian policies, pointing at the redistribution of the property of original factors of production (like land or education and human capital), drove some countries to travel "the whole path from underdeveloped to developed, since the end of World War Two" (2000: 1).

In general, looking at the overall picture in developed countries, we are led to take into account two equally relevant sides of the story. On the one hand, inequality and polarization of earnings can have a strong negative impact on several crucial spheres of the economic systems, such as contractual disputes, social instability and transaction costs. Even the solidity of a stable relationship between different generations, which favor their cooperation to common goals, can be jeopardized, making it more complex to reach agreements at the individual and collective level. Furthermore, inequality can be considered a concurrent cause of decline in the middle-class prominence, which is currently destabilizing the economic and social setting in different countries.

On the other hand, inequality in performance and outcomes can be regarded as an ordinary result of competition in everyday life, not conflicting with a sustainable growth. Therefore, in order to discriminate between physiologic and pathologic inequality and to assess to what extent this trade-off risks to be unbalanced, an order of magnitude has to be ascertained. This is why it is important to take into consideration the notion of MSIT for an economy.

Definition and measurement of this threshold are subject to two conditions. First, it should refer to a kind of inequality which violates equality in opportunities. Second, it should refer to a level of inequality which does not match with economic, social and environmental sustainability.

This issue has been tackled as a rule indirectly by economic theory, in many different ways, even without knowing exactly at what level MSIT is positioned and more than that, even without being able to measure it in a comprehensive way. However, this option also has to be explored.

But this question can no longer be avoided, when no credible solutions exist. And the problem, unhappily, is that this is becoming even truer. In fact, for different reasons and with varying severity, the effectiveness of the three methods generally employed in the past for this purpose dramatically decreased by the end of the twentieth century.[22] And when the main available gateways to the equity issue fail, this, by itself, makes it more necessary to find alternatives: estimating the actual value of MSIT is one among them.

Learning from the models of capitalism theory

Summing up the main conclusions reached in the last two sections, we may focus on four crucial aspects.

(a) The evolution of the globalization process fostered a change in the very nature of inequality and its second phase could facilitate a resurgence of the variety in models of capitalism.

(b) The debate on the foundations of inequality points out its multidimensional nature and recommends high attention to the fact that different concepts and measures of inequality generate even more different results.

(c) The dispute on the determinants of within-country inequality let emerge its multidimensional causes and suggested that a non-secondary role has been played by economic and institutional factors that are internal, area specific and local, together with the global and external ones. This implies that we have to take into account several forces interacting at the micro-, meso- and macro-level.

(d) The study of the effects of globalized and multidimensional inequality shows how crucial its initial level can be for subsequent development. At this layer, the issue concerning the relevance and definition of an MSIT can be raised with significant implications for the sustainability and inclusiveness of economic growth. This threshold can vary in different models of capitalism, but we can also try to devise analytical tools for comparing their specific MSIT in order to assess their degree of sustainability.

Following this way of reasoning, we may conclude that the way in which different economic and social systems evolve in terms of income and wealth distribution paths and, more generally, in terms of sustainable and inclusive development, depends on four pillars:

(a) the baseline, that is the initial economic and institutional structure of each system;
(b) the capacity of each system to cope with and adapt to its 'natural' drift;
(c) the aptitude of each system to face and absorb global shocks; and
(d) the capacity of each system to react and adapt to private strategies and public policies.

On the whole, an appropriate theoretical framework for dealing with such complex phenomena requires starting from the analysis of the interrelated subsystems from which the overall outcomes derive.

The basic idea is that the institutional architecture of each economic system promotes the adoption of some specific change and innovation, while penalizing some others, through the establishment of complementarities involving enterprises and networks, macro-economic regulation and functioning of goods, services and inputs markets, labor markets and channels for human resources education and training. This approach, based on the idea that different models of capitalism determine the existing incentive structure and compete with each other, is theoretically grounded in real economic facts.[23] Tax rates, benefit systems and access to the welfare system in the different models of capitalism can be very influential in determining their performance in terms of inequality.[24]

Varieties of capitalism are originated by variety in interrelated sub-systems, whose main domains are the product markets, the labor markets, the financial markets, social protection, education and innovation. The support of a model able to nourish such an effort at the theoretical level is as much important as the availability of multidimensional indicators at the empirical one.

However, we have to put forward two fundamental clarifications in order to avoid fatal misunderstandings. The models of capitalism theory recognize a fundamental role of institutional structure in explaining the evolution of the economic systems, but, and this is the first warning, it cannot be confused with neo-institutionalism or pan-institutionalism. The neo-institutionalist literature in economics tends to emphasize the endogeneity of institutional rules, the limits of economic policy and the boundlessness of institutional reforms when aiming at improving the performance of national economies. In this way, it tends to ignore the complexity of interactions which determine their performance and swamp into pan-institutionalism. As suggested by Schettkat (2003) and Zenezini (2006), best practices are considered key research questions and dominant prescriptions in the realm of institutional architecture.

Although in the literature on models of capitalism a model cannot be defined without complex institutions, because they shape and regulate the interactions between agents, institutions play the role of resources as well as constraints. This difference can be better assessed if we consider that in the neo-institutionalist literature the economic structure interacting with the institutional one is straightforwardly based on the general equilibrium theory and the theoretical model is neutral with respect to the empirical setting. Therefore, the step of empirical investigation becomes a purely descriptive application of this model, the rules derived from the best practices becomes universal and the 'rule of law' is transferable over all.

This is not true for the literature on models of capitalism theory. In this case, first of all, the institutional complexity is accommodated in the model through the notion of 'interrelated sub-systems' and complementarities are not necessarily positive, leaving ground for failures. Moreover, this literature does not pretend to explain all kinds of performance of the economic systems, and, what is more important, it is based on a different theory of economic structure. Its main assumptions turn out to be the following:

(a) non-optimality of the final configurations (no single best solution can be achieved);
(b) diversity in micro-, meso-and macro-objectives prevails;
(c) redundance and resilience are considered as much important as effectiveness;
(d) real economic interdependences are relevant for describing the economic structure;
(e) income distribution and inequality are not explained completely in an endogenous way.

In this manner, institutional structure and economic structure are always interacting, for at least three basic reasons. First, economic structure and institutional structure relate at the same level of abstraction and institutions cannot be interpreted simply as empirical artifacts or ad hoc elements relevant only when we come at the applied stage of research. Second, the behavior of agents coherent with the economic assumptions is shaped by the action of 'institutional entrepreneurs' (e.g., élites, policy makers at the different levels of government and governance) in the making of institution building. Third, scarcity of economic resources often conditions the constraining character of the institutional rules and affects the way fundamental rights are reshaped by law in books rather than law in action.

The search for complementarities or codetermination between institutional structure and economic structure becomes the core purpose of scientific research based on two methodological assumptions:

(a) institutional rules, legal codes and constitutions are necessary, but not sufficient conditions for cohesion and sustainability of economies and societies;
(b) institutional rules, which are essentially varied and partial, derive from different value judgments associated with different cultures and specific historical backgrounds.

The second warning is tantamount and crucial, since it makes clear that focusing on interrelated sub-systems does not amount to believing that mechanical and deterministic forces control the interactions. Apart from the relevance of the stochastic components, the multiplicity of potential outcomes does not allow the set of the final configurations of each economic system to be enfolded in few and arbitrary categories. This statement can be better understood if we focus on the meaning of complementarity and match it with an applied example.

The notion of complementarity is manifold and, contrary to what may be thought, its most appropriate meaning in models of capitalism theory refers to the occurrence of mutually compensating components rather than of reciprocally reinforcing components or similarities.[25] Therefore, to the extent that balancing characteristics in one way or another are better describing institutional complementarities in the theory of models of capitalism, determinism is prevented from exercising a significant role in it.

The ever-changing taxonomies arranged for describing the different models of capitalism can be interpreted as provisional outcomes of a theory in search of more comprehensive models and of greater ability to work out this challenge. The taxonomy can change in each given point of time and over time because models of capitalism can evolve through the transformation of complementarities.

Concluding comments

Taking into consideration the contribution of traditional economic literature on income and wealth distribution in the light of the globalized and multidimensional nature of inequality suggests that we have to amend several biases and that a new, lengthy and complex research path has to be planned, even more so if we want to reach outcomes that are reliable from a didactic point of view.

Multidisciplinary studies are essential, but they cannot be conceived as short-cuts with respect to the need for new analytical, qualitative and quantitative tools, starting from new appropriate indicators and databases.

On the qualitative side, it is of crucial importance to study how to reintroduce in the economic analysis of inequality and income and wealth distribution a proper theory of class structure. The lack of a theory of a class structure in modern economies helped to marginalize distributional issues in economics. Functional and personal income distribution theories in the neoclassical setting, coupled with the conjecture that Euler's theorem could help in avoiding the study of conflicts on distributional issues, contributed to give support to this neglect.

The unspoken relevance of the middle class as a basic precondition for a sound application of the human capital theory to the interpretation of personal income distribution is a vanishing key factor.

On the quantitative side, it is of crucial importance to study how to implement sound measures of globalized and multidimensional inequality capable of giving actual consistence in economic models to the notions of sustainability and inclusiveness of economic development. This is important both from an analytical point of view and in order to plan ahead for feasible incentive structures and cohesion schemes in local and global communities. In this framework, it can be relevant to devise appropriate indicators of MSIT for comparisons between and within different models of capitalism.

Notes

1 And different paradigmatic models have been developed by different schools of thought all along the history of economic analysis.
2 In institutional contexts totally different from close national systems.
3 In this section I will try to include also less traditionally recognized contributions in the field.
4 In this respect the room left by Piketty (2014) to the contributions of the classical and neoclassical schools cannot be considered appropriate.
5 See also Boike Rehbein and Jessé Souza in this volume.
6 As Amarthya Sen (1997: 77) writes: "It is easy to recognize the contrast between arguments of the kind: 'A should get more income than B since his needs are greater', and those of the type: 'A should get more income than B since he has done more work and deserves a higher reward'. Inequality can, therefore, be viewed not merely as a measure of dispersion but also as a measure of the difference between the actual distribution of income on the one end and *either (i)* distribution according to the needs *or (ii)* that according to some concept of desert."
7 Following the traditional view, four are the main typologies of income and wealth distribution theories that have been developed in the framework of economic analysis (Quadrio Curzio and Pasotti 2011).
8 The so-called Hicks-Marshall laws of derived demand suggest that, other things being equal, the own-wage elasticity of demand for a category of labor is high under the following conditions.

   (a) When the price elasticity of demand for the product being produced is high (scale effect). So when final product demand is elastic, an increase in wages will lead to a large change in the quantity of the final product demanded affecting employment greatly.

(b) When other factors of production can be easily substituted for the category of labor (substitution effect).

(c) When the supply of other factors of production is highly elastic (that is, usage of other factors of production can be increased without substantially increasing their prices) (substitution effect). That is, employers cannot easily replace labor as doing so will lead to a large increase in other factor prices making it useless.

(d) When the cost of employing the category of labor is a large share of the total costs of production (scale effect).

9 The Gini coefficient is an index of statistical dispersion widely used to measure the income or wealth distribution in various types of communities. It is defined as a ratio with values between 0 and 1: the numerator is the area between the Lorenz curve of the distribution and the uniform distribution line; the denominator is the area under the uniform distribution line. The interpretation of a Gini coefficient can raise issues, because the same value may result from many different distribution curves.

10 Another alternative in the allocation of time, concerning time worked not for the market, can be added in the framework of the economics of the family.

11 As clarified by Mark Blaug (1978: 48–9), Adam Smith "traces all differences in wage rates in stationary equilibrium to differences in: (1) the agreeableness of different occupations, (2) the cost of acquiring the skill to carry them on, (3) the degree of regularity of employment, (4) the trust and responsibility imposed upon those employed, and (5) the probability of actually obtaining anticipated earnings given the great uncertainty of success in some lines of employment." The second cause "contains the germ of an idea that is only now being fully exploited, namely, the concept of human capital."

12 See Anand and Sen (1997). Most of the academic literature on the concept of human development is focused on the capability approach. In fact, the writings of Amartya Sen on human capabilities provided the philosophical foundation of human development. However:

> the capability approach explicitly draws on a long lineage of thinkers, including Aristotle, Smith, Kant, Mill and Marx among others. In the more recent past, Sen acknowledges the Basic Needs approach....Whilst acknowledging many authors and sources, the capability approach drew together several aspects only some of which have been stressed in previous approaches. Some of the key features of this work are:
>
> • a focus on people as the "ends" of development; clarity about ends and means. People-centred.
> • a substantive notion of freedom related to well-being (capabilities) and agency (empowerment)
> • a focus on that freedom being "real" – not just paper freedom but an actual possibility
> • a well-being objective that includes multiple capabilities – that need not be unidimensional
> • stable curiosity regarding the causal connections between different dimensions of human development and between economic growth and human development
> • a focus on supporting people as active agents, not passive victims, of development
> • an ability to prioritise capabilities for poor people across time while keeping in view the development of rich persons and of non-material capabilities.
>
> (Alkire 2010: 14–15)

13 See Antonelli and Cainelli (2001).

14 See Autor and Katz (2010).

15 The notion of portability of skills in migration choices (Borjas 1987), that is of a strong positive correlation between earnings in the source and host countries which ensures that skills are portable across countries, can be considered as an important instance of

realization of this need of blending together the notions of human capital and social capital, while taking into account economic structure and embeddedness.

16   The Kuznets curve diagrams show an inverted U curve with inequality, usually measured by the Gini coefficient, on the y-axis and economic development, usually measured by per-capita GDP, on the x-axis.

17   In this case, as also the recent evidence for European Union shows, countries that most ruthlessly cut their budgets see their overall debt loads increase as a share of their GDP.

18   Which, coherently with what we have seen before about the Kuznets curve, is assumed to be positive.

19   See in particular *The Economist* (January 28–February 3, 2017).

20   For further details see Antonelli (1997).

21   And, among them, those implied by the 'robotization' and 'uberization' scenarios.

22   There were three main methods used in the twentieth century to curb inequality. All of these methods were based on long-term processes. Underpinning the efforts at reducing economic inequality in all three cases was a recognition that social equality through equal citizenship had to be created. This meant that equal citizenship was created across genders, religions, castes, ethnicities and regions through law. Countries and societies in which those efforts have been made may not have achieved social equality enshrined fully in law, but that is the official benchmark they have established for themselves. A leading role of middle classes was crucial to this purpose.

The more direct method has been focused on the redistribution of real assets. Therefore, land and educational reforms, nationalization of industries and services were ways to create economic equity, not only in the socialist and communist countries, but also in the emerging capitalist ones.

The second method, prevalent in the capitalist societies, was based on the redistribution of income through progressive taxation. The 'welfare state', by taxing the rich more and spending more on public programs aimed at creating a system of gradual, but sustained reduction in income inequality.

The third method was shifting the burden to ensure equity in the distribution of personal incomes to the mechanism of 'compensating income differentials' through private investment in human capital.

Unfortunately, as mentioned, the performance of these three methods had seriously worsened well before the end of the twentieth century, for different reasons and with differing degrees of severity.

23   A first step in this line of research has been endorsed by authors like Albert (1991) and Prodi (1991). A second and more comprehensive step has been carried out among the others by authors like Amable (2000, 2003) and Aoki (2001).

24   Amable (2003) highlights five different models of capitalism: (1) market-based capitalism (Australia, United Kingdom, United States and Canada); (2) Asian capitalism (Japan and Korea); (3) continental European capitalism (Switzerland, Netherlands, Ireland, Germany, France, Norway, Belgium and Austria); (4) social-democratic capitalism (Denmark, Finland and Sweden); and (5) Mediterranean capitalism (Greece, Italy, Spain and Portugal).

25   As suggested by Crouch et al. (2005: 359–63), these two notions coexist with the notion employed in the economic theory of consumption for distinguishing between substitute and complementary goods and with the general notion of similarity. The first one shares with that focusing on mutually compensating components the notion of completion through compensation.

References

Adelman, Irma (2000) 'Fifty Years of Economic Development: What Have we Learned?', Paper prepared for the World Bank European Annual Bank Conference on Development Economics, Washington, D.C.: World Bank.

Albert, Michel (1991) *Capitalisme Contre Capitalisme*, Paris: Editions du Seuil.

Alkire, Sabina (2010) 'Human Development: Definitions, Critiques, and Related Concepts', Oxford University, OPHI Working paper, No. 36.

Amable, Bruno (2000) 'Institutional Complementarity and Diversity of Social Systems of Innovation and Production', *Review of International Political Economy*, Vol. 7, No. 4: 645–87.

Amable, Bruno (2003) *The Diversity of Modern Capitalism*, Oxford: Oxford University Press.

Anand, Sudhir and Amarthia Sen (1997) 'Concepts of Human Development and Poverty: A Multidimensional Perspective', in *Human Development Papers 1997*, Human Development Report Office, New York: UNDP, 1–19.

Antonelli, Gilberto (1997) 'Broad Production Factors and Technological Systems', in G. Antonelli and N. De Liso (eds.) *Economic Analysis of Structural Change and Technical Progress*, London: Routledge, 86–106.

Antonelli, Gilberto (2013) 'Structural Economic Dynamics and Multi-Dimensional Inequality', Focus Asia Workshop on "Entrenched Inequalities: East and West", Centre for East and South-East Asian Studies, Lund University, March.

Antonelli, Gilberto and Giulio Cainelli (2001) 'Politica Formativa come Politica Economica: Limiti e Efficacia', in M. R. Carrillo and A. Zazzaro (eds.) *Istituzioni, Capitale Umano e Sviluppo del Mezzogiorno*, Napoli: Edizioni Scientifiche Italiane, 221–55.

Aoki, Masahiko (2001) *Toward a Comparative Institutional Analysis*, Cambridge, MA: MIT Press.

Autor, David H. and Lawrence F. Katz (2010) 'Grand Challenges in the Study of Employment and Technological Change'. A white paper prepared for the National Science Foundation, Harvard University and NBER, September.

Balassa, Bela (1989) Exports, Policy Choices and Economic Growth in Developing Countries After the 1973 Oil Shock. Reprinted in Balassa, B. (ed.) *Comparative Advantage, Trade Policy and Economic Development*, New York: New York University Press, 323–37.

Berloffa, Gabriella and Maria Luigia Segnana (2006) 'Trade, Poverty and Growth: Two Perspectives, One Message?', in N. Salvadori (ed.) *Economic Growth and Distribution: On the Nature and Causes of the Wealth of Nations*, Cheltenham: Edward Elgar, 374–412.

Blaug, Mark (1978) *Economic Theory in Retrospect*, Cambridge: Cambridge University Press.

Borjas, George J. (1987) 'Self-Selection and the Earnings of Immigrants', *American Economic Review*, Vol. 77, No. 4: 531–53.

Crouch, Colin, Wolfgang Streeck, Robert Boyer, Bruno Amable, Peter A. Hall and Gregory Jackson (2005) 'Dialogue on Institutional Complementarity and Political Economy', *Socio-Economic Review*, Vol. 3, No. 2: 359–82.

Cunha, Flavio, James J. Heckman and Susanne M. Schennach (2010) 'Estimating the Technology of Cognitive and Noncognitive Skill', NBER Working Paper Series, No. 15664, February.

Heckman, James J. (2013) *Giving Kids a Fair Chance: A Strategy That Works*, Cambridge, MA: MIT Press.

Heckman, James J., John Eric Humphries and Tim Kautz (2014) (eds.) *The Myth of Achievement Tests: The GED and the Role of Character in American Life*, Chicago: University of Chicago Press.

IDS (Institute for Development Studies) (2009) 'After 2015: Rethinking Pro-Poor Policy', Focus Policy Briefing, Issue 09.

Kaldor, Nicholas (1956) 'Alternative Theories of Distribution', *The Review of Economic Studies*, Vol. 23, No. 2: 83–100.

Kaldor, Nicholas (1957) 'A Model of Economic Growth', *The Economic Journal*, Vol. 67, No. 268: 591–624.

Kaldor, Nicholas (1966) *Causes of the Slow Growth in the United Kingdom*, Cambridge: Cambridge University Press.

Kanbur, Ravi and Nora Lustig (1999) 'Why Is Inequality Back on the Agenda?' Paper prepared for the Annual Bank Conference on Development Economics, Washington, DC: World Bank.

Kuznets, Simon (1955) 'Economic Growth and Income Inequality', *The American Economic Review*, Vol. 45, No. 1: 1–28.

Lucas, Robert Emerson (1988) 'On the Mechanics of Economic Development', *Journal of Monetary Economics*, Vol. 22, No. 1: 3–42.

Marmot, Michael (2013) *Fair Society, Healthy Lives*, Florence: Casa Editrice Leo S. Olschki.

McGregor, J. Allister (2007) 'Researching Well-Being: From Concepts to Methodology', in I. Gough and J. A. McGregor (eds.) *Wellbeing in Developing Countries*, Cambridge: Cambridge University Press.

Pasinetti, Luigi L. (1962) 'Rate of Profit and Income Distribution in Relation to the Rate of Economic Growth', *The Review of Economic Studies*, Vol. 29, No. 4: 267–79.

Piketty, Thomas (2014) *Capital in the Twenty-First Century*, Cambridge, MA: The Belknap Press of Harvard University Press.

Prodi, Romano (1991) 'C'è un Posto per l'Italia tra i Due Capitalismi?' *Il Mulino*, Vol. 41, No. 1: 21–33.

Quadrio Curzio, Alberto and Ilaria Pasotti (2011) *Distribuzione del Reddito, Dizionario del liberismo italiano*, Cosenza: Rubettino editore.

Rehbein, Boike and Jessé Souza (2014) 'Inequality in Capitalist Societies', *Transcience: A Journal of Global Studies*, Vol. 5, No. 1: 16–27.

Rodrik, Dani (1997) 'The "Paradoxes" of the Success State', *European Economic Review*, Vol. 21: 411–42.

Rodrik, Dani (1998) 'Globalisation, Social Conflict and Economic Growth', *The World Economy*, Vol. 41: 143–58.

Romer, Paul Michael (1986) 'Increasing Returns and Long-Run Growth', *Journal of Political Economy*, Vol. 94, No. 5: 1002–37.

Schettkat, Ronald (2003) 'Institutions in the Economic Fitness Landscape: What Impact do Welfare State Institutions Have on Economic Performance?' Institute for the Study of Labor, IZA, Bonn, January, mimeo.

Sen, Amartya (1997) *On Economic Inequality*, Oxford: Oxford University Press; enlarged edition with a substantial annexe *On Economic Inequality after a Quarter Century* by James Foster and Amartya Sen.

Sraffa, Piero (1960) *Production of Commodities by Means of Commodities: Prelude to a Critique of Economic Theory*, Cambridge: Cambridge University Press.

Solow, Robert M. (1956) 'A Contribution to the Theory of Economic Growth', *The Quarterly Journal of Economics*, Vol. 70, No. 1: 65–94.

Sumner, Andy and Richard Mallett (2013) 'Capturing Multidimensionality: What Does a Human Wellbeing Conceptual Framework Add to the Analysis of Vulnerability?' *Social Indicators Research*, Vol. 113, No. 2: 671–90.

Thirlwall, Antony Philip (2013) 'The Rhetoric and Reality of Trade Liberalization in Developing Countries', *Rivista Italiana degli Economisti*, Vol. 18, No. 1: 3–24.

UNDP (2013) Humanity Divided: Confronting Inequality in Developing Countries, New York: United Nations Development Programme.

Zenezini, Maurizio (2006) 'Sono Davvero Importanti le Istituzioni del Mercato del Lavoro per Capire la Disoccupazione?' Dipartimento di Scienze Economiche e Statistiche, Università di Trieste, Working paper No. 103.

3 Globalization, capitalism and inequality

Boike Rehbein and Jessé Souza

Few people would dispute that globalization in the twentieth century was linked to colonialism and the expansion of Western capitalism.[1] In the twenty-first century, the connection between globalization and Western capitalism becomes less obvious. On the one hand, very few nation states today cannot be classified as capitalist. On the other hand, the West has lost its dominant role, while societies in the rest of the world are adapting capitalism to their own cultures, structures and institutions. Capitalism in the twenty-first century will be more global in its reach than ever before but it will also be more diverse and shaped by former colonies as much as by the global North (cf. Antonelli in this volume).

Colonialism introduced a dependency structure integrating the colonies into the capitalist world economy (Frank 1969). But this integration did not allow them to generate their own capitalist classes and their own capitalist modes of production. This has changed slowly with independence. The elites of the newly independent nation states experimented with different political and economic systems but most had embraced capitalism by the early twentieth century. This is partly the result of pressures from international institutions dominated by the global North, partly of continuing inequalities in the world market but partly of active decisions by these elites themselves, who have turned into capitalists and joined the group of the global rich. This chapter looks at the three aspects of the capitalist expansion, global inequality and capitalists on a global scale. It will do so with the goal of uncovering the global and national structures of domination, which we consider to be the roots of all three of these issues.

Capitalism and capitalists

David Harvey (2005) has described the expansion of capitalism after the end of colonialism quite convincingly. He links the expansion to neoliberalism and attributes it to a response to the stagflation after the oil crisis and the end of Bretton Woods. The actual reason for the adoption of neoliberalism in the global North, according to Harvey, was the downturn of the profit rates to the degree of becoming negative. This was "a clear *political* threat to economic elites and ruling classes everywhere" (2005: 15). The economic downturn was coupled with considerable bargaining power on the part of the working classes and trade unions in many Western countries because of the Communist threat during the Cold War. The economic and political concessions reduced the share of wealth held by the top one percent considerably. Against this background, Harvey argues, neoliberalism can be interpreted as a Western political project to reinstall the power of the economic elites (2005: 19).

The project began as an experiment by the so-called Chicago Boys in Chile after 1975 and was firmly established by Thatcher and Reagan in the 1980s. Corporate taxes were slashed, salaries stopped experiencing any increase and money supply was strictly controlled. Under the conditions of the ensuing recession, making money in the US and the UK became difficult. Harvey (2005: 27) argues that this was the backdrop for the globalization of neoliberal capitalism. During the domestic recession, American banks turned to financing foreign governments. The US government supported the project by opening the foreign countries, by putting them under pressure through the IMF and by liberalizing the international financial system. Mexico's bankruptcy in 1982 marked the turn, according to Harvey. Until then, lending to governments had been done at the lender's risk but from then on, the regulations shifted the burden to the governments by forcing them to sign contracts that make repayment their first priority (Harvey 2005: 29).

From his account, Harvey draws two conclusions that are relevant in terms of inequality (2005: 33–6). First, he argues that the "financialization of everything" transferred economic power back to the capitalists. Second, this process privileged managers over owners of capital and thereby opened up the opportunity of upward mobility to new entrepreneurs, especially financial wizards. As a consequence, the global expansion of neoliberal capitalism gave rise to a new "class" consisting not only of capital owners but also of individuals occupying leading positions in companies, finance, trade and R&D.

Apart from the fact that Harvey does not define his notion of class, it is evident that he subsumes the owners and the manipulators of economic capital under the "dominant class". We will argue that this account sheds light on some aspects of capitalism and the economy but completely misunderstands the relation between class and domination. This is due not only to the lacking definition of class but also to a reductive reading of Marx, whose theory forms the backdrop of Harvey's argument. Before exploring this issue, we will deal with the implications of Harvey's account for economic inequality.

The extreme concentration of economic capital since the 1970s in all capitalist societies and on a global scale can no longer be denied (Piketty 2014). However, this concentration is much worse than it seems. All analyses of wealth inequality demonstrate that the richest fraction owns more economic capital than the rest of the population. The latest, rather shocking Oxfam report (Hardoon 2017) calculates that the top percent of the world population owns as much as the entire rest combined. But actually, both the number and the term are misleading. More than 99.9 percent of the world population do not own any means that can be used as *capital*, even if they own goods or money. The overwhelming majority of human beings owns very little and those who do own something consume what they own: their private home, their car, their clothes, their luxury goods. They do not own capital. To compare relatively rich individuals, managers and R&D developers with the owners of capital in the same statistic is a category mistake both in Harvey's account and in the Oxfam report.

If we specify who owns economic capital that can be invested for profit, we see an extreme concentration of capital in the hands of very few. The capitalists own basically the *entire* economic capital in the strict sense. According to the Global Wealth Report, 34 million persons, or far less than one percent of the world population, own wealth of more than one million USD (Stierli et al. 2015: 20). In the US, it is five percent of the population, in Western European countries up to two percent and in the poorest of the former colonies only a handful. Western Europe, North America, Japan and Australia host 83 percent of the world's millionaires. Of the millionaires, only four million own wealth worth more than five million USD. In Western Europe, North America, Japan and Australia, much less than five million will be enough to buy a nice house, a summer house, a couple of luxury cars and a boat. That is, even the overwhelming majority of millionaires do not qualify as capitalists. This leaves us with less than 0.1 percent of the world population as actual capitalists, most of whom are citizens of Europe and North America. If we talk about wealth for the rest of the population, we are not talking about economic capital in the strict sense.

A similar picture emerges when we look at the global economy. A lot of companies exist in the world but they do not really compete for economic power. They contribute to production and are most relevant for providing goods and labor but do not yield any significant influence on the global market. Vitali, Glattfelder and Battiston (2011) have studied the network of transnational corporations (TNC) and their ownership. They identified 43.000 TNCs, 295 of which form the core of a global network. Within the core, three quarters of the corporations' shares are held by other TNCs of the core. One hundred forty-seven of them hold 40 percent of all TNC shares. The authors conclude that these 147 TNCs control the global economy and themselves. Actually, they control about a quarter of global GDP. The nation states account for another huge part, which we estimate at 40 percent.

This means that the global economy is controlled by fewer than 200 private companies and a smaller number of large nation states. Both the states and the corporations are primarily located in Western Europe and North America (Vitali et al. 2011: 26). Just as Harvey argues, private investors play a decreasing role, both as managing owners of the TNCs and as shareholders. But they invest via financial institutions, which belong to the core of the above-mentioned network of TNCs. Some of these institutions require a minimum investment of up to 1 billion USD. This restricts the circle of possible investors to a very small group, namely the capitalists we mentioned above.

We define the owners of economic capital in the strict sense as the dominant economic class or the capitalist class. In contrast to Harvey, we claim that they continue to control the global economy even under the conditions of neoliberalism and financialization. It is a very small group of people, mostly citizens of the nation states that were dominant in the twentieth century but also an increasing number of the rich elites in the global South, who have adopted capitalism. Mobility into this group of capitalists is possible, especially under the new conditions of financial capitalism that Harvey described. However, managers and other employees who have to work for their livelihoods are not members of this class.

Economic and social classes

Our main point is that this notion of economic class must be distinguished from that of social class and that social class is more fundamental than economic class. Interestingly, both notions have been developed by Marx, albeit in different phases of his life and not in conjunction. In the *Communist Manifesto* (1964) he distinguishes between the capitalist class, the laboring class, the petty bourgeoisie in between the two and the so-called lumpenproletariat at the bottom. *The Capital* (1953) talks of only two classes, capital and labor. However, it is evident that the other two classes exist even for the later Marx.

We argue that the two systems of class categories make sense only if we interpret capital and labor as economic classes, since *The Capital* mainly deals with the economy, and the four earlier classes as social classes. Harvey does not address this issue. However, it is evident that not every manager, who makes a lot of money, has enough economic capital to act as a capitalist. It is also evident that a football player whose wealth exceeds a couple of million USD does not automatically become a member of the upper class. At the same time, every member of the upper class who does not play the game of capitalism, such as some old nobility, will eventually lose his or her membership of the upper social class.

This illustrates the relationship but also the difference between social and economic class. The upper social class has to reproduce its position in a capitalist society via economic capital. However, other players enter the game of capitalism, who may accumulate enough wealth to become members of the economic capitalist class, while members of the social upper class may go bankrupt. In either case, a change of the social class may be the result of a change in economic class. But more commonly, a member of the upper social class will have enough economic as well as cultural, symbolic and social capital to be in a better position in the capitalist market than any competitor from the lower classes (Bourdieu 1984).

Membership in the upper social class opens up all options for becoming or remaining a capitalist, while membership in the upper economic class without other types of capital only qualifies for being a new rich. Therefore, social class is more fundamental than economic class. This can be verified historically. We can trace Marx's four classes in Western Europe to the present (Rehbein et al. 2015). We do not only find a similar class structure, we also find that most ancestors of the present generation occupied a similar social position. In former colonial societies, the social position can even be traced back to a corresponding social position in the precapitalist hierarchy (Jodhka, Rehbein and Souza 2017). That is, the descendant of a peasant is a member of the lower class today, while the descendant of a noble family is member of the upper class – in Germany just like in Laos.

The notion of social class was first introduced by Max Weber (1972), even though it was already implicit in Marx's early writings. It was more thoroughly explored by Edward P. Thompson. In *The Making of the English Working Class* (1963), he tried to show that the British laborer was not only characterized by relative poverty but also by active and positive traits that were passed on from one generation to the next. He spoke of a working-class culture, which Bourdieu (1984) later referred to as habitus and non-economic capital. Following Michael Vester et al. (2001), who also drew on Thompson, we call the social class with a persisting, albeit ever-changing culture a "tradition line".

In Germany, we can trace the tradition lines from the early Marx and Weber to Geiger in the 1920s (1932) and Vester et al. in the late 1980s (2001) and then to our own study in the 2010s. We see a constant internal and external reconfiguration of the classes but also an internal continuity of tradition lines. And we reach similar results in the global South (Jodhka, Rehbein and Souza 2017). Contemporary social classes are heirs of earlier classes and precapitalist hierarchical ranks. They also bear many characteristics, which are transformations of traits characterizing those earlier forms of the same tradition line.

We argue that the hierarchies in capitalist and precapitalist societies are orders of domination and that the order of social classes in capitalism is more fundamental than the capitalist economy even though it cannot be reproduced independently of it. If you do away with capitalism, domination or the hierarchy of tradition lines remains, but if you remove the order of domination, capitalism as we know it becomes impossible. We have to add this argument to Marx and Harvey in order to make their accounts intelligible.

The social hierarchy has to be sustained by a moral hierarchy, which classifies people into different species with a different value.[2] While it is evident that economic capital entitles you to buy something in a capitalist society, it is not evident that this influences your social value. Social class needs to be coupled with a symbolic dividing line, which distinguishes it from others in a hierarchical and moral way. The higher position of a certain social class and the membership in it have to be legitimate.

Three dividing lines constituting four social classes are especially relevant in contemporary capitalist societies. Two are related to classes already identified by Marx, while the line between the middle classes is different, since the middle classes have changed since then. The most relevant line is that between "worthy" and "unworthy" people. The "worthy" people are socially classified as those who are supposed to contribute to society and thereby live above an invisible line of dignity. They are divided by a second line, which is that of "sensibility" or "expressivity", into a class occupying the leading functions in society and a class beneath consisting of the mere laborers without any "higher goals". A tiny class exempt from any classification and competition is situated above the hierarchy. Aloofness constitutes the third dividing line. The dividing lines between the classes are incorporated actively and passively. They are used to give or deny access to particular functions in society, to assess people, to choose a marriage partner and to guide one's own actions.

Looking at three very different countries from three world regions with very different histories, we can see that they develop similar class structures, which can be explained using the concepts of tradition lines, distribution of capital, class culture and dividing lines. We wish to exemplify this with regard to Germany, Laos and Brazil. A significant part of the explanation for the similarity is that class has a particular relation to labor. In spite of these similarities, the precise configurations of the classes, the persisting structures of precapitalist inequalities and the habitus types differ vastly between the countries.

We refer to the four social classes we identified in contemporary Germany as the marginalized, the fighters, the established and the aloof (Rehbein et al. 2015). The marginalized remain excluded from many sections of society, especially a stable and well-paid profession. They dispose of a small total volume of capital. The class of fighters form the bulk of the laboring population. It consists of two tradition lines, one rooted in the old working class and one in the petty bourgeoisie. We call these the aspiring and the defensive fighters, since the former occupy the technical jobs requiring specific skills, while the latter struggle against declassation. The established carry out the leading functions and dispose of a large total amount of capital. The aloof are aloof in the sense that they are separated from the rest of society and morally as well as financially exempt from labor. They form the dominant social class.

A very different type of social structure is Laos. Here, colonial, socialist and even precolonial social structures persist underneath the capitalist class structure. Within the first, there is a hierarchy of ethnic minorities, peasants in a difficult environment, well-off peasants, urban population and nobility. Within the socialist structure, we can distinguish between village cadres, administration, leading cadres and party leadership; within this structure, there is much greater social mobility than in the other two structures. The capitalist hierarchy comprises the marginalized class, the working class, commercial farmers and traders, the new urban middle class and the capitalists.

The older structural layers slowly transform into a capitalist class hierarchy but the social groups tend to remain on the same hierarchical level. Subsistence peasants, who do not remain peasants, either become commercial farmers or agricultural laborers or they migrate into the towns. The small urban group becomes the new urban middle class. The old elites begin to engage in business and become capitalists. Chinese and Vietnamese reappear – partly in their colonial role as businesspeople but also as farmers, laborers and petty traders. Laos is much more heterogeneous than Germany, since it is undergoing a rapid capitalist transformation. This entails a persistence of precapitalist habitus forms and hierarchies.

Brazil, like Germany, has a long history of capitalism and a cemented class structure. Like Laos and in contrast to Germany, it was constructed by colonial rule. Contrary to Laos, not the entire population was declared equal with independence but slaves, women and ethnic minorities only gained full citizenship over time. These inequalities persist up to this day and inform the Brazilian social structure. We found four classes in Brazil, which differ from the German case. While dominant and marginalized classes of Germany and Brazil can be compared to some degree, the lower middle class in Brazil does not exist in Germany, while the Brazilian upper middle class comprises both of the classes that would be fighters and established in Germany. While the Brazilian marginalized class comprises up to 40 percent of the population, the German marginalized amount to half of that. The Brazilian middle class comprises only around 25 percent of the population, while the two German middle classes reach a total of almost 80 percent. We can trace the two Brazilian lower classes to the descendants of the slaves, the middle class to the administrators and the dominant class to the colonial rulers and landowners.

Since the Brazilian class structure emerged historically out of the hierarchy of a slave-holding society, its internal configuration and composition differs greatly from that of Germany and Laos. However, all three societies are developing similar dividing lines between the classes, namely the lines of dignity, expressivity and aloofness. In Laos, these lines are not yet very pervasive, while even in Brazil and Germany, they do not entirely explain the class structure, since the Brazilian middle class and the German fighter class both comprise two tradition lines and habitus groups do not fully correspond to the order of classes. Old middle classes also exist in Brazil and Laos but are rooted in a very different social order and division of labor. Similarly, the new middle classes in these countries do not clearly divide the established from the fighters. Finally, Laos hosts a rural middle class, which has ceased to exist in Brazil and Germany. These differences will not disappear entirely in the near future, since they are part of the historical heritage and are reproduced both by habitus and by the (international) division of labor.

Structures of global domination

The contemporary world order is a transformation of the colonial world, whose inequalities partly persist and partly have been transformed into capitalist structures. On the global and on the national level, an egalitarian and meritocratic discourse is coupled with a moral legitimation of inequality. All of us are influenced to some degree by modernization theory, which is the capitalist transformation of colonial evolutionism. Modernization theory depicts societies in the Global South as deficient realizations of the North-Atlantic model. Niklas Luhmann (1995) distinguished between "decent" and "corrupt" societies after his visit to Brazil, thereby idealizing North-Atlantic societies. We think of economically less developed societies, which need to implement reforms in order to reach such standards of social organization and institutions, and of developed societies, which have by and large met or even elaborated these standards. Closely connected to this idea is the interpretation of "underdeveloped" societies as corrupt, inefficient, undemocratic and somehow incomplete, while their citizens are regarded as untrustworthy and undisciplined. This idea implies that inequality in North–Atlantic societies is either a transient phenomenon (Kuznets 1955) or a desirable result of a fully developed market economy (Friedman 1962).

Modernization theory argues that capitalism in North–Atlantic societies is decent and developed, while all other arrangements are classified as corrupt and deficient. This view of the world was convincing as long as Europe ruled the colonial world and as long as the United States was the world's superpower. It is less convincing since Singapore has achieved the highest GDP per capita and China the largest volume of trade as well as the second largest GDP. It is quite obvious that these countries have institutional configurations that differ significantly from Europe and the United States and will continue to do so for some time to come (cf. Antonelli in this volume). However, the general framework of modernization theory still prevails. All rankings – from the worthiness of credit to corruption to human development – largely translate the colonial order into an order of development and modernization.

For migrants, the freedom to move, the job opportunities, the value of an educational degree and the symbolic classification largely depend on the relation of their country of origin and the receiving country (cf. Weiß in this volume). This relation is partly determined on the basis of modernization theory. The rankings by the UN, think tanks and governments use indicators as GDP, development of technology, Western education system, bio-medicine, Western democracy and corruption. These are the indicators of modernization theory. However, the order of states determines the outcome of migration only to a certain degree. A university professor and a rural laborer from the same country of origin will occupy very different social positions after migration. Their positions, to a large degree, depend on their capital and habitus.

Furthermore, the world has not become fully globalized. The nation state continues to be the most important framework both for inequality and for sociological research. This entails a contradiction in and for the position of the dominant classes. Their social position is tied to the nation state and can only be reproduced within it; at the same time, their actions and interests are increasingly global. The national roots of the dominant classes tie them closely to their nation state. A university professor can use his or her capital in most nation states to a similar degree and occupies a similar social position before and after migration. This is not the case for members of the dominant class. An Indian billionaire does not automatically become member of the British dominant class after migrating to London. And even if a British billionaire did become member of the Indian dominant class after migrating to India – which is questionable – his or her global position and influence would suffer. For this reason, we see little international migration toward the top end of society (Hartmann in this volume).

The position of the dominant class is linked to the deeper historical contra-diction between capitalism and the nation state. The European nation state was closely entangled with colonialism, which in turn implied the global expansion of (Western) capitalism. The nation state in Europe developed technology, an efficient division of labor and administration in the interior at the same time as colonial expansion and global reproduction of capital. All of this happened under the leadership of the dominant classes in the European nation states. The nation state was an important tool for the expansion of capital and domination, just like Harvey has demonstrated for the US in the late twentieth century.

At the same time, the nation state is a barrier to the expansion of capital and domination. The dominant classes today consist mainly of capitalists, who act globally and strive for economic and political power on a global scale. Their means of action are multinational corporations, international financial institu-tions and tax havens. All of these are limited in their scope by nation states and their regulations – even if these states were founded to pursue the interests of the dominant classes and are still very much influenced by them. The interests of a particular dominant class and its nation state are not necessarily identical but the dominant class can reproduce its social position and secure its interests only by means of the state. Furthermore, the interests of the different national dominant classes may collide. The dominant classes do not pursue one common agenda of global domination.

The increasingly homogeneous order of standardized nation states is com-plemented by an increasingly similar order of classes. Each class has a par-ticular function in the structure of domination and a particular relation to labor: the dominant class monopolizes capital, the established class (functional elites) manages society, the middle class labors, and the marginalized are the "reserve army". We argue that this structure is reproduced within each nation state effectively if it remains invisible and unconscious, since each class is best equipped for the particular social functions.

The dominant classes form a global hierarchy, which corresponds to the hierarchy of nation states. The relation of dominant class and nation state exerts a key influence on the position of the state in the hierarchy of states. The domi-nant class in each nation state has to reproduce its social position by accumulat-ing economic capital, which has to be invested in a profitable way, often against the interests of the nation state. In order to reproduce its social position, it also has to accumulate social capital, which is very much limited to the nation state. Cultural capital is less relevant but also plays an important role in management and family strategy to make the right investment decisions. All three types of capital are also used to directly influence the nation state through corruption, party donations, lobbies, think tanks, media ownership and personal networks.

One of the most important issues in the coming years is the actual glo-balization of the dominant classes. As capitalists (or members of the capitalist economic class), they are already entirely globalized. But their domination is limited to their respective nation state. In both dimensions, the families and net-works within this class are global competitors and need national development.

As financial investors, the dominant classes form a global entity. However, they still do not form a global class, since their position is reproduced only within the nation state. The nation states are not mere instruments of the dominant classes but their relationship explains a large part of global inequality. Half of the members of today's dominant classes are citizens of North America and a quarter are citizens of Western Europe. The dominant class of the US is still in a position of unique global economic power, since it is the richest in total and since its interests largely converge with that of the most powerful nation state. Both strive for global domination. Interests of dominant classes and states tend to diverge more in the smaller countries, since the global action of the dominant class is counteracted by a nationalist agenda of the state.

Conclusion

We have distinguished social from economic classes and argued that the hierarchy of social classes is more fundamental than that of economic classes, since it secures domination, while capitalism is only one means, one particular system of domination. The hierarchy of classes has to be reproduced, on the one hand as a tradition line and on the other by symbolic classification. In a capitalist society, it also has to be reproduced via economic capital. This leads to a particular dialectic relation between domination and capitalism.

Capitalism today is an order of global domination, which consists of dominant classes and nation states. The institution of the nation state was key in the expansion of Western capitalism and in the attempts of dominant classes to achieve regional and later global domination. At the same time, the nation state limits the power of dominant classes – except for those in the dominant nation state. Today, there is no single dominant nation state any more but at least China can compete with the US on an equal footing in many regards. The capitalist economic class increasingly emerges in all nation states. It is possible that this will decrease the relevance of the nation state. But as long as the dominant social class has to reproduce its position within the nation state, this institution will remain important and will continue to influence the structure of global inequality.

Notes

1 This chapter is partly based on Surinder S. Jodhka, Boike Rehbein and Jessé Souza (2017) *Inequality in Capitalist Societies*, Singapore and London: Routledge, chapter 6. Material used by permission.
2 The theoretical foundation and the empirical manifestations of the dividing lines between capitalist classes are explained in detail by Souza in this volume.

References

Bourdieu, Pierre (1984) *Distinction*, Cambridge, MA: Harvard University Press.
Frank, André Gunder (1969) *Latin America – Underdevelopment or Revolution*, New York: MR Press.

Friedman, Milton (1962) *Capitalism and Freedom*, Chicago: University of Chicago Press.

Geiger, Theodor (1932) *Die soziale Schichtung des deutschen Volkes*, Stuttgart: Ferdinand Enke Verlag.

Hardoon, Deborah (2017) *An Economy for the 99 Percent*, Oxford: Oxfam International.

Harvey, David (2005) *A Brief History of Neoliberalism*, Oxford: Oxford University Press.

Jodhka, Surinder, Boike Rehbein and Jessé Souza (2017) *Inequality in Capitalist Societies*, Singapore and London: Routledge.

Kuznets, Simon (1955) 'Economic Growth and Income Inequality', *The American Economic Review*, Vol. 45, No. 1: 1–28.

Luhmann, Niklas (1995) 'Kausalität im Süden', *Soziale Systeme*, Vol. 1: 7–28.

Marx, Karl (1953) *Das Kapital* (3 volumes), Berlin: Dietz.

Marx, Karl and Friedrich Engels (eds.) (1964) 'Das Kommunistische Manifest', *Werke*, Vol. 4, Berlin: Dietz, 459–93.

Piketty, Thomas (2014) *Capital in the Twenty-First Century*, Cambridge, MA: Harvard University Press.

Rehbein, Boike, Benjamin Baumann, Lucia Costa, Simin Fadaee, Michael Kleinod, Thomas Kühn, . . . Ricardo Visser (2015) *Reproduktion sozialer Ungleichheit in Deutschland*, Constance: UVK.

Stierli, Markus, Anthony Shorrocks, Jim Davies, Rodrigo Lluberas and Antonios Koutsoukis (2015) *Global Wealth Report 2015*, Zurich: Crédit Suisse.

Thompson, Edward P. (1963) *The Making of the English Working Class*, Harmondsworth: Penguin Books.

Vester, Michael, Peter von Oertzen, Heiko Gerling, Thomas Hermann and Dagmar Müller (2001; second edition) *Soziale Milieus im gesellschaftlichen Strukturwandel*, Frankfurt: Suhrkamp.

Vitali, Stefania, James B. Glattfelder and Stefano Battiston (2011) 'The Network of Global Corporate Control', *PLoS ONE*, Vol. 6: 1–18.

Weber, Max (1972; fifth edition) *Wirtschaft und Gesellschaft*, Tübingen: J.C.B. Mohr.

4   Lower classes

Jessé Souza

The lower classes in this world seem to be much less likely candidates for a potentially global class than the upper classes.[1] It is well-known that they suffer much more from legal and factual constraints to movements across national borders. Even though that is certainly the case, the international migration of the lowest classes is relevant and surprising. There is much more international mixture in the lowest classes than we might expect. However, the main characteristic of the lowest classes as opposed to the upper classes is their fragmentation. Their life-worlds, social conditions, world views and life histories have little unity and conformity when compared to the upper classes. This is even true for their families.

At the same time, we have to acknowledge that the principle that generates a lower class is the same in all capitalist societies. In this regard, one can speak of the lower class as a global phenomenon. It is the class that lives below the line of dignity. The nation states differ in the size and the internal composition of this class. Whereas it is relatively small in the rich countries of the global North and comprises around 20 percent of the population in Germany (Rehbein et al. 2015), it accounts for at least one third of the population of Brazil (Souza 2009) and up to twice that proportion in some African countries. Thereby, it is the largest class and includes almost as many human beings as all other classes combined.

This chapter focuses on the symbolic and moral construction of this class. I claim that the principle of this construction, namely an invisible dividing line between the "worthy" and the "worthless" persons, is valid for all capitalist societies. I will discuss the incorporation of this dividing line into social practice and also illustrate it with regard to the empirical case of Brazil.

Dividing lines and legitimation of inequality

Capitalism claims to be egalitarian and fair, and because of this develops a complex of formal equalities that populates the constitutions and legal systems of contemporary nation states. Since the perception of inequality and injustice created by the inequality of inheritance of socially relevant capital and habitus has to be suppressed (cf. Piketty 2014), there comes into play a hierarchy "felt" by everyone in his or her everyday life, yet at the same time, never addressed openly, never reflected on and never portrayed as a hierarchy. This is an effective hierarchy which is based on class and not on formal equality under the law.

Even though this principle is valid for all capitalist societies, whether in the global South or the North, some societies have come closer to justice defined as equality than others. The abyss between the real hierarchy and formal equality is much smaller in Northern Europe than in Brazil. Unlike the ridiculous "inherited cultural belief systems" (da Matta 1981) with which we explain the difference between the global South and the North, the criteria of the greater or lesser difference between the dream of egalitarian justice and its practical realization is a much better instrument for measuring this distance, which is real.

The idea of an "inherited value stock", a superficial interpretation of Max Weber's *Protestant Ethic* (2011) which modernization theory turned into common sense everywhere, is a kind of unreflected presupposition of every thought on this matter not only for intellectuals and world organizations. The "public opinion" in the Global North gladly accepted this idea out of sheer narcissistic motives used by the ruling classes for political legitimation. The "empirical test" can be made by everyone. A decent, not openly racist American, German or French has always to make an "effort" to treat a Latin-American or an African "as if" he or she were equal as the political correctness demands. In the global South, the idea of the inherited value stock is also used by the ruling classes to demonize lower classes seen as "support" of the national inferiority. The ruling classes in those countries see themselves as "European" even though they are not treated as Europeans by the Europeans themselves.

In fact this idea replaces the racism of color of the skin which was regarded as "science" well into the twentieth century exactly as the "inherited value stock" is today. Both do exactly the same job of splitting the world and the single nations of the global South in two: those who are human beings and those slightly under this level. It is always easier to oppress those who lack "humanity" itself – that is, the "spirit" – and can be reduced to "bodies" and therefore "animalized".

We have to break with this idea by clarifying how invisible hierarchies work. How are these invisible hierarchies constructed everywhere and felt by everyone, built upon inequality as the major principle in relation to the formal equality that everyone swears they pursue? We address this central question in two stages. First, we try to show how contemporary capitalism constructs the invisible moral hierarchies that enable the repositioning of inequality as the foundation of a type of society which sells itself as being egalitarian and fair. Then we study the incorporation of the hierarchies.

A moral hierarchy pervades contemporary societies. However, in everyday life and in received wisdom, we only see the effect of money and power. Thereby, classes are constructed on the basis of income and wealth. But money and power need to be legitimized in everyday life by moral standards, otherwise they cannot produce their effects. On the other hand, we also feel emotions we are unable to explain and which do not necessarily have anything to do with money and power, such as remorse, guilt, envy, resentment and admiration, which to a large extent explain our concrete actions in the world.

Although we are blind to this dimension of the world, we are able to recon-struct it through actions and reactions of people in the practical world. A well-constructed and well-conducted empirical study can reconstruct the practical relevance of these moral hierarchies for our concrete behavior, although we are hardly ever conscious of them. In fact, our conscious perception is much less important than the way in which we act and behave in practice. Normally, what we think we are is, to a large extent, the fruit of the need to justify and legitimize the life we lead. It does not necessarily reflect the "truth" of our behavior. As various critical thinkers have demonstrated, the primary need of human beings is not the truth. Our primary affective need rather is to justify and legitimize the life we lead.

What is important here is to highlight that it is possible to demonstrate beyond any reasonable doubt the effect of these moral hierarchies or lines of social classification, despite being invisible in everyday life, where we perceive only the workings of money and of power. In fact, these moral hierarchies can be observed in their effects on the practical actions of people, even though "in our heads" we do not have the least idea of their existence. The fact that we are not conscious of the causes of the moral sentiments and of the moral hier-archies which are their source, only makes them stronger, as in this way we are unable to obtain the necessary reflexive distance from them.

Pierre Bourdieu was a pioneer in demonstrating the influence of these invis-ible dividing lines created by the moral hierarchies in modern society. In his most important work, *Distinction* (1984), Bourdieu was able to demonstrate that equality in France, based on state education for all, was a fiction. Not in the sense that the republican and egalitarian French effort was a failure, far from it. What Bourdieu demonstrated is that in spite of having set the standard for common "dignity" of all French people, which does not exist in societies such as Brazil, French society as an example to all other modern societies con-structed alternative and subtle forms, hardly perceptible to anyone immersed in the perspective of common sense, of justification and legitimation of inequality and of privilege.

Bourdieu's classic work analyzes aesthetic taste as an invisible mechanism of production of social distinction, in the sense of legitimation of the perception of superiority of some, and of inferiority of others. This is easily illustrated. For people who drive expensive cars, wear fashionable clothes and drink special wines, this kind of consumption does not only mean that they have more money than others who cannot afford such things. It also means that they have "good taste", which implies a superiority that is not just aesthetic, but also *moral*. The good aesthetic taste is a matter of spirit, education and humanism. Those who do not have it are perceived as mere bodies, having needs just like animals, and are therefore inferior in the aesthetic and moral senses.

Everyone who sees him- or herself as representative of the spirit develops a solidarity with one's peers and a prejudice against those who do not share their vision of the world. In fact, taste is not restricted to isolated consumption, but defines an entire lifestyle. It is not just the special wine, but also the kind of food one eats, the clothes, the holidays, the friends and the entire life-world, as Bourdieu (1984) has demonstrated. These are shared lifestyles that imply a feeling of superiority. The majority without such access suffers the mostly unconscious prejudice of not just being poor in the economic sense, but also of not having "spirit" and of exemplifying a degraded form of human existence.

The invisible lines of social classification and disqualification, based on moral hierarchies invisible for received wisdom become the basis of solidarity and of prejudice in capitalist societies. The distinction by good taste is a decisive element both in understanding the solidarity between the members of the upper classes as well as their prejudices in relation to the lower classes. Although it is ubiquitous in society, it serves primarily to legitimize the difference and the privileges of the middle and high classes in relation to the "people".

This argument is inspired by the Canadian philosopher Charles Taylor. Taylor (1989) has argued that in contemporary societies, two value-ideas control our lives: the notions of authenticity (or expressivity) and of dignity. Both reflect a process of learning, which is its moral dimension, and a process of distinction and legitimation of social domination, which represents its intercalation with the pragmatic dimensions of money and of power. In the end, every human action is intercalated in this double dimension which is both utilitarian and moral. What changes in each individual is the greater strength in relation to one aspect or the other.

The dimension of authenticity is more recent, historically speaking, and only in the twentieth century, especially in the context of the counter-culture of the 1960s, did it reach a truly popular dimension. Before this it was something restricted to the intellectual elites. Authenticity means the absorption in social life of the moral principle of the "sensitive human being" as the value-guide for one's everyday life. The important thing is that this idea is not just to have money or power, but rather to live life in accordance with feelings and affections that are particular to each person as an individual.

The notion of authenticity refers to "reflected feelings", which are not to be confused with blind and animal passions. It is a sublimation and spiritualization of our affective dimension. It is precisely this notion of authenticity or expressivity that Bourdieu calls "good taste", as an invisible mechanism producing class solidarities and prejudices. However, Bourdieu does not perceive the possible learning that inhabits authenticity as a moral dimension, seeing it solely as a producer of social distinction to oppress the lower classes. Taylor, in turn, does not see the potential hierarchy- and prejudice-producing effect of this principle.

My point is that it is both, the "possibility of learning" and the producer of "social distinction". This principle becomes important when it is institutionalized in universities, museums and in the arts, as well as in the capitalist culture industry. The entire history of Western culture lives in the big box-office films, self-help books, best-selling novels and soap operas. These products are not supposed to educate and stimulate critical thought, but rather to reproduce conformist and stereotyped versions of an authenticity to be readily sold. In this way, one does not have to consider that sensibility is only authentic if it is discovered and constructed individually through hard effort. However, the very success of this industry of pastiche is only possible because the notion of sensibility has already taken hold of the popular imagination, even of those who have not constructed an authentic sensibility and are obliged to buy it. In this way, we can perceive the social efficacy of an idea, when it dominates us all, whether we want it or not, whether we perceive it or not.

The late historical construction of the notion of authenticity or of the sensitive human being takes place through opposition to the other great source of moral hierarchy in the West, which is the notion of dignity of the useful producer. "Dignity" is not to be confused with the imprecise notion we give it in received wisdom. This notion is much older and begins to be constructed with the Christian ethics of control of desire and the passions by the spirit, linked to the value of social respect as deriving from "productive work in favor of the common good", as Taylor (1989) explains. As continued productive labor requires discipline and self-control, the idea of dignity in successive stages comes to be perceived as the capacity to discipline and control desires and passions that make discipline impossible.

Protestantism deepened the notion of discipline. If Christian ethics in the broad sense constructs the idea of the spirit as superior to the body and therefore of having to control desire and the passions, Protestantism makes labor "sacred" (Weber 2011). Labor becomes the path to God and to salvation in the other world. Although in the secular world reference to God is no longer obligatory, labor continues to be the principal reference of every individual through concretization of the abstract idea of God which is transformed into the idea palpable more as the "common good". The greater or lesser respect and admiration we have for other people comes to depend on their performance in labor. Whether we like it or not, we admire people, even if we envy them, for their good performance on the job. This is concrete proof which anyone can test in everyday life of the strength of moral ideas which constrain us. This means that the source both of self-esteem of the individual in Western capitalism and of social respect due to it, is intimately linked to useful labor. Just as we admire those who work well, we despise or feel pity for those who perform no useful labor, such as the parked car keepers in the large Brazilian cities. Anyone reflecting on what really matters to them will discover these two moral hierarchies. Although we are blind to this practical efficacy of the moral hierarchies in our lives, as we can only see the most obvious action of money and of power, it can be shown in its effects and consequences in each one of us, providing we reflect a little.

Bourdieu and Taylor, however, suppose that the "dignity of the useful producer" were something generalized in modern society. After all, in Western nation states, the vast majority of the population is "worthy", i.e. has access to the social conditions of dignity in the sense formulated here. Although

Bourdieu has analyzed the marginalized of Algeria, he, and every other European or American thinker, tends to perceive of the phenomenon of marginality as a transient trait, in the case of the transition from dispossessed farm-worker to the city, as they effectively were transient in Europe and the United States. But the existence of entire social classes below the line of "dignity" is a permanent phenomenon. In Brazil and in large parts of the world there is a social class, which is notable for its absence of the very conditions to carry out useful activity in the present context of the knowledge society (Souza 2009). This unknown class exists in all capitalist societies but its size is larger and its living conditions are worse in the global South.

The starting point was Bourdieu's insight into the practical power of the invisible line of social distinction and legitimation of privilege, the idea of aesthetic taste in France. In the same way that the French case can be generalized for all modern societies wrapped up in the challenge of covering up unjust privileges by subtle and imperceptible means, the idea of "dignity" in Brazil can be generalized, to a large extent, to all societies with large numbers of marginalized and excluded people. Therefore, the final section of this chapter is devoted to a case study of Brazil.

As capitalist societies make claims of being fair and meritocratic, these are the two "invisible lines" that legitimize the separation between those that are noble and superior and those who are inferior and vulgar in society. Even if the two lines of "authenticity" and of "dignity" become mixed up and are fluid at their borders, the dividing line of "authenticity" separates, above all, the classes of privilege from the lower classes. The line of "dignity" distinguishes the lowest class, or the "unworthy", from the rest. The line of "dignity" dividing individuals and entire social classes into worthy and unworthy of respect and the capacity of performance in the labor market helps us to see both the dividing line between the working class and the socially excluded as well as the redoubled and amplified prejudice of the upper layers of society in relation to the latter.

The incorporation of dividing lines

Even the rich need some cultural capital to be accepted in their group. Without it, the access to social capital is at risk. An uneducated rich "savage" cannot make any alliances with important peers, nor a profitable marriage to increase the capital accumulated. At least some overlap in taste and behavior is necessary, even though the role of high culture and authenticity in the global South is much less pronounced than in Bourdieu's (1984) France. Building some cultural capital of "distinction" in relation to the other classes to show that money is the fruit of a supposed innate good taste is also vital for the dominant class. Cultural capital is also required for business deals, understanding the economy and passing on one's legacy.

The inverse happens with the middle class in its various kinds. Although its privilege is based on incorporation of cultural capital, some economic capital is necessary so that they can buy, for example, free time with their children.

Unlike the children of the lower classes, who have to study and work from adolescence onwards – which almost always implies doing neither one nor the other well – the children of the middle class can dedicate themselves just to studies. This allows them to concentrate on the more highly valued cultural capital for the employment market, which they will enter later on. This basic fact is overlooked when defining social classes by means of external attributes such as income.

In fact, human beings are formed by internalization, or the unconscious incorporation of forms of behavior of the parents or caregivers. The most important relationship of the socialization process of any human being is therefore primarily emotionally affective. In short, we are what we are because we imitate those we love. Children "incorporate" their parents' characteristics in silence and invisibly (Who has not enjoyed watching a child of two or three walking beside the father with the same sway of the body?) and this is the most relevant fact for us to understand the reproduction of the social classes over time.

If economic capital is transmitted by inheritance and property titles, cultural capital is transmitted by an invisible inheritance, which requires the heirs to develop the same emotional and affective structure that enables the correct inheritance (Bourdieu 1984). This inheritance may include curious facts, such as the father's way of walking and speaking, but also includes other aspects that determine success or failure in social life. Family generations receive the baton from the previous one and specialize in creating all the right conditions so that they are "winners" first in school and then in the labor market. There is a bond, almost never perceived, whether in received wisdom or in the official social sciences, which links family socialization to school, and to the labor market.

Since these bonds are forged during family socialization, in the family home and at a tender age, they are not thought of as privilege. It is for this reason that the middle class becomes the class par excellence which believes in the meritocracy. As most of the stimuli are incorporated unconsciously during childhood socialization, it is as if they had been born with them. An illusion is thus created of individually attained merit instead of inherited privilege. While middle class children play with toys that stimulate their creativity, hear stories from the mother full of fantasy that stimulate their imagination and see the father reading every day, which stimulates their liking for and perceived importance of reading, the everyday experience of the lower classes is very different.

The son of a construction worker plays with his father's wheelbarrow and learns to be an unqualified manual laborer. He perceives his mother's praise for schooling as lip service, since the mother's schooling has helped her little or not at all. It is the real practice that constructs classes as winners or as losers, when they enter school at the age of five. Because of this, understanding the different family socializations between the classes is so important. Without it, we do not realize privilege acting as it most likes to act, that is in silence and invisibly, and we reproduce all kinds of prejudice as if there were people who chose to be poor and humiliated.

In the lower classes the distinction between laborers and the excluded, which is quite fluid, becomes one of degree and not of quality. Poor families are not just poor, and their misery is not just economic. They reproduce an everyday life of cognitive want that tends to prolong the moral and affective misery. Even in the families that are still able to maintain the family model with a loving father and mother, taking care of their children in adverse circumstances, the parents are only able to transmit their own social maladaptation. One cannot, after all, teach what one has not learnt. We see mothers worried about their children's schooling, but as they know that school has made no difference to their own lives, they do not effectively perceive and teach how it can make any difference to them.

When we interviewed adult members of the lowest class in Brazil about their school experience (Souza 2009), we were surprised about the generalized affirmation that they had "spent many hours looking at the blackboard without learning anything". We discovered that the capability to concentrate, which enables learning, is not a natural given of any "normal" human being, like having a head and a belly. Without stimulation to read and without reading as a part of everyday life, there is no capacity of concentration. Without capacity to concentrate, in turn, there is no real learning, and it becomes intelligible why the state schools for the poor largely churn out functional illiterates. Worse still, in our interviews, the poor socialized in this precarious schooling of precarious pupils felt guilty for their supposed "innate stupidity". Imagine having had the chance of going to school and not having taken advantage of it. The cycle of domination is closed when the victims of abandonment see themselves as the cause of their own misfortune.

The dividing line between the two lower classes reflects the possibility of differential appropriation of what we call "cultural capital". Although the cultural capital at play here it is not the kind of valued and recognized cultural capital incorporated by the middle classes, any labor under the conditions of competitive capitalism requires incorporation of knowledge. Furthermore, we see in the example of the middle classes that there is no incorporation of knowledge without the pre-requirements of relative educational success being fulfilled. The fluid line between the working class and the excluded class is constructed by the greater or lesser possibility of incorporation of the affective and emotional pre-requirements that enable the avoidance of complete educational failure. What separates the laborer from the excluded is that he or she is able to incorporate a minimum amount of knowledge useful in the competitive market. With family socialization and schooling a bond is produced that afterwards enables the selling of what was learned beyond muscular energy and physical strength.

The definition of useful labor produced through knowledge or through "manual effort" (not very different in this sense from animal power) is fluid. Formal jobs, as construction worker or sugar cane cutter, are in reality a mixture of the two dimensions. Even so, it is possible to separate the types of family socialization by social class – whether it enables or disables one to learn at school and afterwards to exercise productive functions in the competitive labor market. None of us are born with the attributes of discipline, of prospective thought and the capacity of concentration. These attributes are privileges of class. Some classes have them "from birth", such as the middle class, others construct them precariously, like the laborers in the global South, and others still never construct them in any suitable amount, like the population of the excluded, the lowest class.

The reality of the lowest class is rendered invisible by the two dominant discourses: on the one hand, the liberal conception of society, which universalizes the middle class and extends it to the lowest class, whose members can thereby be blamed for their failures; and, on the other hand, the notion of "political correctness", which takes the discourse of the underclass itself at face value. However, the description by the socially excluded of his or her own situation is necessarily reactive. One tends to subjectively deny the lack of dignity, which characterizes one's life objectively. Creating a reflexive distance from one's own situation is possible only for persons who have the means to change it. Those who lack access to different options are left with no option but to deny or euphemize their reality. However, in most studies of the lowest class, this reality is not acknowledged and the "politically correct" perspective is unconsciously adopted.

The case of Brazil

In Brazil, the lowest class is sometimes called an "under-proletariat", a mere residual concept of proletariat that explains nothing. In a certain sense, what should be explained is swept beneath the carpet. Even worse is the European term "precariat", which implies something like failure. Precarious for Europeans is that group, which no longer enjoys the guarantees and security of the European social-democratic pact which is now on the defensive. This has nothing to do with the Brazilian case, which has never had a social-democratic pact. While the Brazilian left speaks of a "precariat" or "under-proletariat", the conservatives apply the scheme of income classes. The lowest class becomes a mere arbitrary number, as classes E and D, intending to circumscribe a reality that cannot be understood. The differences between individuals and classes are supposed to be captured by such superficial criteria – which are more an effect, than a cause of poverty.

This now dominant pseudo-explanation does not explain the main point: how and why do countless individuals find themselves in this situation of such misery whilst others are not? It is this, in the end, that is so necessary to understand. In the case of Brazil, the greatest single difference is the historical construction of a class of "disqualified", forgotten, abandoned and despised by the whole of society, whose main attribute is precisely the partial or complete absence of the condition and capacity that define "dignity". Obviously, this lack of dignity is produced by a perverse, foolish and unequal society. It is perverse because of the apparent culpability of the victim of abandonment, as if anyone chose to be poor and humiliated, and foolish and unequal because the importance of a long term inclusive strategy is not perceived for the wealth and well-being of the whole of society.

In an empirical study of the lowest class in Brazil (Souza 2009), we looked at the relationship between the "material" dimension and the "symbolic" dimension of deprivation. The following paragraphs summarize a few results from this study that are of relevance to the argument outlined in the preceding sections. In order to understand the symbolic dimension of social exclusion and the persistence of material, existential and political deprivation, we have to refer to the incorporated moral hierarchy. It is only the symbolic legitimation of inequality that makes it acceptable and its reproduction possible.

The study of social exclusion of large segments of the population in countries like Brazil may contribute to understanding the same issue in countries of the center, where the proportion of excluded groups is smaller. Analytically, however, the process of social exclusion and marginalization does not differ between Brazil and the global North. It is the lack of capital, especially economic and cultural capital, that reduces the persons concerned to mere bodies, which are sold on at low prices to deliver socially despised services. Typically, the men do "three d" jobs (dirty, dangerous, and demeaning), while the women do domestic and sexual work. These are people who have failed to incorporate the capabilities necessary for success in competitive markets. As a result of this lack, they live below the line of dignity.

In our research on Brazil, we developed a methodology which comprised sequential interviews with the same individuals. This allowed us to deal with their natural resistance to being interviewed and to explore the same issues in increasing depth, rather than focusing on different issues in each interview. The informants were chosen according to a typology developed during the process. Typically, in the first interview informants would present their family life as an idyll. In succeeding interviews, inconsistencies appeared and deeper inquiry into certain issues became possible. Caring and loving parents turned into sexually abusive and mostly absent fathers and instrumental mothers. On this basis, we were able to reconstruct some of the most important characteristics of the lowest class in Brazil as well as to uncover the line of dignity.

An important characteristic of the lowest class in Brazil – but probably everywhere – is the lack of fundamental capabilities for acquiring cultural capital of any kind. Talking about their experience at school, many of our interviewees reported having attended class without learning anything. As this type of report was frequently repeated, we began to understand that these children had failed to internalize the ability to focus – an ability that members of the middle classes usually regard as "natural", as if one was born with it. However, children of the lowest class failed to develop this ability. Even in more structured families of this class, in which parents had not separated and tried to implement a caring and affectionate relationship with their children, we observed traces of social neglect. As the children had never seen their parents read and had never interacted with written material at home, their success at school was expected to be limited. This "failure" is not entirely irrational, since an educational title is not sufficient to leave this class. Our interviewees pointed to examples in their families or circles of friends, where a person had completed school but had still become a drug addict or an unskilled laborer.

School as an institution is irrelevant in this context because the children already start school as "losers", while middle-class children, on the basis of effective examples and incentives, begin as "winners". In addition, the public education system promises upward mobility through education, but actually translates social neglect into individual failure. With the state's seal and society's agreement, school officially labels children from the lowest class as stupid and lazy. Many adolescents from this class who we interviewed perceived themselves as unable to focus and stupid. And they considered this to be their own fault. School as an institution and as part of a life-world incessantly reconfirms that the existentially and economically deprived class is in fact "worthless". The exclusion of its members is thus objectified and naturalized.

The same context explains the political impotence of this class. Our study revealed a dividing line between the so-called honest poor, who are willing to sell their muscle power for little money, and the so-called delinquents who react against the structure that condemns them. We found the same division in Germany (Rehbein et al. 2015). In no other social class is this division as pronounced as in the lowest class. The everyday drama unfolding in the majority of the families we studied is focused on the issue of "honesty". The realm of "honesty" is reckoned to be a safe haven in a sea of delinquency, prostitution, alcohol and drugs. The issue of honesty constitutes a division in the underclass that renders internal solidarity within this negatively privileged class difficult. Practically every family that we studied comprised some 'delinquent' members. The dominant moral hierarchy, with the concept of 'dignity' at its core, blames the assumed lack of dignity on the individual and thus divides the entire class, as well as each family and each neighborhood, into irreconcilable foes.

Another important characteristic of the lowest class is the reproduction of the 'de-structured' family, something to which the dominant discourse is blind. The naturalization of sexual abuse by the elders in the family was shocking to our research team. This issue never appears in the media. It is part of a universal instrumental attitude that is pervasive in this class and even extends to the immediate family. Florestan Fernandes (2008) had already pointed to this phenomenon in a study conducted in São Paulo during the 1950s. It is not hard to imagine the kind of wounds this practice inflicts on the self-respect of members of the lowest class. It is reproduced from one generation to the next by a tacit understanding between the victim and the perpetrator. The model of the bourgeois family, with its stress on mutual obligations, is reproduced only to a very limited degree here. The complete neglect of these families existing in a mode of exclusion seems to be a decisive factor in the reproduction of this class.

The construction of Taylor's dignified self is unlikely from the outset in this class, since the "moral and emotional economy" which is supposed to be incorporated during socialization is almost completely lacking. Without discipline, self-control and planning, the socially produced ability to concentrate fails to be incorporated along with mutual trust, solidarity and cultural capital, first in the school and then in the ongoing learning process that is increasingly relevant in any labor market in the world. These deficits help to explain why this entire class has been ruled out of competition in any formal or valued dimension of the market, and is instead relegated to muscular, sexual or other kinds of "three d"-jobs purchased cheaply by the privileged classes.

In recent years, a public debate has emerged whether a new middle class has emerged in Brazil. This has been exploited politically for the claim that Brazil is becoming a society of the First World. We also studied this class and found it to be a working class of financial capitalism rather than a new middle class (Souza 2010). Its members work 10 to 14 hours a day and regard themselves as autonomous and independent workers. They have a comparatively small amount of cultural and economic capital and mostly work under conditions of little legal protection and without paying taxes. They are also mostly individuals with two jobs, or people who work by day and study at night.

This class is separated from the lowest class by a solid work ethic, due mostly to family background and religious socialization. In the cities, religious socialization occurs mostly later in life and, in the great majority of cases, reflects the influence of Pentecostalism. A sizable proportion of this class consists of people who have risen out of the lowest class by breaking the vicious circle of unstructured family life and precarious work conditions. As with the Brazilian lowest class, this new class should not be conceived as a purely national phenomenon, but one which is spreading worldwide. In these groups, finance capitalism seems to have found its ideal "supporting class", especially in heavily populated countries like China, India, Brazil and Russia, lacking strong traditions of working-class struggle and with vast numbers of people willing to work hard in any conditions. However, this class is located above the line of dignity and should therefore be distinguished from the lowest class.

Conclusion

The Brazilian case is particular in some regards, for example the structure of colonial society and its impact on contemporary society, the industrial policies in the mid-twentieth century and the social policies after the turn of the century lifting millions of people out of the lowest class. Some aspects of violence and sexual exploitation within the lowest class may also be more pronounced than in the lower classes of other nation states. But the combination of the invisible line of dignity with the incorporation of the characteristics associated with it seems to apply to all capitalist societies (Jodhka, Rehbein and Souza 2017). It produces the lowest class, which would not exist otherwise.

This has implications for political action and further research. Lifting members of this class out of poverty does not change their class position. Research and policies directed at economic indicators will contribute to the invisibility of the mechanisms producing and the lowest class and thereby to its reproduction. Any meaningful endeavor has to address the moral hierarchy and its incorporation. This, however, would threaten the foundations of domination in capitalist societies.

Note

1 This chapter is partly based on Surinder S. Jodhka, Boike Rehbein, Jessé Souza (2017) *Inequality in Capitalist Societies*, Singapore and London: Routledge, chapter 4. Material used by permission.

References

Bourdieu, Pierre (1984) *Distinction*, Cambridge, MA: Harvard University Press.

DaMatta, Roberto (1981) *Carnavais, malandros e heróis*, Rio de Janeiro: Zahar.

Fernandes, Florestan (2008) *A integração do negro na sociedade de classes*, São Paulo: Globo Editora.

Jodhka, Surinder, Boike Rehbein and Jessé Souza (2017) *Inequality in Capitalist Societies*, Singapore and London: Routledge.

Piketty, Thomas (2014) *Capital in the Twenty-First Century*, Cambridge, MA: Harvard University Press.

Rehbein, Boike et al. (2015) *Reproduktion sozialer Ungleichheit in Deutschland*, Constance: UVK.

Souza, Jessé (2009) *A ralé brasileira*, Belo Horizonte: Editora UFMG.

Souza, Jessé (2010) *Os batalhadores brasileiros: Nova classe média ou nova classe trabalhadora?* Belo Horizonte: Editora UFMG.

Taylor, Charles (1989) *Sources of the Self: The Making of Modern Identity*, Cambridge, MA: Harvard University Press.

Weber, Max (2011) *Die protestantischen Sekten und der Geist des Kapitalismus*, Munich: C.H. Beck.

5   Middle classes

Florian Stoll

In the last decade, a new debate on "middle classes"[1] emerged that focused mostly on the Global South.[2] While there were debates on rising inequality and the decline of the middle classes in Northern countries like the United States (Searcey and Gebeloff 2015) and Germany (Schimank, Mau and Groh-Samberg 2014), the "middle classes" in the Global South are a new phenomenon that has received so far little attention, particularly in the social sciences. In contrast, international media and development institutions have identified the rise of the "middle classes" in developing and emerging countries as one of the most important trends in poverty reduction. The United Nations (2015: 4) point out in their Report on the Millennium Goals that the number of those having more than 4 USD per day has tripled between 1991 and 2015, with half the workforce in developing areas in this middle-income stratum. At the same time, the number of extremely poor with less than 1.25 USD per day decreased from 1.9 billion persons to 836 million.

As a consequence of the political and economic rise of countries in Asia, South America and Africa since around the year 2000, a considerable share of their populations could improve financially. In particular, countries like China and India in Asia, and Brazil and Chile in South America, but even many African countries grew economically in the new millennium. Many millions of individuals succeeded in rising out of poverty or in stabilizing their positions. Economic institutions and development agencies began, subsequently, a debate on "global middle classes" (Banerjee and Duflo 2008; Kharas 2010; Birdsall 2010) which collects economic data on these new groups in developing and emerging countries. However, the only criterion for "middle class" is daily income or expenditure which makes it more of a middle-income stratum as it provides no information on values, political positions or lifestyles as the notion "middle class" implies. In addition to international debates, there were national and regional discussions such as those about the "nova classe media" in Brazil (Scalon and Salata 2012; Pochmann 2014) or "the African middle class" (African Development Bank 2011).

Similar to previous debates on development and modernization, the "middle-class" narrative evokes hopes on economic progress and democratization. The underlying assumption is that a socioeconomic middle class of a significant size leads to certain political structures as well.

It is fundamental for an understanding of the new debate that economic definitions of "middle class" (Neubert and Stoll 2017) are purely descriptive as they often examine only relational middle share of the population. For example, Easterly (2001: 10) studies the middle 60 percent between the poorest and the richest 20 percent; another approach aims at the group between 75 percent and 125 percent of the median income of a nation state (Birdsall, Graham and Pettinato 2000: 3). A different economic definition considers absolute numbers such as purchasing power per person. The entry levels for "middle class" differ strongly, and one can find, for instance, 10–100 USD (Kharas 2010: 9, 12) for the Global South or regionally adapted values such as 2–20 USD for Africa (African Development Bank 2011). Income and consumption rates point at economic developments but they are only vague orientations and cannot describe in detail if and how living conditions have changed and if these living conditions justify the label "middle classes". Absolute numbers seem to suggest that it is possible to define "middle classes" clearly by dollars and even cents. Nevertheless, economic definitions are being set according to the subjective estimates of economists and what they consider as adequate, as the variety of definitions show. Economic numbers give a vague idea of financial possibilities but they do not tell anything about the concrete living environments such as local living costs, positions in symbolic orders and sociocultural influences. Or, to put it simpler: data on daily consumption give a rough orientation if someone is above the poverty line but they do not show much more.

Development institutions, financial organizations and academics do not only study economic growth rates, but they ascribe certain features to them and propose even changes of development aid. The United Nations (2015: 4) formulate, for instance, the growth of the "middle classes" as part of their first goal, the eradication of poverty and hunger. While this sounds plausible, it can comprise a shift from the poorest parts of the population to better off strata which might result in different support strategies. Similarly, the influential development economist Nancy Birdsall (2010) considers the rise of "middle classes" as a success and suggests a shift of priorities in development policies from the focus on the poor to the creation of "middle classes". In these and many other economic reports it remains, however, unclear what characterizes these "middle classes" in empirical settings. There are only plausible but unfounded assumptions that the existence of "middle classes" drives economic growth and democratic developments. Furthermore, it is highly questionable if a monthly income of 120 USD qualifies individuals even on an economic basis to be "middle class", in particular, as the notion evokes inevitable references to European and North American middle-income strata.

It is a fundamental problem of the debate that "middle class" is being defined only on an economic basis and that attributions to this group have a weak empirical and theoretical foundation. Chiefly, authors in this debate do not distinguish socioeconomic stratification and sociocultural differentiation in countries of the Global South, namely, middle-income strata without further specification from middle classes with shared characteristics. Another shortcoming of the debate is the little attention that authors dedicate to established as well as new inequalities. The question of inequality is particularly important as different forms of globalization in the last decades have reshaped economic and social relations, both in the Global North and in the Global South (Rehbein and Schwengel 2008). This new, globalized world did, on the one hand, help many millions of people to improve their financial situation. On the other hand, the transformations led to new processes of exclusion and socioeconomic inequality and extreme political reactions, for instance, by supporting populist and xenophobic politics. In contrast to the focus of the debate on "global middle classes", this article considers the so far neglected inequalities as well.

One important conceptual distinction that clarifies differences between structural and sociocultural analysis, is the contrast between the approaches of "middle stratum" or "middle-income stratum" (Mittelschicht) and "middle class" (Mittelklasse). The conceptual differentiation originates from German Sociology (cf. Geissler 2006: 93–120; Neubert and Stoll 2017). A middle-income stratum is a descriptive analysis on the basis of empirical findings in a certain income range without presuppositions or assumptions about shared characteristics. Middle class is, in contrast, a socioeconomic group in a certain income stratum that share, additionally to similar income, certain characteristics, values, political convictions and possibly even a class consciousness. The theoretical background are class theories by influential sociological authors such as Marx, Weber and Bourdieu that can explain conceptually why the members of a class share certain characteristics. In these theories, class position is also the reason for certain values, positions in political conflicts and lifestyles, as in the societies these authors examined class positions and cultural aspects mostly overlapped. In contrast to descriptive studies, class theories do not only point at empirical findings but they offer an explanation as well. As a third approach this article introduces the concept of social milieus that studies social units on the basis of shared sociocultural characteristics and does not presuppose a similar income.

The international debates on "middle classes" in the Global South ignore, by and large, the analytical distinction of "middle-income stratum" and "middle class" on the one hand, and the analysis of sociocultural differentiated milieus on the other. Both perspectives are, however, helpful tools for understanding the impact of recent changes and the situations of so called middle classes in emerging and developing countries (for Africa: Neubert and Stoll 2017).

The next sections show by examples from Brazil and Kenya how diverse the economic and sociocultural differentiation of middle-income strata in two countries of the Global South are, and by which concepts it is possible to consider the particularities (cf. Rehbein and Stoll 2017). Societies in the Global South differ strongly and there are countries such as Brazil which are to a high degree vertically stratified and where even the "middle classes" must be understood with reference to a vertical order. In particular, in Brazil exist a privileged upper-middle income stratum and an established middle-income stratum which are both in an economically and symbolically better position than the social climbers of the "nova classe media" in the lower middle-income stratum. In contrast, in Kenya it is not convincing to distinguish social units along a vertical order as, namely, the middle-income strata are in their value systems and lifestyles very diverse. Additionally, constitutive sociocultural characteristics of social groups are not necessarily limited to the middle-income strata. Consequently, the particular forms of stratification and sociocultural differentiation show if it makes sense to talk about middle classes or, on a more descriptive basis, middle-income strata.

An analysis of middle-income strata must consider the most relevant qualitative aspects in a certain setting and cannot determine a priori a relative or absolute share of "middle classes". Similarly, the sociocultural differentiation of milieus in a society depends from particular local conditions. It is necessary, therefore, to study on an empirical foundation how social structure and cultural differentiation are embedded in political and economic systems of a society. Brazil and Kenya are two cases that differ strongly and can therefore provide theoretical insights as well. There is a high correspondence between the socioeconomic position and sociocultural aspects in Brazil that makes a description of Brazil as a highly stratified or even "class"[3] society rather plausible. In contrast, in Kenya one encounters, in spite of the high inequality, a multiplicity of sociocultural influences and lifestyles that makes it difficult to draw conclusions from the socioeconomic positions or to speak of a "class" society. Particularly, the middle-income stratum in Kenya is not homogenous.

Theoretical background

Inequality and middle classes/middle strata

The background of the debates on "middle class", "middle-income strata" or "middle strata" are developments in Europe and North America, mainly in the nineteenth and twentieth century (Rehbein and Stoll 2017: 114–17). The notion "middle class" implies more than being part of a certain income range and it contains connotations about related values, political orientations and lifestyles (Neubert 2014). Using the "middle-class" concept in the Global South necessarily carries many connotations into new settings. Connotations such as the hope for development and democracy are responsible for the attractiveness of the "middle-class" concept of the Global South to the Northern public. It is, however, unclear, which of these connotations can be verified for emerging countries through data and which are the projections of journalists, consultants and academics.

The debates on middle classes in the Global North are connected to the emergence of democratic political systems in Europe and America. Additionally, middle classes are situated in debates on stratification and inequality. In economics, Adam Smith (2007) established the widely accepted imagination that inequality is inescapable in capitalist societies and that it is, therefore, a necessary part of society. In contrast, most sociologists treat inequality in the tradition of

Marx (1953) as the major problem of capitalism which is the result of social conflicts and negotiations. The next sections summarize classical approaches to inequality from economics and sociology.

In the decades after the Second World War, inequality seemed to lose its importance in comparison to earlier phases of Northern capitalism. Instead of sharp social contrasts, the socioeconomic indicators pointed at the growing importance of average incomes and of middle classes. For this development, Simon Kuznets (1955) formulated a "law" that assumed inequality would increase in the formation process of early capitalism and decrease in the later periods. Since the 1990s this "law" has lost much of its appeal and there were less and less data that supported it. This seems to show that it is not economic growth itself but the particular social framing of market societies that influences inequality. Consequently, one of the most famous living economists, Joseph Stiglitz (2012) argues that an enduring economic growth is only possible if inequality does not become too high. Similarly, economy as a discipline has taken up in the recent past the question why social inequality has risen by all indicators and why the growth of the Global South had no moderating effect. As a striking example, Branco Milanovic's *Worlds Apart* (2005) examines how inequalities between all individuals and between rich and poor have grown.

Classic economic approaches have not explained inequality and did not even aim to look for explanations. Inequality was considered a consequence of the economy that mathematical models can calculate and predict. Nevertheless, prognoses from the 1990s have not been correct. The theoretical models and their corresponding calculations have been developed for data of the past and it is, therefore, not surprising that they did not succeed in making predictions. By introducing more and more indicators, economic theories intend to develop an improved analysis of inequality on the basis of quantitative data, most prominently in the programme of the World Bank (2015).

Since the 1950s, the majority of sociologists shared the economists' belief in the reduction of poverty and inequality as a function of social development. With social differentiation and modernization theories as theoretical foundations, including professions and education, inequality seemed, in line with a certain reading of Max Weber, to be the mere result of social processes on a macro level of society. Subsequently, most theories of stratification equated the question of social order with the study of the division of labour. For instance, John Goldthorpe's (2007: 104, Volume II) model of social stratification divides the populations of countries in the Global North into seven to eleven classes in different versions of his work. These classes are professional groups and apart from the little attention to social struggles, they ignore the majority of a population, such as students, housewives/-men or retired persons. This model is as well not able to integrate persons with several or changing sources of income. In addition, the model is purely descriptive and it cannot explain theoretically why and how the professional groups differ as the model suggests.

In sociological debates on stratification, Max Weber (1972) prepared the ground for a multidimensional analysis that has been widely considered as an opposing model to Marx's materialism. Theodor Geiger (1932) succeeded Weber and became highly influential in Germany's sociology after the Second World War. Geiger distinguishes groups of mentalities and separates these analytically from the study of socioeconomic positions which is a very different approach than Marxism's deduction of consciousness from class.

Weberian multidimensional approaches lead to approaches as the analysis of social strata ("Schichten") in Germany or status attainment theory (Blau, Duncan and Tyree 1967) in the United States that brought research on inequality close to economics as they took income, professions and corresponding social status as stratifying dimensions. This model implies that the distribution of income or wealth on a descriptive basis is sufficient. In contrast, the sociology of Pierre Bourdieu has a more complex understanding of class and inequality that also carries a critical impulse by showing hidden mechanisms of power and class domination. Similar to Marx, Bourdieu considers inequality in *Distinction* (1984) as a class society whose reproduction must be understood. However, he constructs in a comparable way as Weber and Geiger a multidimensional frame. The reproduction of inequality and social positions is the result of the symbolic justification of hierarchies which can range from professions to taste. Being part of a class includes forms of behaviour, access to different types of social circles and particular cultural ways of doing things. Consequently, for Bourdieu someone's class origin determines the whole amount of available resources, so called capitals, and a certain "habitus", a specific view on life and a way that bears practices. Growing up in a certain social class does not only determine education, work and income but taste and general orientations towards life as well. This "habitus" is the result of someone's social environment but it structures practices in new settings and has, for Bourdieu, the function to explain the reproduction of inequality in changing social conditions. For instance, the middle classes in 1960s France imitate on the one hand – with moderate success – the legitimate taste of the upper classes but they do not acquire the same symbolic position as they miss important trends and are often too late. On the other hand, members of the middle classes distinguish themselves from the working class whose members do not identify with high-class aesthetics and values but who distance themselves and make "out of necessity a virtue" by developing a working-class taste.

Bourdieu's approach goes beyond the focus on financial aspects and takes a new look at inequality by emphasising the importance of culture. Nevertheless, Bourdieu's focus on reproduction and class were in the center of several critiques as well. Jeffrey Alexander (1995) criticises, among other things, that the habitus is mainly a derivé from class position and determines at the same time someone´s practices. Consequently, Alexander misses an adequate study of meanings and the symbolic dimension of actions because Bourdieu reads them necessarily through the lens of social class. Similarly, Michèle Lamont (1992) has shown in a study on upper middle-class men in France and the United States that processes of distinction have a different cultural foundation and that the focus on taste from Bourdieu's *Distinction* is not universal. In contrast,

North American upper middle classes distinguish themselves rather through work ethics than through displays of taste as their French counterparts do. Both of these critiques are important for the study of middle strata in the Global South where living conditions differ to a higher degree from France than they do in the US. In addition, it is not possible everywhere to speak of classes as the socioeconomic position and elements of lifestyle do not necessarily overlap everywhere in the same way.

Sociocultures and milieus

All class theories presented in the previous section focus for their interpretation of inequality on economic factors and study vertically stratified units (cf. Rehbein and Stoll 2017: 117–19). In spite of integrating other dimensions of life, even Bourdieu considers economic differences as most relevant influences. Similar to other authors he considers professions as main criteria for the study of social positions. The focus on professions and other economic indicators is economistic because it excludes a variety of other aspects. The concentration on income and profession is, therefore, rather a distraction than a legitimate focus for the study of middle income classes. In particular, with the rise of middle-income strata in the Global South the scientific more European than North American ideal of a life-long occupation loses much of its legitimacy due to rising inequality, informal labour relations and frequent job changes in developing and emerging economies. The idealized, Eurocentric equation of occupation, social position and realities of life cannot do justice to the more complex living conditions of middle-income strata in different regions of the Global South.

As a consequence, this article recommends paying more attention to sociocultural aspects that are an integral part of inequalities in capitalist societies. In contrast to an economistic understanding capitalist modernity consists of more social and cultural dimensions that cannot be deducted from positions in the division of labour or the income distribution.

Unquestionably, the study of contexts in Africa, Asia and South America requires approaches that consider historical particularities and contextual differences. Examining sociocultures and milieus is an alternative to the study of classes and strata.

In contrast to the analysis of social classes and socioeconomic strata, milieu analysis does not take professions or income as the element of social groups. Instead, milieu studies examine sociocultural phenomena such as core values, forms of actions, preferences in taste and consumption as well as crucial meanings and non-economic activities of social units. This approach has a strong empirical focus and can, consequently, consider particularities such as the relation to the extended family, ethnic ties and forms of colonial history. The reconstruction of social groups on an empirical basis is open to regional specifics and is, for this reason, a powerful tool for studies in the Global South. Societies in Africa, Asia and South America are very heterogeneous but they have in common a history that is different from the classical European one with the sequence of feudalism, the emergence of industrial capitalism and nation-states since the eighteenth century. Correspondingly, countries in the South have not experienced similar processes of class formation like European countries where a large number of workers and farm workers faced a minority of large scale entrepreneurs and land owners in the nineteenth century. Additionally, the growth of significant middle classes and the rise of inequality in the twentieth century was particular for Europe as well.

If one follows the definitions of Marx, Weber and Bourdieu then classes are historically grown, hierarchically separated lines of traditions. These lines of traditions are not being reproduced without minor or major transformations as their societal environments permanently change. Classes as lines of traditions have, therefore, necessarily a strong generational dimension. Differences, ruptures and conflicts between the parents' and the children's generation are the result of upbringings in different social conditions.

Lines of traditions do not, however, necessarily take the shape of vertically separated classes. Instead, the study of milieus as groups with shared mentalities and lifestyles has the potential to cover alternative group formation. The empirical outlook can describe the emergence of new groups under rapidly changing societal, cultural and economic conditions. The flexible milieu approach is, therefore, particularly useful in Southern countries where the influences of a globalized economy and new technologies clash with forms of living and customs that have been established for a long time. Finally, it is an open question which shape social milieus in the different countries of the Global South take. Only empirical research can answer this question. Under certain societal conditions it is possible that milieus take the shape of highly stratified societies, as the example of Brazil demonstrates in the following section.

In contrast, middle-income milieus in urban Kenya are neither homogenous nor are they limited to the middle strata. Data from ethnographic research show that divisive lines follow different patterns than class theory assumes. For instance, the extended family is for certain milieus the most probable household unit and not the individual or the nuclear family.

Middle-income strata in Brazil and Kenya

Brazil

After economically difficult decades in the 1980s and 1990s, the Brazilian economy grew between 2000 and 2011. Tens of millions of Brazilians could improve financially and move, at least in statistics, out of poverty and a precarious existence into what economists called "nova classe media" (Neri 2008), Brazil's new middle class. Additionally, some economically rather modest welfare programs for the elderly and handicapped (*Benefício Assistencial de Prestação Continuada*), a more known welfare program (*Bolsa Família*) for the poorest families contributed to a significant reduction of inequality (Boekle 2010: 436).

In spite of these and more changes since the year 2000, Brazil is still a paradigmatic example for a highly unequal and vertically stratified society. It is possible to distinguish social layers in a vertical hierarchy that differ in income and wealth, access to education and professions as well as in everyday culture with typical lifestyles or ways of consumption. The correspondence of structural positions and cultural characteristics in a vertical order has its roots in the history of Brazil. Since the beginnings of Portuguese colonization, Brazil has been highly unequal with slavery lasting until 1888 and with little participation of the poor majority in the immense growth of the country in the twentieth century. Although Brazil had the highest growth rates worldwide between 1930 and 1980, the politics mainly of authoritarian regimes did not aim at redistribution and excluded continuously the marginalized, mainly Afro-Brazilian former slaves and their descendants.

Since the 1930s, Brazil followed an economic model of state-led capitalist development that favored mainly the upper and middle strata (Pochmann et al. 2006). From the 1950s to the 1970s a considerable, almost exclusively white share of the population rose into socioeconomic positions of established middle- and upper-middle strata who received comparable incomes like their European and North American counterparts. At the same time, the rural and urban poor had to survive under extremely precarious conditions. The economic crisis of the 1980s lead to a restructuring of the economy and improved only after another painful decade that included massive job losses for significant parts of the middle strata and the poor in the 1990s (Pochmann et al. 2006: 32–7). Marcio Pochmann emphasizes, however, that the re-creation of the job market fell together with a new divide of different sections into upper, middle and lower middle-strata. In contrast to the struggling lower and the middle strata, the majority of the upper middle stratum could significantly improve their social position, in particular, through cooperation with international companies in jobs as professionals, lawyers or journalists.

Only against the backdrop of these changes is it possible to understand the economic boom of Brazil between 2000 and 2010. When the 2000s finally brought macroeconomic improvement and tens of millions of new jobs, this was on the basis of two decades of crisis in one of the most unequal countries worldwide. Undoubtedly, the new stability helped many million Brazilians to rise out of poverty. Nevertheless, the discussion about the "nova classe media" (new middle class) was an effective branding of economists and journalists who coined the term according to the five income class A–E of the official Brazilian statistics.

While there are several methodologies that use different estimates about the borders and the size of income brackets, the approach of the institute DIEESE is a rather realistic example how to identify income strata according to the accumulated minimum wage of family households (880 Reais; 260 Euros in December 2016). The institute distinguishes the income stratum E for the "miserable" with 1 minimum wage or less, the stratum D "low" with 1–2 minimum wages, the stratum C "lower middle class" with 2 to 6 minimum wages, the stratum B with 7–19 minimum wages, the stratum A2 "upper middle class" with

20–30 minimum wages and the "upper class" A1 with more than 30 minimum wages. Rehbein and Souza estimate that up to half of the Brazilian population is poor (2014). This matches with my own estimates (Stoll 2012: 109) that put the marginalized in the lowest stratum at about 20 percent, "workers" at about 20 percent, the lower middle stratum at around 30 percent, the middle stratum at around 20 percent, the upper middle stratum at around 8 percent and the rich at 2 percent of the population.

The income differences between the strata are striking, as the upper end of the "upper middle class" has 15 times the family income of the "lower middle class". The large gaps between the strata mirror the high inequality in Brazil and the fundamentally different living conditions. However, the discovery of a "new middle class" was a hype produced by economists (Neri 2008; Lamounier and de Souza 2010) and mass media that resulted in massive critique by trade unions and social scientists (Souza 2009; for an overview over the debate see Scalon and Salata 2012) who criticized that the so-called new middle class was rather a statistical construction and that the modest improvements do not justify the classification as middle class.

The true part of the label "new middle class" is that many million Brazilians have been able to improve their socioeconomic position significantly since the year 2000 and that they formed a clearly identifiable group of social climbers. However, the critique is justified as the living conditions of the "nova classe media" are often vulnerable and they must still struggle like the lower strata to satisfy even basic needs. Their improvement, especially in the economic crisis since 2010, remains highly insecure. In addition, their financial possibilities are far away from the upper middle classes who have similar incomes like European and North American middle strata. Even in the Brazilian context, the new middle classes are not a symbolically legitimate middle class but the public opinion puts them, partly due to their limited economic possibilities, close to the lower strata.

Ethnographic research in Brazil (Stoll 2012) has shown that the lifestyles of social milieus overlap to a large degree with their position in the socioeconomic and socioprofessional stratification. This means that members of a certain stratum in Brazil share, with a high probability, typical basic orientations in life, values and lifestyles. The high inequality makes it plausible to speak of Brazil as a class society as, for instance, Rehbein and Souza do (2014). It may, however, contribute to a better understanding of the Brazilian social reality considering in a first step social milieus with particular conducts of life and basic orientations independent from positions in stratification. This approach is particularly insightful in comparison to the second example of middle-income milieus in urban Kenya where socioeconomic and socioprofessional stratification are not the main criteria for different conducts of life in spite of a high socioeconomic inequality.

Ethnographic research and interviews have revealed that typical conducts of life and basic orientations of milieus with the socioeconomic positions. For instance, the use of time, forms of consumption and taste overlap to a high degree with the socioeconomic position. This is not surprising as Brazil had been highly stratified for generations and typical mentalities of milieus have evolved and reproduced without the postmaterialist tendencies of many North-ern countries in which the conducts and orientations of the social middle from industrial workers to white-collar workers have been intermingling for some decades. In Brazil, however, there is a small but clearly identifiable group of rich and super-rich who have some connections to the upper middle milieu. This upper-middle milieu consists of primarily white graduates who are with the rich in the privileged top 10 percent of Brazil and who have a distinct lifestyle and a high symbolic position. They work as professionals, entrepreneurs and in the liberal professions as leaders and experts in companies and public service. They have a privileged symbolic position and they earn similar salaries like European and North American middle classes. Their standard of living includes several cars, apartments in prime areas, travels to Europe and North America, private schooling for their children and the means for several domestic employ-ees. Members of the middle-middle milieu have significantly different conducts of life, symbolic and economic positions than the upper middle even though members of both milieus sometimes interact.

Similarly, members of this group differ in most cases clearly from the lower-middle milieu that has much less stable living conditions and shares many char-acteristics with the lower strata. The middle-middle milieu consists of small entrepreneurs, employees with good education or employees in public service in middle positions. In spite of negative effects of the economic changes since the late 1980s for this milieu, their living conditions, practices of consumption and basic orientations in life show still some signs of privilege. With a relative stability in their professional life, members of this milieu usually have household help, live in protected apartments and own a car. Their lifestyle has similarities with North American middle classes as they have sufficient financial possibili-ties and considerable time for leisure time activities. This difference in lifestyle activities and mentalities describes a strong boundary line between the middle and the lower-middle milieus who are in an insecure situation and who strug-gle often in a comparable way like workers or the marginalized. While there are employees in this lower middle-milieu, there are as well qualified workers in the formal economy and micro-entrepreneurs who run a small business with-out employees. Their life is still characterized by the struggle to make a living; many of them work in the same jobs as individuals from lower strata, in the formal and informal economies.

Moreover, there are many resemblances in mentalities, housing and aesthetic preferences with the lower income groups. In spite of moderate consumption, the lower middle-milieu has few similarities with European and North Ameri-can middle classes. The majority of the "new middle classes" has risen into this milieu and, consequently, carries typical characteristics. For instance, there is a whole economy of shops like Ponto Frio or Casas da Bahia who make a large share of their turnout with products such as stereo systems and refrigerators for the "new middle classes", namely, by selling the products on credit with very high interest rates that can amount up to 20 percent per month or even more. In spite of the high interest rates, buying on credit is often the only possibility to finance consumption, for members of the low middle milieu as well as for workers and the marginalized.

All in all, there is a high correspondence between the socioeconomic position and the sociocultural milieu affiliation in Brazil. While race is highly relevant as well, it is not identical with stratification but overlaps to a high degree as Afro-Brazilians are overrepresented in relation to their share in the whole population in the lowest strata and are strongly underrepresented in the upper strata. The middle-income strata, i.e. the "middle classes", are like the whole Brazilian society in itself clearly stratified. The example of middle classes in urban Kenya shows that there are fundamental differences and that sociocultural differentiation does not necessarily overlap with socioeconomic and professional stratification.

Kenya

The middle-income stratum of urban Kenya is, in contrast to Brazil, socioculturally highly diverse and it is, therefore, hardly possible to study it convincingly with a vertical approach (cf. Rehbein and Stoll 2017: 125–8). Instead, empirical research (Neubert and Stoll 2015) has shown that different basic orientations and values lead to a variety of social milieus. While it is plausible to speak of "middle class" or "middle classes" in Brazil, the middle-income stratum in urban Kenya is too diverse and relevant forms of differentiation are too complex to put them in a vertical order of high and low groups.

Many of the crucial sociocultural influences have already existed or started to develop under British colonial rule. Namely, these significant impacts are ethnic ties, the relation to the extended family or the membership in churches. Similarly, in colonial times a group of well-educated Kenyans emerged who were mostly employed in public service. These employees were in a better position than the poor majority who lived on farming. After independence in 1964, new groups of entrepreneurs, commercial farmers and individuals in other professions emerged who were in a much better position than most Kenyans.

For almost all Kenyans the relationship to the extended family, the connection to a certain ethnic, regionally founded group (Kikuyu, Luo, Luhya, etc.) and religion are significant orientations (Berg-Schlosser 1979). The intensity of these and other sociocultural influences differs strongly in each milieu. It is a widespread phenomenon to share one's income with the extended family or the local community. Consequently, data on individual consumption do not explain the factual income distribution but they are at best a vague orientation. According to the data of the African Development Bank (2011: 5) 16.8 percent of the Kenyan population were in the year 2010 part of the "middle class", or rather middle-income stratum with a daily income between 4 and 20 USD per head. This share of the middle-income stratum rises to 44.9 percent when the data include the "floating class" (African Development Bank 2011) as well.

This text considers the income range between the poor and the rich as middle-income group to study the diverse basic orientations and conducts of life in milieus. This is necessary as Kenya has never been a stratified class society in the sense of Marx and Weber like most European states or North America in which persons in a similar socioeconomic position shared similar professions with a comparable status and particular cultural features like values or leisure time activities. Sociocultural characteristics such as ethnicity, the relation to the extended family, persisting urban-rural-ties and more influences like religion and different basic orientations lead to varying conducts of life that categorizations founded on income, professions and status cannot describe sufficiently. One reason is that economic activities frequently change and several income sources exist as it is often necessary to overcome financially insecure periods. Likewise, the nuclear family is, unlike in Europe, in most cases not the household unit. Financial support for distant relatives and contributions for school fees or hospital bills are very common and part of a security network.

In contrast to Brazil, the majority of Kenya's population lives in rural areas. The differentiation of milieus in urban areas is much stronger but it offers an orientation for rural areas as well. The realities of life in the urban middle stratum are socioculturally diverse and it makes, therefore, no sense to apply class concepts. Empirical research in Nairobi has shown the existence of the following milieus (Neubert and Stoll 2015; Stoll 2016; Rehbein and Stoll 2017: 126 f.):

- Members of the *neo-traditional milieu* have intense contact with relatives on the countryside beyond their nuclear family and with members of their ethnic group, including frequently political positions that favor their ethnic community. Moreover, members of this milieu feel obliged to share their income with their extended family.
- *Social climbers* have very long working hours and they focus on saving with the aim of improving their individual socioeconomic position and the living of their nuclear family. They save for starting their own business or for fees to acquire a degree.
- The *pragmatic domestic milieu* has, in comparison to other milieus, no strong aspirations but tries to maintain their standard of living including moderate consumption. Mostly, they spend their leisure time at home.
- Members of the *cosmopolitan-liberal milieu* combine a career ambition with a strong orientation towards civil values and against tribalism. As a result of their liberal and democratic convictions, they are active in human rights or environmental groups and are involved in campaigns against corruption and the oppression of women.
- For those in the *Christian milieu* religious norms and the participation in church-related activities are central. Activities like the participation in bible circles, counselling of needy members of their congregation and attending church services take a lot of the free time apart from family life. Religious convictions normally include striving for economic wealth and are seen as God's favor.
- In contrast, *young professionals* are a highly urban milieu with hedonistic consumption, international orientation and career ambition in economically

well-paid fields. Members of this milieu are between 20 and 35 years old, are mostly from families in the upper or upper middle strata, work in well-paid positions and have usually few or no connections to their relatives in rural areas.

In addition to these milieus there are other Muslim or Hindu (micro-)milieus which have been partially researched but which are considerably smaller than, for instance, the *Christian milieu*. It is so far not possible to give exact numbers for the percentage share of each milieu as there are no reliable quantitative data on sociocultural differentiation. Furthermore, it is not always possible to assign a person to a certain milieu. In contrast to milieu studies in Germany (Hradil 1987; Schulze 1992; Vester et al. 2001) the research in Kenya has not always shown clearly distinctive characteristics of members of milieus as it is often a gradual difference of ethnic and rural ties, religious activities or aspirations that lead to varieties in conducts of life. Likewise, there are strong influences of the urban environment on the composition of milieus and the results from Nairobi must be adopted to the situation in other cities. For instance, the *young professionals* exist as a milieu of a considerable size only in Nairobi and even other milieus like the *Swahili* in Mombasa are bound to the local setting (Stoll 2017).

With regards to the debate on global and African middle classes, the results of research in urban Kenya show that there is not "the African middle class" (AfDB 2011). Even in one place there is a large sociocultural variety of milieus with distinctive values and orientations that do not add up to one class. Vertical approaches like those of Marx, Weber and Bourdieu are, in contrast to Brazil, not adequate to study social units in Kenya as they assume a high correspondence of socioeconomic positions, professions and sociocultural characteristics.

Conclusion

While there are discussions on shrinking middle classes in Europe and North America, the debate on middle classes in the Global South reflects recent changes in the world economy (cf. Rehbein and Stoll 2017: 128–30). Since the year 2000 a considerable share of the Asian, South American and African population could economically improve, according to the United Nations (2015) has the size of the middle strata tripled. An exclusively economic definition of "middle strata" or "middle classes" is, however, highly questionable as these groups are often only constructs and it is not always clear which criteria separate them from the poor. This and other problematic points in the debate lead to new questions. Can we really call these groups "middle classes" or do we need another definition? Are these "middle classes" mainly constructs, in spite of some economic improvements? Has there been some redistribution or have certain parts of the populations in the Global South lost some ground in the recent economic changes? These and more questions stimulate discussions on the interpretation of economic data.

The main argument of this text on the relation of middle classes, on inequality in the Global South focused, however, on qualitative and theoretical aspects. In particular, the examples of middle strata in Brazil and Kenya have demonstrated that there are very different middle groups as political, social and economic structures differ strongly. Universal explanations miss necessarily the distinctive relation of socioeconomic structure and sociocultural differentiation in both case studies. Brazil's historically long-established inequality led to a social structure of social groups in a vertical order where life-worlds of milieus overlap to a high degree with economic strata. There are, for this reason, good arguments to consider Brazil as a class society. Data from Kenya have, likewise, shown that a correspondence of economic strata and milieus is not necessarily the case. On the contrary, the statistical construction of individuals in very different realities of life ignores the sociocultural heterogeneity and makes people with fundamentally different orientations and aims in life look like a relatively homogeneous class. This argument is not just a theoretical remark but it has practical consequences as many authors believe that "the global middle class" will be the carrier of good governance (Kharas 2010), economic market orientation and, therefore, development (AfDB 2011; United Nations 2015). An analysis of middle strata as middle classes must be empirically founded and theoretically correct in order to show convincingly the present situation and possible changes. For instance, the argument that the middle class is pro-democratic and favors good governance is as plausible as the argument that the middle class benefits in many contexts from clientelist structures and is, therefore, against good governance and political reforms. Only a clear definition of concepts and empirical studies of political orientations can reveal which positions are prevalent and if there is a connection between the middle-income stratum and a particular positioning. The examples of Brazil and Kenya as well as of other countries like Laos (Rehbein 2007; Rehbein and Stoll 2017) demonstrate that it is more important to understand culture and complexity before it is possible to develop arguments about common traits of middle classes in the Global South.

Notes

1 This text distinguishes a narrative about "middle classes" (for this reason in quotation marks: mainly in the Global South) as they are often being equated with recently grown middle-income strata from middle classes in the Global North which have a comparatively high income and stability of living conditions.

2 I am thankful for the support of the support of the German Ministry of Research for the project "Middle Classes on the Rise" which was part of the Bayreuth Academy of Advanced African Studies and for the support of the Volkswagen Foundation for a Postdoc-Scholarship at the Center of Cultural Sociology, at Yale University. The article was written in Bayreuth and at Yale. It develops ideas that were first put forward in Rehbein and Stoll (2017).

3 Due to the different uses by many authors, "class" appears here in inverted commas. Here, "class" describes how adequate a vertical analysis of social groups is, i.e. to which degree structural socioeconomic positions and culture of "class" members overlap.

References

AfDB (African Development Bank) (2011) 'The Middle of the Pyramid: Dynamics of the Middle Class in Africa', Market Brief, April 20, available at www.afdb.org/fileadmin/uploads/afdb/Documents/Publications/The%20Middle%20of%20the%20Pyramid_The%20Middle%20 of%20the%20Pyramid.pdf (02.04.2015).

Alexander, Jeffrey C (1995) *The Reality of Reduction. The Failed Synthesis of Pierre Bourdieu in Alexander, Fin de Siècle Social Theory*, London, New York:Verso, 128–217.

Banerjee, Abhijit V. and Esther Duflo (2008) 'What Is Middle Class About the Middle Classes Around the World?', *Journal of Economic Perspectives*,Vol. 22: 3–28, available at http://pubs.aeaweb.org/doi/pdfplus/10.1257/jep.22.2.3 (02.04.2015).

Berg-Schlosser, Dirk (1979) *Tradition and Change in Kenya*, Paderborn: Ferdina Schöningh.

Birdsall, Nancy (2010) *The (Indispensable) Middle Class in Developing Countries*, Washington, DC: Center for Global Development.

Birdsall, Nancy, Carol Graham and Stefano Pettinato (2000) 'Stuck in Tunnel: Is Globalization Muddling the Middle?' Center on Social and Economic Dynamics Working Paper No. 14, DOI:10.2139/ssrn.277162.

Blau, Peter M., Otis Duncan and Andrea Tyree (1967*) The American Occupational Structure*, New York: Free Press.

Boekle, Bettina (2010) 'Soziale Ungleichheit und Brasiliens Politikantwort in den neunziger Jahren: Ein Rückblick', in Sérgio Costa et al. (eds.) *Brasilien heute: Geographischer Raum, Politik, Wirtschaft, Kultur*, Frankfurt:Vervuert Verlag, 429–39.

Bourdieu, Pierre (1984) *Distinction:A Social Critique of the Judgement of Taste*, Cambridge, MA: Harvard University Press.

Easterly, William (2001) 'The Middle Class Consensus and Economic Development', *Journal of Economic Growth*,Vol. 6: 317–35.

Geiger, Theodor (1932) *Die soziale Schichtung des deutschen Volkes*, Stuttgart: Enke.

Geissler, Rainer (2006) *Die Sozialstruktur Deutschlands*, Wiesbaden:VS.

Goldthorpe, John H. (2007) *On Sociology*, Stanford, CA: Stanford University Press.

Hradil, Stephan (1987) *Sozialstrukturanalyse in einer fortgeschrittenen Gesellschaft: Von Klassen und Schichten zu Lagen und Milieus*, Opladen: Leske + Budrich.

Kharas, Homi (2010) 'The Emerging Middle Class in Developing Countries', Paris, OCED Development Centre Working Paper 285.

Kuznets, Simon (1955) 'Economic Growth and Income Inequality', *The American Economic Review*,Vol. 45: 1–28.

Lamont, Michèle (1992) *Money, Morals, and Manners. The Culture of the French and American Upper-Middle Class*, Chicago: University of Chicago Press.

Lamounier, Bolívar and Amaury de Souza (2010) *A classe média brasileira: Ambiçoes, valores e projetos de sociedade*, Rio de Janeiro: PUC.

Marx, Karl (1953) *Das Kapital*, Berlin: Dietz.

Milanovic, Branko (2005) *Worlds Apart: Measuring International and Global Inequality*, Princeton, NJ: Princeton University Press.

Neri, Marcelo (2008) 'The New Middle-Class', available at www.fgv.br/cps/classe_media/ (01.02.2017).

Neubert, Dieter (2014) 'What Is "Middle Class"? In Search for an Appropriate Concept', available at http://dx.doi.org/10.17192/meta.2014.2.1330 (24.07.2016).

Neubert, Dieter and Florian Stoll (2015) 'Zur Analyse soziokultureller Differenzierung von Mittelschichten im Globalen Süden: Eine exemplarische Analyse von Milieus in Nairobi', Verhandlungen des 37: Kongresses der Deutschen Gesellschaft für Soziologie, available at http://publikationen.soziologie.de/index.php/kongressband/article/view/51/pdf_77 (24.07.2016).

Neubert, Dieter and Florian Stoll (2017) 'The "Narrative of the African Middle Class" and Its Conceptual Limitations', in Lena Kroeker et al. (eds.) *The African Middle Classes* (in preparation).

Pochmann, Marcio (2014) *O mito da grande classe média: Capitalismo e estrutura social*, São Paulo: Boitempo Editoria.

Pochmann, Marcio, Alexandre Guerra, Ricardo Amorim, and Ronnie Silva (2006) *Classe media. Desenvolvimento e crise*, São Paulo: Boitempo.

Rehbein, Boike (2007) *Globalization, Culture and Society in Laos*, London and New York: Routledge.

Rehbein, Boike et al. (2015) *Reproduktion sozialer Ungleichheit in Deutschland*, Konstanz: UVK.

Rehbein, Boike and Florian Stoll (2017) 'Mittelschichten und Ungleichheit im Globalen Süden', in Hans-Jürgen Burchardt et al. (eds.) *Entwicklungstheorie von heute – Entwicklungspolitik von morgen*, Baden-Baden: Nomos, 111–32.

Rehbein, Boike and Hermann Schwengel (2008) *Theorien der Globalisierung*, Konstanz: UVK.

Rehbein, Boike and Jessé Souza (2014) *Ungleichheit in kapitalistischen Gesellschaften*, Weinheim: Beltz Juventa.

Scalon, Celi and André Salata (2012) 'Uma nova classe média no Brasil da última década? O debate a partir da perspectiva sociológica', *Sociedade e Estado*, Vol. 27: 387–407.

Schimank, Uwe, Steffen Mau and Olaf Groh-Samberg (2014) *Statusarbeit unter Druck? Zur Lebensführung der Mittelschichten (Interventionen)*, Weinheim: Beltz Juventa.

Schulze, Gerhard (1992) Die Erlebnisgesellschaft: Kultursoziologie der Gegenwart, Frankfurt: Campus.

Searcey, Dionne and Robert Gebeloff (2015) 'Middle Class Shrinks Further as More Fall Out Instead of Climbing Up', *New York Times*, January 25.

Smith, Adam (2007) *The Wealth of Nations*, Petersfield: Harriman House.

Souza, Jessé (2010) *Os batalhadores brasileiros: Nova classe média ou nova classe trabalhadora?* Belo Horizonte: Editora UFMG.

Souza, Jessé et al. (2009) *A ralé brasileira*, Belo Horizonte: Editora UFMG.

Stiglitz, Joseph (2012) *The Price of Inequality*, New York/London: Norton.

Stoll, Florian (2012) *Leben im Moment? Soziale Milieus in Brasilien und ihr Umgang mit Zeit*, Frankfurt and New York: Campus.

Stoll, Florian (2016) 'Lebensweisen von Mittelschicht-Milieus in Nairobi: Eine Analyse mit Randall Collins' Interaction Ritual Chains', in Antje Daniel, Sebastian Müller, Florian Stoll and Rainer Öhlschläger (eds.) *Mittelklassen, Mittelschichten oder Milieus in Afrika? Gesellschaften im Wandel*, Baden-Baden: Nomos, 195–216.

Stoll, Florian (2017) 'Cities as Second Nature? Local Characteristics of Middle Class Milieus in the City of Nairobi as Urban Human-Environment Relations', in Michael Hauhs and Georg Klute (eds.) *Human-Environmental Relations and African Natures: Modern Africa* (in preparation).

United Nations (2015) 'The Millenium Development Goals Report', available at www.un.org/millenniumgoals/2015_MDG_Report/pdf/MDG%202015%20rev%20(July%20 1).pdf.

Vester, Michael, Peter von Oertzen, Heiko Geiling, Thomas Hermann and Dagmar Müller (2001) *Soziale Milieus im gesellschaftlichen Strukturwandel*, Frankfurt: Suhrkamp.

Weber, Max (1972) *Wirtschaft und Gesellschaft*, Tübingen: Mohr.

World Bank (2015) *World Development Report 2016*, Washington, DC: World Bank.

6 Elites

Michael Hartmann

The global elite – a myth

Since the early 1990s, the notion of a global or transnational elite has become surprisingly popular in public discourse as well as in the social sciences. Among the proponents are well-known journalists, such as Chrystia Freeland and David Rothkopf, and famous sociologists like Rosabeth Moss Kanther, long-standing President of the Harvard Business School, Manuel Castells, Ralf Dahrendorf and Ulrich Beck. However, the notion of an elite is rarely defined. Those researchers, who, in contrast to the above-mentioned authors, present empirical work and clear definitions of the notion of elite, refer mostly or exclusively to the economic elite. This is even true for William Carroll. Among the proponents of a global or transnational elite, he has published the most thorough and comprehensive analysis. In his study of board members of the 500 largest global companies, in 1996 and 2006, he concludes that it is justified to speak of a "global corporate elite". Between 1996 and 2006, the transnational network of top managers had become more tightly, instead of loosely, knit. But he adds that the network of the "transnationalists" is not really global but encompasses only the North Atlantic. It comprises Europe and North America with an increasing emphasis on inter-European connections. This network, however, is highly integrated (Carroll 2009: 295–8; Carroll 2010: 34).

In recent years, a number of empirical studies focusing on the economic elites of several countries have been published that cast doubt on the notion of a global economic elite or present empirical material which is incompatible with the notion (Bühlmann, David and Mach 2012; Bühlmann, Davoine and Ravasi 2017; Davoine and Ravasi 2013; Dudouet, Gremont and Vion 2012; Ellersgaard, Larsen and Munk 2013; Hartmann 2007, 2009a, 2010, 2015; Heemskerk 2013; MacLean, Harvey and Chia 2010; MacLean, Harvey and Kling 2014; Pohlmann 2009; Schmid, Wurster and Dauth 2015; Schneickert 2015; van Veen and Marsman 2008; van Veen and Elbertsen 2008; van Veen and Kratzer 2011; Timans 2015: Yoo and Lee 2009). But these studies only refer to regional notions and often also functionally limited samples of the economic elites.

Lately, I have completed the first study of all CEOs of the world's 1,000 biggest companies as well as the board members of the largest companies located in the most important countries of Europe, North America and Asia (Hartmann 2016). The results are unambiguous. Only 126 of the 1,002 CEOs were born abroad, which means one out of eight. If we exclude those companies that have their legal headquarters in another country for tax reasons or are binational with two headquarters, the percentage drops to less than ten percent. There are significant differences between the nation states. By far the highest percentage of foreign CEOs work in Swiss corporations (72 percent). Australian and British companies follow with about 45 percent. The percentage of foreign CEOs in Canadian, Dutch and German enterprises is between 15 to less than 30 percent. We have to take into account, however, that some of the corporations in the Netherlands, Great Britain and Switzerland have their actual headquarters in other countries.

In most countries, less than ten percent of the CEOs are from abroad. The percentage for the US is eight percent, for France four, and for Japan two. In the largest Chinese, Italian, Russian, Spanish and South Korean corporations, no CEO is from another country. Furthermore, two thirds of the foreign CEOs are from a culturally similar country. A foreign CEO in an Anglo-Saxon company would typically be from another Anglo-Saxon country, while a foreign CEO in Germany would be from Switzerland, Austria or the Netherlands. As far as experience abroad is concerned, the numbers increase. Of the native CEOs, 22.5 percent have spent a period of at least six months abroad. But this is not really a convincing argument for the internationalization of economic elites either, since more than three quarters of the native CEOs have never been abroad for a longer period of time (Hartmann 2016: 31–4, 53–61).

If we restrict our analysis to the 100 largest companies of Germany, France, Great Britain, the US, Japan and China, we see that internationalization has increased significantly during the past two decades only in German and British corporations, increased very slowly in US and French corporations and even slightly decreased in Japanese and Chinese corporations (Hartmann 2015). Looking at the 100 largest British companies, the share of foreign CEOs drops to one third as opposed to 44 percent for the 50 British companies within the 1,000 largest companies of the world (Hartmann 2016: 65). We may infer that the percentage of foreign CEOs is highest in the sample of the 1,000 largest corporations. It might decrease considerably if we look at a larger number of companies.

Among other elites, the internationalization is far less pronounced. We can confirm this with reference to political elites by studying the European Union, which is the only institution in the world that is able to produce transnational political elites imbued with actual power. The European Union is presently characterized by centrifugal and not by homogenizing tendencies. Even in the administrative elite of the EU, national connections remain far more important than is commonly assumed. Among the 33 general directors of the European Commission (all of whom but three come from the old EU member states) only one third has had a European career, i.e. a career that after the first four years was spent exclusively within European institutions. Thirteen general directors switched from a national to a European career after the first ten years or even later. The remaining third switched from a national to a European career during a period of between four and ten years. Only 6 of the 38 vice-directors have moved into a European career after four years of professional life or earlier, whereas 21 spent at least their first ten years in their country of origin. This means that 17 directors can be classified as having a European career and exactly twice as many as having an overwhelmingly national career. The European College in Bruges, supposedly *the* recruitment center of the European bureaucracy, does not play a major role in this regard. Only 5 of 71 directors have studied there, all of them after completing a university in their country of origin. All other directors have studied exclusively at national universities, the French and British directors mostly at renowned elite institutions. The national type of elite formation remains dominant in all realms.

The three dominant national types of elite formation

We can divide the national types of elite formation into three general types on the basis of two core characteristics, namely vertical and horizontal social integration. In principle, the homogeneity of elites decreases with its vertical integration, i.e. with its ties to the rest of the population, and increases with its horizontal integration, i.e. with the ties between its parts. This means that elites are most homogeneous where recruitment is not only socially exclusive but also draws on elite educational institutions and consists of individuals who shift between the different elite sectors, e.g. between politics and business. In Europe, the French case is the only one that fully fits this model, outside of Europe, the Japanese case is very close to it.

The second type is represented by Great Britain. Recruitment is also exclusive and draws on special educational institutions but there is little exchange between the elite sectors. The US is a good example of this type outside of Europe. Most industrialized countries can be subsumed under the third type. There is little mobility between the sectors and there are no special educational institutions. Therefore, elites of this type are likely to be more heterogeneous than those of the other two types. However, the degree varies strongly with the social recruitment of elites, which can be rather different between the nation states. The following sections outline a few examples for the prevailing three types.

Elite universities and circulation between the sectors

To reach an elite position in France is almost impossible without attending one of the famous elite universities in the country, the *grandes écoles*. This is easily visible in the economic elite. More than half of the native CEOs of the 100 leading French corporations (or 50 out of 96 CEOs) have attended one of the three most famous *grandes écoles* – ENA, Polytechnique or HEC – even though these host a total of 0.5 percent of all students in France. A significant portion of the top CEOs completed their studies at one of five other elite universities like Sciences Po or École Centrale. A total of two thirds are alumni of these eight schools. Their significance for the French business elite has not changed for many decades (Hartmann 2016: 173).

Something similar is the case in politics, and the administrative and legal systems. In the governments of Valls and Cazeneuve similar to the preceding cabinets, about 40 percent of the ministerial positions have been occupied by alumni of ENA and Sciences Po. President Hollande and two of his immediate predecessors (Giscard d'Estaing and Chirac) have also graduated from ENA. The same holds true for 21 of the 42 directors and vice-directors of the *cabinets ministériels*. Another eight had studied at the Polytechnique and three more at the other famous *grandes écoles*. These are numbers that have hardly changed since the 1990s (Hartmann 2010: 293–4). The highest administrative and financial courts are equally exclusive. 47 out of 50 presidents and vice-presidents of the highest administrative court are alumni of the ENA. This is true for nine of the eleven most powerful positions at the highest financial court, namely seven of the eight presidents, one of the two secretary-generals and the general attorney. The other two have studied at other *grandes écoles*.

After attending a *grande école*, one has to take another hurdle, the *grands corps*, which are the elite institutions of public administration. There are five administrative *grands corps*, the *Conseil d'État*, *Cour des comptes*, *Inspection des finances*, *Affaires étrangéres* and *Corps préfectoral*, and two technical ones, the *Corps des mines* and *Corps des ponts et chaussées*. They are basically reserved for the best French graduates of the ENA and the Polytechnique. Access depends on graduate ranking. Graduates can choose their destination based on their rank position. Almost all of them will inevitably choose a position in the *grands corps*. The ten best ENA graduates are likely to choose the *Inspection des finances* and the ten best Polytechnique graduates would pick the *Corps des mines*.

These two *corps* offer the best prospects for a business career. Every fourth French CEO was a member of one of these *corps*. An alternative itinerary leads through the ministries. Twelve of the top-100 CEOs have worked in a ministry, usually as a member or director of a cabinet *ministériel*, the immediate entourage of a minister. These positions are less formally defined than the *grands corps* and also accessible through other *grandes écoles*. A related example is a former minister of the economy, who had worked in the ministry of education for four years in the early stages of his career. Almost every second CEO (42 percent) of the 100 largest French companies has spent some time working in a government administration or in politics (Hartmann 2016: 178–80). The French even have a specific term for this pattern, *pantouflage*. The combination of *grandes écoles* as a condition for access to an elite position in all sectors with the common shift of individuals from one sector to another results in a uniquely high level on a global scale of horizontal integration of the French elites.

In terms of vertical integration or social recruitment, the French elites are the most exclusive among all industrialized countries as well. Seven of the eight presidents of the Fifth Republic have their social origin in the upper or upper middle class. Their fathers belonged to the top four percent of the population. Merely Pompidou was middle class. Three quarters of the 20 prime ministers and 50 to 80 percent of the cabinet members (depending on the ruling party) have their origins in the upper middle and upper class. Ninety percent of the CEOs of the 100 largest companies have the same social origin. One of the main reasons for this exclusive recruitment is the social exclusivity of the *grandes écoles*. A regular person is very unlikely to pass the entrance exam. Less than ten percent of students belong to the lower 90 percent of the French population. These schools are dominated by upper middle and upper class children (Bourdieu 1996: 36–7, 74, 137–41, 169, 246–8; Hartmann 2010: 296). This leads to the extreme and globally unique exclusivity and homogeneity of the French elites.

Apart from France, two other industrialized countries have similar systems of elite education. These are Spain and Japan. Spain does not have elite universities that would compare to the *grandes écoles* but an elite corps of public administration, which is organized according to the French model. Its members occupy the majority of the highest administrative positions. In 2005 and 2015, every fifth CEO of the 30 largest Spanish companies had occupied such a position earlier in life. This means that there is movement between the sectors similar to France. However, this becomes less common. Before the government of Rajoy, a quarter of the cabinet members had moved through the *elite corps*, in this government we do not find this type any more. However, it comprises two former CEOs, which means that there is some exchange between the economic and the political elite.

In Japan, the movement between leading positions in different sectors is common as well, usually from high position in the government bureaucracy into politics and business. Just like in France, there is a special term for this, "*Amakudari*" (descending from heaven). But the Japanese system differs fundamentally from the French *pantouflage* in one regard. Movement takes place on the second or third levels but only rarely between top positions. Only one of the 98 Japanese CEOs of the 100 largest Japanese companies had worked in the high ministerial bureaucracy prior to becoming a CEO. Japanese business careers almost exclusively remain within one company: 95 out of the 98 CEOs of the 100 largest corporations have never worked in another company (Hartmann 2016: 181). In politics, where *Amakudari* used to be common even in top positions, movements from other sectors have become rare as well. Only three of the twenty cabinet members in the Abe administration had worked outside of politics before. In the 1990s, it was one third (Colignon and Usui 2003: 150–4; Hartmann 2010: 318; Schmidt 2005: 180–2).

Japan, however, shares the same significance held by elite universities in France. The so-called top five, including the oldest and most famous university, Todai, have hosted most of the leading politicians and businesspeople. Eight of the twenty members of the Abe government have studied there, four at Todai alone, and 52 of the 98 leading CEOs, 22 of whom at Todai (Hartmann 2016: 173). Even though the relevance of elite universities has declined for a political career, albeit not for a business career, they can still be compared to the *grandes écoles*.

As far as social recruitment is concerned, the Spanish elites are similar to the French but not quite as exclusive (Hartmann 2010: 298). Data on Japanese CEOs is insufficient in this regard. However, among the last five prime ministers, three have an upper-class background. Nine of the twenty cabinet members of the Abe government come from the same class. Their fathers have been prime minister, minister, president of parliament, governor, high ministerial bureaucrat or CEO. At least for the political elite, it is safe to say that its recruitment is rather exclusive. It is likely that this also holds true for the economic and administrative elites, since the elite universities, especially Todai, are socially very selective, even if not quite as exclusive as the French *grandes écoles* (Schmidt 2005: 93).

Elite universities without circulation

The recruitment of elites in Great Britain has traditionally been very similar to that of France and Japan but individuals have not shifted between the different sectors of politics, business and administration. There used to be a clear educational pattern. Most members of the elites studied at highly exclusive institutions. First, they attended a private school, usually a renowned public school, then they studied at Oxford or Cambridge. This pattern has changed during the past two decades, especially as far as the economic elite is concerned. Only 23 or one third of the 67 British CEOs of the largest 100 British companies are alumni of Oxford or Cambridge. Twenty years ago, it used to be almost 50 percent (Hartmann 2016: 173). If we compare the conservative cabinets of Cameron and May with that of John Major, we see a similar picture. Under Major, almost 80 percent of the ministers had studied at Oxbridge. Today this is true for 50 percent.

For the high administrative and legal positions, Oxford and Cambridge are still highly relevant. Two thirds of the 114 highest judges in the country are graduates of these two universities. This is less than in the 1990s, when the percentage was three quarters. In contrast, we see no change for state secretaries. Around 70 percent are alumni of Oxbridge (Hartmann 2010: 299). Still, Oxbridge has lost some of its power to connect the British elites across sectorial boundaries.

Even more relevant is the declining relevance of private schools, especially the renowned public schools. These used to be much smaller than Oxbridge and therefore produced fewer graduates and were more exclusive. Therefore, they constituted the nucleus linking elites across sectors to each other. In contrast to Oxbridge, they were also relevant for the education of the leading representatives of the military. In 1995, about three quarters of the 93 CEOs of the 100 largest companies had attended a private school, in the financial sector even more than 80 percent. Eleven had gone to Eton, the most famous public school, and more than 25 percent to one of the Clarendon Nine, the nine most exclusive public schools in the country, including Eton (Hartmann 2010: 298–9).

This has changed significantly during the past two decades. Today, only three graduates of Eton and six graduates of the Clarendon Nine in total remain among the top CEOs. The share of private school graduates has declined from three quarters to one third. If we include non-British CEOs, the percentage is even lower (Hartmann 2016: 186–8). Private schools, and especially public schools have lost much of their formerly outstanding relevance. This is partly due to the massive restructuring of the financial sector, which has been dominating the British economy for more than a century. The classic private banks, all of which were led by Clarendon alumni, mostly Etonians, have been swallowed by large foreign banks. The private banks used to occupy a central position in the City of London and within the British upper class. On this basis, they also dominated the recruitment of leading managers for the other financial enterprises and, to a lesser degree, the rest of the economy. This pattern belongs to the past, along with the overwhelming influence of the renowned public schools. In my opinion, the deregulation and globalization of London as a financial center, which the protagonists in politics and business considered inevitable, is responsible for this decline.

This decline mainly concerns the key positions in the economy but also extends to other elite sectors, even if not to the same degree. Two thirds of cabinet members under John Major have attended a private school and one-eleventh of them had gone to Eton. Eton still is relevant, since three of the forty-four cabinet members of the Cameron and May Governments are Etonians but overall, only 40 percent of the ministers have attended a private school. We can observe a similar development among the state secretaries. Whereas 75 percent of them had attended a private school in the 1990s, this is true for only 40 percent today. The percentage of the Clarendon Nine merely declined from 14 to 12 percent. The situation is no different for the leading judges. The share of those who have attended a private school decreased from around 80 to 50 percent, the percentage of the Clarendon Nine from more than one fourth to 14 percent (Hartman 2010: 299). Even though every seventh high judge today is a graduate from one of the Clarendon Nine, private and especially public schools are far less relevant today.

Public schools no longer connect the elite segments in the economy and in the other sectors, even though they have not disappeared (Commission on Social Mobility and Child Poverty 2014). However, the social recruitment of British elites has not been affected significantly by this development. Eighty percent of the CEOs, 60 percent of the members of the Cameron and May cabinets, a large chunk of the legal elite and most state secretaries have their roots in the upper middle and upper class.

The structure of the elites in the US resembles that of Great Britain. Almost one third of the 93 US citizens among the CEOs of the 100 largest companies have studied at an Ivy League university, especially Harvard (Hartmann 2016: 170, 173). This is also the case for one half and one third of the cabinet members of the Obama and Trump administrations, respectively. The social recruitment fits the educational structure. Three fourths of the CEOs, which is the same percentage as ten years ago (Hartmann 2007: 237), and half of the cabinet members (and about two thirds of the eight most important ones) have an upper or upper middle class background. Two of the ministers, Penny Pritzker in the Obama and Betty DeVos in the Trump Administration, are among the richest women of the US. Social recruitment under the Obama administration is less obvious than under Reagan and Bush senior, when around 85 percent of the cabinet members had an upper or upper middle class background. But it is more coherent than under Bush junior and much more so than before Reagan, when only a minority of the most important cabinet members came from these two classes – namely between one fifth (under Carter) and two fifths (under Truman and Kennedy) (Hartmann 2009b: 293).

The US-elite has always differed from the British in one regard, however. There has been a significant circulation between the leading positions in politics and the economy. Every fourth member of the administrations since the Second World War had led one of the top-500 companies in the US (Hartmann 2009b: 293). At present, this is true for only one of eight. Possibly the structure of the US-elites is moving toward the British model. Even in the past, not too many CEOs had had a top position outside of the economy before. Around 95 percent had always worked in business, which is true up to this day. Most of the few outsiders had held intermediate positions before entering business.

Neither elite universities nor circulation

In most industrialized countries, the third type of elite formation prevails. It differs from the other two types insofar as access to elite positions does not depend on attendance of elite educational institutions. And it is distinguished from the first type by the relatively clear boundaries between the elite sectors. This type also tends to be less socially exclusive, albeit not in every case.

Members of the elites corresponding to this type are recruited from a great variety of universities. Old and prestigious universities prevail but there is no concentration on a few elite institutions. The economic elites of Germany, Denmark and the Netherlands illustrate this. One third of the German CEOs of the 100 largest companies in the country studied at one of ten universities but these ten institutions host almost 20 percent of the general student population anyway. This is a large percentage combined with the less than one percent of the French student population attending the leading *grandes écoles*, three percent studying at the Ivy League universities, five percent at the top five in Japan and eight percent at Oxbridge. The numbers are similar for the Danish and the Dutch CEOs (Ellersgard, Larsen and Munk 2013: 1057; Timans 2015: 164–5), and they do not differ much in the other sectors. We do not see a focus on a small number of exclusive universities. Furthermore, the preferred universities differ according to the sector. In the economy, technical universities play an important role but not in the other sectors. In the juridical and also in the administrative elite, a degree in law prevails, which is usually not attained at a technical university.

Career patterns are usually restricted to one sector. Not even five percent of German CEOs have worked outside the field of business. The number is twice as high for Denmark and the Netherlands (Ellersgrad, Larsen and Munk 2013: 1061; Timans 2015: 237; Hartmann 2016: 178). This still means, however, that nine out of ten CEOs have spent their entire career in business. The picture is similar for elites in the other sectors, even though we can observe a slightly higher percentage of people working in more than one sector and an increase in elite circulation over the past years. In spite of this, movement from a leading position in one sector to a leading position in another is rare. Sector changes are usually restricted to the early phases of the career (Hartmann 2010: 303–6; Hartmann 2013: 90–9).

In contrast to educational and career patterns, social recruitment differs vastly between the countries. A glance at the economic elite illustrates that. Just like their British or Spanish colleagues, four fifths of the German CEOs have an upper or upper middle class background. Among Italian CEOs, this number decreases to two thirds, and among Danish and Dutch CEOs even a bit less. Only half of Swedish, Swiss and Austrian CEOs are recruited from these two classes (Ellersgaard, Larsen and Munk 2013: 1053; Hartmann 2010: 308–12; Korom 2013: 124–6; Timans 2015: 161).

The contrast is similar with regard to elites in the juridical and the administrative systems. Two thirds of the top positions in Germany are occupied by members of the two highest classes. The political elite is more accessible in all of the countries of this type, even though it is more open in Switzerland, Sweden and Austria than in Italy and Germany. About half of the members of the German executive branch at the federal level can be classified as upper middle or upper class (Hartmann 2007: 222; Hartmann 2010: 308; Hartmann 2013: 48, 65). It is likely that the differences are rooted in national traditions, such as the egalitarian culture in Scandinavia, in the differing sizes of the large companies in each country and the relative influence of lower-class parties.

Conclusion

The prevalence of national elite formation systems and the concomitant huge differences between the elites of different nation states show that we are a long way from something like a transnational elite. In some states, the economic elites have proceeded a bit along this way but even there, truly international patterns are rare. An analysis of the richest individuals on earth confirms this assessment. Only ten percent of the 1,000 richest individuals live abroad. Even less have studied abroad (Hartmann 2016: 120–8, 161–6).

The internationalization in those nation states that do not belong to the group of the fully industrialized countries seems to be even less pronounced. Very few of the CEOs in those countries come from abroad. This includes Brazil, China, India and Russia. However, we have to acknowledge that they developed different patterns of elite formation, which cannot be fully sub-sumed under the three types outlined above. The CEOs of the 100 largest Chinese companies have studied at a great variety of universities without any significant focus on the most famous institutions, such as Tsinghua or Jiao Tong. In this respect, China resembles Germany. However, every third leading CEO has spent several years of his or her career in the state sector, albeit usually on an intermediate level. This means that Chinese career patterns correspond nei-ther to the German nor to the French type but are characteristically Chinese. Therefore, the formation of a transnational elite becomes even more dubious if we include the global South.

References

Bourdieu, Pierre (1996) *The State Nobility: Elite Schools in the Field of Power*, Cambridge: Polity Press.

Bühlmann, Felix, Thomas David and André Mach (2012) 'The Swiss Business Elite (1980–2000): How the Changing Composition of the Elite Explains the Decline of the Swiss Company Network', *Economy and Society*, Vol. 41: 199–226.

Bühlmann, Felix, Eric Davoine and Claudio Ravasi (2017) 'European Top Management Careers: a Field Analytical Approach', *European Societies* (forthcoming).

Carroll, William K. (2009) 'Transnationalists and National Networkers in the Global Corpo-rate Elite', *Global Networks*, Vol. 9: 289–314.

Carroll, William K., Colin Carson, Meindert Fennema, Eelke Heemskerk and J. P. Sapinski (2010) *The Making of a Transnational Capitalist Class: Corporate Power in the Twenty-First Century*, London and New York: Zed Books.

Colignon, Richard A. and Chikako Usui (2003) *Amakudari: The Hidden Fabric of Japan's Econ-omy*, Ithaca, NY: Cornell University Press.

Commission on Social Mobility and Child Poverty (2014) *Elitist Britain?* London: CSMCP.

Davoine, Eric and Claudio Ravasi (2013) 'The Relative Stability of National Career Pat-terns in European Top Management Careers in the Age of Globalization: A Comparative Study in France/Germany/Great Britain and Switzerland', *European Management Journal*, Vol. 31: 152–63.

Dudouet, François-Xavier, Eric Gremont and Antoine Vion (2012) 'Transnational Business Networks in the Euro-Zone: A Focus on Four Major Stock Exchange Indices', in Geor-gina Murray and John Scott (eds.) *Financial Elites and Transnational Business: Who Rules the World?* Cheltenham: Edward Elgar, 124–45.

Ellersgard, Christoph Houman, Anton Grau Larsen and Martin D. Munk (2013) 'A Very Economic Elite: The Case of the Danish Top CEOs', *Sociology*, Vol. 47: 1051–71.

Hartmann, Michael (2007) *Eliten und Macht in Europa*, Frankfurt: Campus.

Hartmann, Michael (2009a) 'Die transnationale Klasse – Mythos oder Realität?', *Soziale Welt*, Vol. 60: 285–303.

Hartmann, Michael (2009b) 'Politische Elite und Einkommensverteilung in den USA seit 1945', *Leviathan*, Vol. 37: 281–304.

Hartmann, Michael (2010) 'Elites and Power Structure', in Stefan Immerfall and Göran Therborn (eds.) *Handbook of European Societies*, Springer: New York, 291–323.

Hartmann, Michael (2013) *Soziale Ungleichheit – Kein Thema für die Eliten?* Frankfurt: Campus.

Hartmann, Michael (2015) 'Topmanager 2015. Die transnationale Klasse – Mythos oder Realität Revisited', *Soziale Welt*, Vol. 66: 37–53.

Hartmann, Michael (2016) *Die globale Wirtschaftselite: Eine Legende*, Frankfurt: Campus.

Heemskerk, Eelke M. (2013) 'The Rise of the European Corporate Elite: Evidence From the Network of Interlocking Directorates in 2005 and 2010', *Economy and Society*, Vol. 42: 74–101.

Korom, Philipp (2013) *Die Wirtschaftseliten Österreichs*, Konstanz: UVK.

MacLean, Mairi, Charles Harvey and Robert Chia (2010) 'Dominant Corporate Agents and the Power Elite in France and Britain', *Organization Studies*, Vol. 31: 327–48.

MacLean, Mairi, Charles Harvey and Gerhard Kling (2014) 'Pathways to Power: Hyper-Agency and the French Corporate Elite', *Organization Studies*, Vol. 35: 825-55.

Pohlmann, Markus (2009) 'Globale ökonomische Eliten – Eine Globalisierungsthese auf dem Prüfstand der Empirie', *Kölner Zeitschrift für Soziologie und Sozialpsychologie*, Vol. 61: 513–34.

Schmid, Stefan, Dennis J. Wurster and Tobias Dauth (2015) 'Internationalisation of Upper Echelons in Different Institutional Contexts: Top Managers in Germany and the UK', *European Journal of International Management*, Vol. 9: 510–35.

Schmidt, Carmen (2005) *Japans Zirkel der Macht*, Marburg: Tectum Verlag.

Schneickert, Christian (2015) *Nationale Machtfelder und globalisierte Eliten*, Konstanz: UVK.

Sklair, Leslie (2001) *The Transnational Capitalist Class*, Oxford: Wiley-Blackwell.

Timans, Rob (2015) 'Studying the Dutch Business Elite', PhD thesis, Rotterdam: Erasmus Universiteit Rotterdam.

Van Veen, Kees and Janine Elbertsen (2008) 'Governance Regimes and Nationality Diversity in Corporate Boards: A Comparative Study of Germany, the Netherlands und the United Kingdom', *Corporate Governance: an International Review*, Vol. 16: 386–99.

Van Veen, Kees and Jan Kratzer (2011) 'National and International Interlocking Directorates Within Europe: Corporate Networks Within and Among Fifteen European Countries', *Economy and Society*, Vol. 40: 1–25.

Van Veen, Kees and Ilse Marsman (2008) 'How International Are Executive Boards of European MNCs? Nationality Diversity in 15 European Countries', *European Management Journal*, Vol. 26: 188–98.

Yoo, Taeyoung and Soo Hee Lee (2009) 'In Search of Social Capital in State-Activist Capitalism: Elite Networks in France and Korea', *Organization Studies*, Vol. 30: 529–54.

Part III
Dimensions of inequality

7 Gender and inequality

Emanuelle Silva

The category of gender has been closely associated with that of inequality right from the start. It was also closely linked to the political scene, since it was mainly promoted by feminist movements. We can distinguish three overlapping phases of the feminist movements, which relate to three different concepts of gender inequality. The first phase, starting in the nineteenth century, consisted of the emancipatory movements against limits of democracy and connected struggles against male domination with those against racism, colonialism, capitalism and others. The second phase rendered the discussion more academic and specialized. This also led to more sophisticated approaches to gender inequality. The third phase reconnects gender to other dimensions of inequality but also questions the assumptions of the earlier phases of the discussion.

The category of gender was only developed in the course of these discussions, first as a means to distinguish the social construction of gender from the biological category of sex. It became evident, however, that this simple distinction had all kinds of theoretical implications and rested on problematic assumptions itself. Against this backdrop, the debates about gender have produced a great deal of literature that is relevant to the epistemology, political framing, methodology and empirical body of inequality research.

This chapter will not summarize the history of research on gender. Neither will it give much attention to the political realm. It will rather focus on the theoretical implications of the discovery of the category itself and the debates around it. The first section deals with the concept, the second develops the social construction of gender, the third studies how this social construction is incorporated, while the fourth relates the notion of gender to that of class. The final section summarizes important aspects of contemporary debates about the concept of gender.

The concept of gender

Gender, as a concept, emerged in the mid-1970s (Rubin 1975) and spread rapidly in the social sciences during the 1980s. The concept distinguished sex – an analytical category marked by biology and an approach anchored in the biological – from the gender dimension that emphasizes features of historical construction, society, and above all policy, and involves relational analysis. As a proposal for a classification system, the category "gender", in its most pervasive and widespread form, has mostly been conceived of as a binary to refer to the differences between: female and male, men and women and also between homosexuality and heterosexuality.

The concept of gender was developed and conceptualized as the social construction of sexual identities and as an object of feminist studies. It constituted a breakthrough in feminist studies to include universal trends in relation to the male and female with historical and cultural specificities (Sardenberg 2004: 24). The term sex, in contrast, implied a biological foundation of gender differences and addressed psychological dimensions, social and cultural rights of femininity and masculinity, from this perspective.

Gender is a relational concept that considers the relations of power between men and women and indicates that the roles and subjective attitudes are both social constructions. The book *Second Sex*, originally published in 1949 by Simone de Beauvoir, can be considered the starting point of gender studies with the sentence: "No one is born a woman, but becomes a woman." This phrase actually represents the only consensus that exists among feminists about gender. In her book *Second Sex*, de Beauvoir sought to deconstruct the naturalization of being a woman, showing that certain biological traits are not more important than the social and political determinations in the process of "becoming a woman".

After many academic publications about women and feminism (Matos 2008), Gayle Rubin in 1979 conceptualized a sex/gender system against the background of a debate with theories such as Marxism and psychoanalysis. The sex/gender system concerns the ways in which a society transforms biological sexuality into products of human activity that become conventional and come to be seen as "natural". The author also argues that this process often results in the oppression of women. Rubin highlights the sexual division of labor, the social organization of sexuality, sexual coercion of women, compulsory heterosexuality, and patriarchy as forces that maintain the oppression of women.

An important contribution was the emphasis on the performative dimension of gender. Gender is not only socially constructed, it also has to play out in social practice. Zimmerman and West (1987) have therefore introduced the notion of "doing gender". The "doing gender" perspective helps us understand the social constructionist aspect to gender and how gender identities are not static, but rather fluid entities that are continually in the process of formation during social interactions. Gender may be fundamental, institutionalized, and enduring, but because actors "do gender" as a process in social settings gender meanings and identities are always capable of and ripe for change. This perspective aligns with identity theory's idea of gender identity commitment and salience, which will be discussed shortly. The more one "does gender" among others in interactions, the more likely one's gender identity will become more committed, and thus salient within the self.

The concept of gender is attributed to social construction, which makes women and men unequal. Its use was a counterpoint to biologistic interpretations that link sexual difference to hierarchically different social positions of women and men. The contemporary understanding of the world has changed this setting, especially from the first attempts to overcome social inequalities between men and women. Using the design dichotomous nature versus culture, or sex versus gender, Bruschini (1998: 89) exposes the concept as:

> Principle that transforms the biological differences between the sexes in social inequalities, structuring society on the asymmetry of the relationship between men and women. Use "gender" for all references to social or cultural, and "sex" for those to biological issues.

There are also those who think that even sex is socially constructed. For ethnomethodologists, sexual categorization is a habit, rarely questioned (Wharton 2005). They believe that sexual categories and the "natural attitude" are social constructions as well as biological and physical realities. This concept brings us to the idea of the immutability of sex, defended by French scholars of the early twentieth century. They refused to separate the social and biological spheres, as well as the concepts of gender and sex.

The first essays and studies on the inequalities between women and men focused on the female aspect of the body and sexuality (cf. Saffioti 2004: 185). The biological characteristics, among them, the lesser physical strength and even the lower weight of the brain, were the center of this discussion in an attempt to explain that the feminine "nature" as weak and the male "nature" as strong. Those biological explanations just helped to emphasize common assumptions previously held of what is the "natural place" for women in the house, in "women's jobs" and in "care for the family" and the "male natural place" in the marketplace or workplace with, possibly, a powerful position outside the household. This idea of the human condition is nothing more than a response to legitimize social inequalities.

For Judith Butler (1990: 29), gender is a shifting and contextual phenomenon, which does not denote a being but a relative convergence point between specific sets of cultural and historical relations. From this perspective, there is no gender identity behind the expressions of gender, since identity is developed. Gender deconstruction theory (Butler 1987: 142) claims that "we become our gender and not our gender". This idea is often cited as a reason for a departure from feminist studies in favor of so-called queer theory. In a view similar to Butler's (1987), Fraser and Nicholson (1990) argue that the rapprochement between feminist theory and postmodernism would drop the idea of gender as the subject of the story, replacing the unitary notions and female generic identity with social identity concepts that are plural and complex, with gender only one relevant trait among others.

Adriana Piscitelli (2002: 7) has pointed to the epistemological consequences. She adopted the concept "campo de genero" (gender field) to criticize dichotomies and binaries in gender studies (Lauretis 1990; Louro 1997). Through meanings and interpretations published and shared in the new analytical perspective and cutting across class, size, age, race, and sex, gender has played the key role in the human sciences to denounce and even unmask the modern structures of colonial oppression, economic, generational, racist, and sexist, operating for centuries in spatiality and temporality.

Social construction of gender

In her essay "The Traffic in Women", Gayle Rubin mainly remembers the later 1970s for having drawn the distinction between sex and gender, providing elements for the elaboration of the concept of gender. The aspects of the text that seem important to highlight point to an intriguing aspect of reproduction and sexuality. Feminists, reflecting on the subordination of women, were pioneers in questioning the direct relationship between reproduction and gender. One of the effects is to confuse sexuality and gender. But over the decades, and in parallel with the rapid growth of sexuality studies within the field of reproductive health, including those aimed at AIDS, these thought-provoking reflections seem to have been diluted. Rubin's "Traffic" was central to these questions.

When developing the idea of a sex and gender system, Rubin shows how the relationship between reproduction and gender permeates certain analytical frameworks and how it is anchored in the assumption that tends to appear in a more veiled manner: the naturalness of heterosexuality. She bases her theory on several authors, including Lévi-Strauss. In particular, the concept of the synthesizing family (1980) is relevant here. Society must ensure that marriage is a fundamental need. That would be secured through a device establishing a reciprocal state of dependency between the sexes: the sexual division of labor. Just as the principle of sexual division of labor established a mutual dependence between the two sexes, forcing them to start a family, the prohibition of incest established a mutual dependence between families, forcing them to perpetuate themselves and create new families.

The conclusion is that the difference between the human world and the animal world lies in the fact that the human family could not exist without society, i.e. a plurality of families willing to recognize that there are other ties beyond consanguineous ones, and that the natural process of descent can only be carried out through the process of social affinity. Rubin says, with reference to Lévi-Strauss, kinship establishes the biological difference between the sexes. Kinship systems involve the social creation of two dichotomous sexes, a particular sexual division of labor, the interdependence of men and women, and social regulation of sexuality, prescribing or repressing other arrangements than heterosexuality.

Thus, the suppression of the homosexual component of human sexuality and, according to Rubin, the oppression of homosexuals, are products of the same system whose rules and relations oppress women. In this sense, the relationship between homosexuality and kinship is particularly interesting, raising several questions. One question refers to the process of destabilizing this assumption and how that would affect the distinction (and relationship) nature/culture. A second question refers to thoughts about how gender would operate if it took into account the relationship between kinship and homosexuality.

Joan Scott offers us one of the most important theoretical contributions to the use of gender. For all human symbols, such as words and concepts, have a history. This includes the term gender (Scott 1988). In this way she rejects words that could foster the notion of biological determinism and stresses the relational character of feminism and masculine settings. Scott argues that the concept of gender was created to oppose a biological determinism in relations between the sexes, giving them a fundamentally social nature. Gender also emphasizes the relational aspect of definitions of femininity (Scott 1988: 5). This relational aspect comes from the concern that some women's studies focused on women too narrowly, so the notion of gender would realize that women and men were defined in reciprocal terms and could not be understood separately. Scott (1988) also highlights gender as an analytical category, like race and class. She promoted the inclusion of the oppressed in history, but has also enabled the analysis of the meaning and nature of their oppression and academic understanding that inequalities, given the power, are related at least to these three elements: gender, race, and class.

The incorporation of gender

As main components of social structure, status and roles allow us to organize our lives in consistent, predictable ways. In combination with established norms, they prescribe our behavior and ease interaction with people who occupy a different social status, whether we know these people or not. There is an insidious side to this kind of predictable world. When normative behavior becomes too rigidly defined, our freedom of action is often compromised. These rigid definitions are associated with the development of labels – oversimplified assumptions that people who belong to the same group have certain traits in common. Although stereotypes can include positive traits, they most often consist of negative ones that are then used to justify discrimination against members of a given group.

The status of male or female is often stereotyped according to the traits they are assumed to possess by virtue of their biological makeup. Women are stereotyped as flighty and unreliable because they possess uncontrollable, raging hormones that fuel unpredictable emotional outbursts. The assignment of negative stereotypes can result in sexism, the belief that the status of female is inferior to the status of male. Males are not immune to the negative consequences of sexism, but females are more likely to experience it because the status sets they occupy are more stigmatized than those occupied by males. Compared to males, for example, females are more likely to occupy roles inside and outside their homes that are associated with less power, less prestige, and less or no pay. Beliefs about inferiority due to biology are reinforced and then used to justify discrimination directed toward females.

The socialization process into gender roles begins at birth: families usually treat newborns differently according to their sex. Families begin to socialize gender roles even in the delivery rooms – boys are dressed in blue, while girls are dressed in pink (or other colors that are symbolically attached to gender). From the moment that a baby enters the world, it is inundated with symbols and language that shapes its conception of gender roles and gender stereotypes. Language used by families to describe boys is often centered on physical characteristics and such themes as strength and agility, while language appropriated to girls by families might address affection, expressivity, daintiness, or fragility.

These different approaches and treatment of babies by the family serve to shape behavior patterns and define boundaries. These boundaries are eventually internalized and become *identity standards* – the references in which interactions, settings, and contexts are used to compare the self to others. Literature in this area examines the mechanisms that differentiate what is considered acceptable for male and female behavior, and how such behavior evolves over time.

Boys and girls learn and develop in gendered subcultures, which influences the character of their social networks and future interactions. For example, when a father teaches a son to be aggressive and encourages playing sports and doing activities that involve negotiating with others, the son will likely learn that appropriate behavior is to interact with a wide range of people in heterogeneous groups. When a mother encourages a daughter to interact intimately with others and encourage more one-on-one play, the daughter will likely internalize messages and cues that promote similar behavior later in life. These identities that are internalized early during child socialization – both from the family and from other sources – serve to create highly differentiated worlds of acceptable behavior.

Gender, class, and Marxism

Criticism directed at postmodern theories, among them deconstructivism and poststructuralism, claims that feminist theory "exaggerates" differences. In this sense, Piscitelli (2002: 32–3), expounding on the objections to these approaches by some feminists, says:

> In addition to dissolve the political subject "Women", the deconstructivist outlook is also accused of re-establish distances between the theoretical reflection and political movement. . . . Today, they say, the theoretical perspectives they result "of little use", inaccessible, esoteric, difficult to understand, too detached from practice and leading to paralysis.
>
> (translation by the author)

The accusation is that feminists are turning their studies toward esoteric theories, while the reality of the living conditions of female workers remain enormously precarious. And despite this instability, many do not realize that their womanhood is subordinated and exploited in this society, which means these women do not acknowledge the need for organization to fight for a new social order.

The problem triggered by new approaches to gender studies is, therefore, a gap between the theoretical discussions and the real-life struggle of women, which demonstrates that these theories are meaningless, in a practical sense, and limited to academia. The "gender studies" referenced by postmodernity eventually create a dichotomy, as shown by Moraes (1996).

Class status determines how these various expressions of oppression will be experienced by subjects. A woman belonging to the ruling class exploits a working-class woman, a young woman can exploit an elderly woman, and a white woman can exploit a black woman. Leftist critique of postmodern gender studies, therefore, have postulated that feminism has to have a class struggle as its core. What is defended here, is not the neutralization or cancellation of differences, but the perception that the feminist movement should converge with certain political and social objectives. Otherwise, feminism would just fragment women, which does not contribute to the fight undertaken by other movements. The "biggest mistake" is to put the emphasis on "differences", just as cultural constructions, not analyzing, with an overarching perspective, that these cultural expressions have common roots in a class society and denote a clear interest on the part of the ruling class to perpetuate subordination of others for their own ends.

From this perspective it has been argued that Marxism, unlike postmodernity, does not result in a confused and barren theory, without clear political developments. Marxist theory is fundamentally focused on the transformation and overcoming of bourgeois society. It has, therefore, explicit objectives of policy intervention intended to instigate a revolutionary process through the commitment and the interests of the working class. Marxism provides a critical analysis of the social relations pertaining to gender through a perspective of totality that does not fragment the reality, seeking to understand it beyond the appearance of "representations".

So-called "culturalist feminism" reframes materialism in the so-called "culturalist materialism" theory, rejecting a "systemic analysis, anti-capitalist and the relationship between the history of culture and the construction of meanings in a social class system" (Hennesy, Castro and Lavinas 1995: 102). The "culturalist feminism" goes against the demands that historical conditions put to confront social inequalities, to marginalize "analysis of work and gender in favor of cultural practice, body meanings, pleasures" (ibid.).

Another critique of blindness to class from a very different perspective has been offered by Nancy Fraser (1997, 1999). She became internationally known for her scathing criticism of the philosophical work of Habermas, especially his concept of the "Public Sphere". The latter had its origin in the structural change in the sphere of work, Public (1984), in which Habermas discussed the genesis and transformation of the "bourgeois public sphere". Fraser (1999) pointed out the moment for the emergence of "subaltern publics", those social groups that, because of the design of a national and homogeneous public sphere, would be excluded from public deliberations, such as women and ethnic minorities.

118 Emanuelle Silva

The main points of critique can be summarized as follows: 1) the different actors in the public sphere cannot put on hold their status differentials and act as if they were equal, confirming the implicit assumption that social equality in liberal models and bourgeoisie is not a necessary condition for democracy; 2) there are multiple competing public spheres and this does not necessarily represent a departure from democracy, on the contrary, the multitude would be preferable to the existence of a single, comprehensive public sphere; and 3) the public sphere would be the voting place about the common good and all other issues that are relevant to the collective would be negotiated in the public sphere; this includes the articulation of private interests (since the "private is also political"). Finally, Fraser says that the public sphere model developed by Habermas presupposes a rigid separation between civil society and the state, which would not always be realistic or even desirable. Turning to the issue of equality, Fraser argued that, despite the lack of formal impediments to participation in public debate, some informal obstacles still persist.

Queer theory

Queer theory emerged in the United States in the late 1980s in critical opposition to sociological studies on sexual and gender minorities. Appearing in departments not usually associated with social investigations – such as philosophy and literary criticism – this theoretical current gained recognition from some conferences at Ivy League universities, which exposed the object of its analysis: the dynamics of sexuality and desire in the organization of social relations. The critical tension with regard to social sciences boosted queer enterprise and the establishment of a dialogue that was already apparent when, in a collection of books on contemporary social theory, the title *Queer Theory/Sociology* (1996) appeared.

The dialogue between Queer Theory and Sociology was marked by estrangement, but also by affinity in the understanding of sexuality as a social and historical construction. The queer-strangeness dialogue in relation to social theory derived from the fact that, at least until the 1990s, the social sciences treated the social order as synonymous with heterosexuality. The heterosexual assumption in sociological thought prevailed until the appearance of investigations into non-hegemonic sexualities. Despite their good intentions, minority studies ended with maintaining and naturalizing the heterosexual norm.

Theoretically and methodologically, queer studies arose from the encounter between a tradition of Philosophy and American Cultural Studies with French poststructuralism, which criticized classical concepts of subject, identity, agency, and identification. Central was the break with the Cartesian concept (or Enlightenment) of the subject based on ontology and epistemology. Although there are variations between several authors, it is clear that the subject of poststructuralism is always seen as temporary and circumstantial. Queer theorists found in the works of Michel Foucault and Jacques Derrida concepts and methods for a more ambitious undertaking than the theoretical undertakings so far by social scientists. In general, the two philosophical works that have provided its foundations were *History of Sexuality: The Will to Know* (1976) and *Of Grammatology* (1967), both published in English in the second half of the 1970s.

Based on these publications, theoretical scholars like Eve K. Sedgwick, David M. Halperin, Judith Butler, and Michael Warner began to undertake social analysis based on Foucault, studying sexuality as a historical device that still exists in modern Western societies and is sexualization of human drives and social regulation (Foucault 1978: 99–100).[1] "Queer" studies highlight the centrality of social mechanisms related to binary operation, heterosexual and homosexual, to the organization of contemporary social life, giving more critical attention to a policy of knowledge and difference. In the words of sociologist Steven Seidman, queer studies deal with "that knowledge and those social practices that organized 'society' as a whole, sexualizing – as heterosexual or homosexual – bodies, desires, acts, identities, social relations, knowledge, culture, and social institutions" (Seidman 1996: 13).

Queer theorists understand sexuality as power. A device is a heterogeneous set of discourses and social practices, a true network that is established between such diverse elements as literature, scientific statements, institutions, and moral propositions. Originating predominantly from cultural studies, queer theorists have given greater attention to discursive analysis of films, artistic and media works in general. Contemporary interpretations of "queer" can be understood as a critical response to globalization and North American models of heterosexual identity, but also of liberal feminism and integrationist gay culture (Preciado 2007: 387), in other words, as a theory, which resists an Americanized, white hetero-gay and colonial world (ibid.: 400).

Given the origin and centrality of desire and sexuality in the development of Queer Theory, some ask, what distinguishes it from the sociology of sexuality. To begin with, it is not institutionalized, so does not have a canonical form and discussion of their differences is always risky. Sociological studies on sexuality and queer theory can be cautiously compared. They both seek to understand sexuality as a social construction, but from different perspectives and proposed methodological procedures that mark not only the results of their research but the very way queer theory and sociology are defined scientifically and institutionally.

Sociologists, and other social scientists, often took sexuality as a given and abandoned socially hegemonic models, which resulted in enlightening research on sexual behavior, relationships between men and women, and the social construction of masculinity and femininity but that, by taking as a starting point normative forms of relationships, tended to reinforce the positive provisions of sexuality denounced by Foucault and provide a language that often approached an updated sexology. Queer theory focused on the theoretical analysis of the speech producing sexual knowledge through a deconstructivist method. Instead of focusing research on the social construction of identities, empirical studies of sexual behaviors that led to classifying them or understanding them, queer developments stem from a distrust of sexual subjects as stable and focus on normalizing social strategies of behavior. By putting into question the coherence and stability that characterize the constructivist model, which provides a comprehensive and standardized framework of sexuality, queer studies provide a sharper look at the standard-setting social processes that create classifications, which, in turn, generate the illusion of stable social identities and consistent and regular behaviors.

Conclusion

Gender studies have contributed to our understanding of inequality on many levels. Important are the inquiries into the social and symbolic construction of differences that are used as unequal classifications. Many assumptions that had been taken for granted by the social sciences were subjected to scrutiny and critique. Much of this critique was developed within the field of gender studies itself and has not been sufficiently acknowledged by the mainstream of the social sciences. At the same time, many scholars within gender studies have not sufficiently evolved with the development of the field itself.

It is highly relevant to repeat that gender studies will remain inconsequential and outdated if they do not seek the connection with other dimensions of inequality and with the political field. This is the main point of intersectionality. This current within gender studies is associated with an influential paper by the legal scholar Kimberlé Crenshaw (1989) who argued that a white woman and a black man are both privileged in comparison to a black woman. The study of the intersections of inequality remains one of the most important tasks.

Note

1   The list of queer theorists is extensive and there are difficult to place names, such as the cultural anthropologist Gayle Rubin. Her *Thinking Sex* (1984) is one of queer references, but the author distances himself from textual analysis objects and various methodological procedures associated with them. His critical position in relation to queer is noticeable in an interview with Butler.

References

Bruschini, Cristina (1998) *Tesauro para estudos de gênero*, São Paulo: Fundaçao Carlos Chagas.
Butler, Judith (1987) 'Variações sobre sexo e gênero: Beauvoir, Wittig e Foucault', in Seyla Benhabib and Drucilla Cornell (eds.) *Feminismo como crítica da modernidade*, Rio de Janeiro: Rosa dos Tempos, 139–54.
Butler, Judith (1990) *Gender Trouble*, New York: Routledge.
Crenshaw, Kimberlé (1989) 'Demarginalizing the Intersection of Race and Sex', *University of Chicago Legal Forum*: 139–67.
De Beauvoir, Simone (1949) *The Second Sex*, New York: Rowman & Littlefield.
Derrida, Jacques (1976) *Of Grammatology*, Baltimore, MD and London: The Johns Hopkins University Press.
Foucault, Michel (1978) *The History of Sexuality: An Introduction*, New York: Pantheon Books.

Fraser, Nancy (1997) 'Heterosexism, Misrecognition and Capitalism', *Social Text*, Vol. 15: 52–9.

Fraser, Nancy (1999) 'Social Justice in the Age of Identity Politics: Redistribution, Recognition, and Participation', in L. Ray and A. Sayer (eds.) *Culture and Economy After the Cultural Turn*, London: Sage, 25–52.

Fraser, Nancy and Linda Nicholson (1990) 'Social Criticism Without Philosophy', in Linda Nicholson (ed.) *Feminism/Postmodernism*, London: Routledge.

Habermas, Jürgen (1984) *The Theory of Communicative Action Vol. 1: Reason and the Rationalization of Society*. Boston: Beacon Press.

Hennesy, Rosemary, Mary G. Castro and Lena Lavinas (1992) 'Do Feminino ao gênero: a construção de um objeto', in Albertina de Oliveira Costa and Cristina Bruschini (eds.) *Uma Questão de gênero*, Rio de Janeiro: Editora Rosa dos Tempos, 100–110.

Lauretis, Teresa (1990) 'Feminism and Its Differences', *Pacific Coast Philology*, Vol. 25, No. 1/2: 24–30.

Lévi-Strauss, Claude (1980) *A Família, origem e evolução*, Porto Alegre: Editorial Villa Marta.

Louro, Guacira Lopes (1997) *Uma perspective pós-estruturalista*, Petrópolis: Vozes.

Matos, Marlise (2008) 'Movimento e Teoria Feminista: é possível reconstruir a teoria feminista a partir do sul global', *Revista de Sociologie e Política*, Vol. 18: 67–92.

Moraes, Maria Lygia Quartim (1996) 'Vinte anos de feminismo: Campinas', Thesis in Sociology, Campinas: Universidade Estadual de Campinas.

Piscitelli, Adriana (2002) 'Re-criando a (categoria) mulher?', in Algranti (ed.) *A Prática Feminista e o Conceito de gênero: Textos Didáticos*, Sa~o Paulo, IFCH/Unicamp, 32–3.

Preciado, Beatriz (2007) *Mujeres en los márgenes*, Madrid: El País.

Rubin, Gayle (1975) 'The Traffic in Women: Notes on the "Political Economy" of Sex', in Rayna Reiter (ed.) *Toward an Anthropology of Women*, New York: Monthly Review Press, 157–210.

Rubin, Gayle (1984) 'Thinking Sex: Notes for a Radical Theory of the Politics of Sexuality', in Henry Abelove (ed.) *The Lesbian and Gay Studies Reader*, London, New York: Routledge, 143–79.

Saffioti, Heleieth I. B. (2004) *Gênero, patriarcado, violência*. 1st ed. São Paulo: Fundação Perseu Abramo.

Saffioti, Heleith (2005) 'Gênero e patriarcado', in Márcia Castillo-Martín and Suely de Oliveira (eds.) *Marcadas a ferro: Violência contra a mulher, uma visão multidisciplinary*, Brasília: Secretaria Especial de Políticas para as Mulheres.

Sardenberg, Cecília M. B. (2004) 'Estudos Feministas: um esboço crítico', in Célia Gurgel (ed.) *Teoria e práxis dos enfoques de Ggnero*, Salvador: REDOR-NEGIF, 17–40.

Scott, Joan (1988) *Gender and the Politics of History*, New York: Columbia University Press.

Seidman, Steven (1996) *Queer Theory/Sociology*, Oxford: Blackwell.

West, Candace and Don H. Zimmerman (1987) 'Doing Gender', *Gender and Society*, Vol. 1: 125–51.

Wharton, Amy (2005) *The Sociology of Gender: An Introduction to Theory and Research*, Oxford: Blackwell.

8   Inequality and migration

Anja Weiß

In the eyes of economists, inequalities in resource distribution are driving the economy. In the eyes of sociologists, unequal resource distribution creates a problem, social inequality, if differences in resource endowment affect the capabilities of human beings. Poverty seen as a lack of resources as well as a very unequal distribution of resources precludes the equal interaction of people. This is interpreted as problematic for political self-organization. For example, if one citizen owns a newspaper and another can neither read nor write it is virtually impossible to see these two as building a political community together. Thus, in sociology, observation and critique of inequalities implicitly connect with the normative assumptions of citizenship. This explains why economy and sociology are often criticized as methodologically nationalist. Both disciplines presume that the borders of a fully developed nation-state bound the collective in which comparison is meaningful.

Scholars of social inequality therefore have trouble when dealing with migration and cross-border economic linkages. In theory, it is clear that supply and demand chains, financial markets, educational systems and even some kinds of governance traverse national borders. Still, the fact that some people live and work, earn and consume in more than one nation state continues to challenge analysts of social inequality. The value of migrants' resources differs between countries and they might belong to more than one political community. This results in the social sciences treating migrants as an exception to the rule. Exceptionalism is often justified with respect to migrants' low numbers: Migrants comprise about one tenth of the population in the Global North (International Organisation for Migration 2013: 59) and just three percent of the world's population live outside their country of birth.

Yet, mere numbers do not adequately grasp the problem. Migration structures inequalities not only when persons migrate, but also when persons *might* migrate or have migrants in their household. Figures of persons born outside their country, i.e. international migrants, omit internally mobile populations, even though their experience can be very similar to that of international migrants, e.g. in the Chinese *hukou* system (Jieh-Min 2010). While the number of migrants may appear to be low, in qualitative terms the decision between "exit, voice, and loyalty" (Hirschman 1970) results in a global social structure in which claims for equal participation extend beyond nation-state borders.

This chapter discusses classic theories relating migration and inequality and it sketches a more comprehensive model, in which the impact of socio-spatial autonomy on world social structure is explained (Weiß 2005, 2017, in print). We start with a review of theories on migrants' position in the country of origin and of arrival, respectively. In the second part, paradoxical class relations between positions in several countries and transnational social spaces are discussed and the argument is expanded to include sedentary populations. Both migrants and non-migrants are positioned relative to multiple contexts in which they acquire and use resources. Spatial fixation and geographical mobility are functional alternatives for attempts to improve one's capabilities. As such, sedentariness can express the privilege to stay in a well-endowed context or the result of social exclusion. Socio-spatial autonomy, i.e. the ability to migrate without loss to one's resources, clearly adds to the value of resources even and especially for those who can choose to stay at home.

Migrants moving between nationally bounded labor markets

Classic migration theory argues that migration responds to income differentials, i.e. inequalities between countries. Migrants are "pushed" abroad by a lack of economic opportunities (and instability) in their country of origin or "pulled" by attractive conditions in another country. This is a classic and important contribution to migration studies, but it overlooks many other ways in which migration and inequalities are related. These ways are usually "social" or "collective", i.e. migrants do not act as individuals, but are embedded in intergroup relations structuring their positioning strategies (Portes and Sensenbrenner 1993). For example, after the 1986 Southern enlargement of the EU, Spanish and Portuguese citizens stayed put despite significant differences in income and employment opportunities. Migration decisions are embedded in complex political situations that evolve over time (de Haas 2011). It follows that the relation between migration and inequalities is complex, too.

This being said, several distinct theories explain most of the inequalities migrants face. One of these theories concerns the selectivity of migration in the country of origin. Migration is a risky endeavor. Therefore, it is the relatively young, healthy, strong and educated who leave a country. As potential migrants need some economic capital in the first place in order to move abroad, migrants stem from the relatively deprived classes, but not from the absolute poor.

The fact that migrants compare well with the people they leave behind receives additional support from economists of the household arguing that it is a rational strategy for extended families to pool their resources in order to send some members abroad (Massey 1990). Extending risk across more than one political entity increases security for everyone. Ideally, the emigrated family members send remittances and serve as pioneers that smooth the path for further emigration. One stable income can matter a great deal for families who remain in a fragile environment in which the economic situation of the family and/or country may suddenly change for the worse. The emigrant, on the other hand, can hope for a wealthy old age "at home" where he or she will profit from familial support.

Even though migrants are endowed with more resources than their compatriots, they tend to be relatively poor once they arrive in a foreign country. For the most part, this is due to income and purchasing power differentials they experience elsewhere. Even members of the middle classes in emergent economies turn into paupers after they have passed the currency exchange and read some price tags in an average store (Korzeniewicz and Moran 2009). This is even more so for immigrants whose family had to pool resources, who come from very poor countries or who had to overcome multiple barriers to immigration.

The pattern governing economic capital also explains cultural capital differentials, with some notable differences. In the case of educational credentials, it is not only a lack of education, but also the discrediting of educational credentials that account for the relative poverty of immigrants in the country of arrival. Since educational systems are organized nationally, schools in poor countries tend to offer a poor education and they do not give access to everyone. In addition, local and national resources and preferences structure curricula with significant differences between centers and peripheral regions in the world. This said, even the poorer countries do have (privately funded) schools and universities whose educational outcomes compare well with that of rich states. The curricula of "international" schools and tertiary education emulate those abroad. Yet migrants who have been able to secure an internationally valid degree find that expectations in the country of arrival do not give them credit (Nohl et al. 2014). Lesser outcomes are also due to signaling effects (Spence 1973) and statistical discrimination (Arrow 1973) by employers who do not value foreign credentials even after the credentials are formally recognized.

In terms of social capital, migrants lose some of the connections they had in their country of origin and replace them with new transnational networks in the country of arrival. As migration tends to strengthen ethnic identity and solidarity, migrants may actually have an advantage over the sedentary population. For example, poor migrants may be able to get credit from compatriots (Portes and Sensenbrenner 1993). For migrant employers it may be easier to exploit cheap labor given a limitless supply of young people in the home country who would love to go abroad.

Yet, ethnic solidarity comes at a price. Given most migrants' relative poverty in terms of financial and educational resources, their network contacts in the country of arrival tend to lack important resources. If they make up for the lack of resources by "enforced solidarity", i.e. by stricter rules and social closure, the more aspiring members of the community and the descendants of migrants may find themselves in a so-called "ethnic mobility trap": Ethnic networks connect with the networks of ethnic majorities in the less favored segments and locations. This can impact negatively on educational aspirations and economic success in the younger generation (Zhou 1997) thereby discouraging individual social mobility.

Finally, the negotiation power of migrants is reduced by migration legislation and the particulars of their boundary spanning position. Newly arrived migrants rarely have access to full citizenship and welfare rights. Restrictions range from complete exclusion from formal employment, as is the case for undocumented migrants, to the obligation to stay in specific labor market segments as is the case for professionals who are either forced to remain in a particular profession (e.g. scientists) or barred from their profession (e.g. doctors). Some restrictions affect employment chances negatively while others enforce employment at any cost (Nohl et al. 2014). In both cases, migrants cannot be choosers in terms of pay, security and career potential when they are looking for a job. Providing for family members in the country of origin creates additional pressure to make as much money as they can as soon as possible. Employers know this, which results in the ethnic segmentation of labor markets (Bonacich 1972). Temporary visas result in a limited time frame which reduces incentives to invest in education with the resulting differences in resource endowment.

Most of the theories relating to migration and inequality use economic (functionalist) reasoning and build on political theories that validate the nation-state. They accept the national organization of educational credentials, the legal exclusion of foreigners or the rationality of banks who offer bad terms to those whose collaterals are located abroad. This is different for discrimination theories (Feagin and Feagin 1986). Theorists of discrimination point out that the value of resources is socially determined and thus negotiated. In their view, the economic poverty of migrants does not only result from purchasing power differentials but is also due to migrants being charged higher prices for lesser value. The education of migrants does not only lose value because employers cannot understand foreign credentials but also because they assume that "our schools are the best in the world". Migrants are reduced to ethnic networking because of ethnic and racial discrimination and politically they can neither vote nor organize without basic citizenship rights. From a macro-regional perspective global relations of racial and gender inequality that were invented during early colonialism take the form of exclusionary citizenship regimes today (Boatcă 2015).

Strategic use of manifold context relations

Most migration theories focus on the state of origin or the state of arrival. Recently, the networks that connect migrants to specific locations have been a focus. Network theories can explain why persons who want to migrate opt for destinations in which friends or at least compatriots reside. Migrant transnationalism has argued as well that the connections migrants build between plural locations in the world matter not just for their identities, but also for more material matters.

Take the earnings of migrants as an example. For the reasons mentioned above, the majority of migrants make less than the average in the country of arrival. They are reduced to three-D jobs: dangerous, dirty and demeaning. Scholars of class therefore debate whether migrants are the "new underclass", the new "precariat", and so on, and they are amazed by migrants with conservative political tendencies (Levitt and Glick Schiller 2007). How can the poorest of the poor express middle class sentiments and follow parties that stabilize the status quo?

Migrant transnationalism has an answer to that riddle. The same migrants who appear to be destitute without rights from a country-of-arrival-perspective have experienced paradox class mobility (Parreñas 2001) from a transnational perspective. It is true, that their above average qualifications have not earned them qualified jobs, which is a kind of downward mobility they suffer from. At the same time, their earnings often translate into an above average income in their country of origin. They send remittances, thus enabling their family to invest in education and real estate and support a middle-class position there. This in turn impacts on the social structure in the country of origin (Nieswand 2011): If educated and striving persons who stayed at home are outdone by the success of less educated (but also striving) migrants who work 3-D jobs abroad, this challenges and/or transforms order in the country of origin.

Migrants live, learn, work, earn and consume in more than one country and sometimes in more than one (transnational) social field. This has an impact on their class position, which then appears to be a "paradox" from a nation-state perspective. A more transnational lens in studies of inequality accepts that migrants' class position evolves in relation to at least two nation-states as well as further, more transnational, fields of contestation. In the case of highly skilled migrants this means that they are not only "Iranians living in Germany", but also persons that are part of a transnational professional network of doctors and of epistemic communities applying universal standards of knowledge to situated problems (Weiß 2016). Their social positions are connected to and situated in more than one social context.

This argument can and should be expanded to more sedentary parts of the population. As argued above, the experience of internal migrants might be similar to that of international migrants, for example in the Chinese *hukou* system distinguishing between rural and urban citizens. Some sedentary groups, notably elites, have formed resource networks and fields of contestation that cross national borders. And even those who do conform to the idea of locally bound immobility have to face competition by people with more versatile social connections. This results, as I have argued (Weiß 2005, 2017, in print), in a global social structure in which socio-spatial autonomy plays a significant role.

In the sociology of social inequality, three schools of thought connect persons with the contexts in which their resources are validated: First, aspects of persons become valuable as resources in differentiated social systems. Bourdieu's (1986) differentiation of economic, cultural and social capital is one way to grasp the ways in which persons gain capabilities. In a similar vein, Luhmannian systems theory argues that systems observe aspects of persons and include them in their functioning. Since Luhmann's systems span national borders even more than Bourdieu's fields it places the above mentioned high skilled migrants in a diversity of national and transnational social contexts. For example, an IT-professional working for a global player in Dubai operates in a global labor market and not in the nation-state in which she is residing. Her networks may have a focus on India as well as her (post-)colonial Commonwealth and her cultural capital might stem from India and the United States.

Second, differentiated social relations are reframed in the political system and relations of symbolic hegemony. By highlighting ascribed criteria political systems fix persons to (imagined) places irrespective of their functioning in socially differentiated fields. As a female from India the above-mentioned IT-professional is in a politically precarious position in Dubai, but the precariousness is offset by her ability to move abroad at any time.

Third, persons are also body-actors in a territory offering a specific infrastructure and specific action settings. This is not important for the IT-professional who will be wooed by most nation-states in the world, but it could matter for her Syrian domestic workers when considering a move across the Mediterranean onwards toward the EU. For undocumented migrants whether they can reach a territory where they might become legal residents is decisive, or where purchasing power is so high that even incomes in the informal sector translate into large remittances.

Empirically, the three kinds of context relations intertwine and partially compensate for or add to each other. For example, the Syrian domestic worker in Dubai may be able to pass as local. This may not help in terms of political rights, but in terms of symbolic recognition and connections to local networks. Also, context relations interact with the resources a person holds which results in a model of social structure in the world where social positions are characterized not only by the quantity and quality of their capital, but also by the socio-spatial autonomy of their person and resources.

This enables us to expand our argument from migrants to the general population. Sedentary people can improve their position through socio-spatial autonomy, too. For example, in the upper classes of the world, status high passports and universally recognized financial and cultural capital add to the value of their resources through socio-spatial autonomy. Among the less favored of the world the ability to build transnational migratory networks and to pluralize risk through boundary spanning families improves their capabilities.

For other people, restrictions in socio-spatial autonomy reduce the value of the resources a person holds. As Bauman (1998) and others have argued, globalization has resulted in heightened barriers to mobility for those who are considered to be dangerous (Shamir 2005) or to enjoy inferior rights (Weiß 2010). Persons of African descent are often ascribed an inferior status, even when they own many resources and a status high passport. For people who are physically or symbolically bound to less endowed contexts or whose resources do not transport well, capabilities will depend on the quality of the contexts to which the person and her resources are bound.

The same principle of spatial fixation applies to persons who are bound to a wealthy national welfare state. This is not obvious, as they will generally enjoy better capabilities than a person who is bound to a badly equipped infrastructure. Among the sedentary population, differences in socio-spatial autonomy can explain cleavages between factions in a field. Hartmann (in this volume) shows that most of the corporate elite is educated in national institutions and remains inside the nation state. Yet, a fraction of boundary spanners hold a seat in a directorate in more than one country or even continent (Carroll 2009). For this transnational fraction, socio-spatial autonomy structures their social position. Depending on circumstance, they may pose a threat to those who do not know how markets work elsewhere.

The cleavage in the EU and the US between younger, educated and internationally socialized people on the one hand and older people in economically more precarious positions who favor a strong national welfare-state can be understood against this background. Those who enjoy socio-spatial autonomy both as a person and with respect to their transnationally recognized capital, have good reason to espouse open borders. For others, who depend on a protectionist state and whose fate rises and falls with their state's position in the world, open borders are a much more ambiguous achievement.

Conclusion

Socio-spatial autonomy matters for the social positions of migrants and sedentary people alike, both in the Global North and the Global South. It matters most for migrants who move across strong national borders. This relatively small group of three percent in the world and ten percent in the wealthy North finds that their resources lose value after they have crossed a border. Many theories explain why this is so, ranging from a functionalist acceptance of nationally segmented labor markets to the critique scholars of discrimination voice against national closure.

The mere possibility of migration affects a much larger part of the world's population. For elites, the ability to compete across borders may be a comparative edge that translates into larger symbolic and other capital. For the social structure in migrants' country of origin, changes are likely since emigrants are usually younger, more educated and at least a bit wealthier than those who stay. When migration offers a viable alternative to for example, education with an uncertain reward at home, this changes educational aspirations and status systems in countries of emigration (Nieswand 2011). And, even for those citizens of wealthy nation-states who are neither migrants nor directly competing with migrants, the existence of global economic competition is a concern. If they see the national welfare state on which their privilege depends as threatened this may result in re-nationalization. This again, has consequences for the position of immigrants in their country, which may then deteriorate.

I have argued that resources can in principle work across national borders but this depends on the specifics of the plural contexts in which they are to be recognized. Social positions in the world are not only structured by resources but also by how people fare with respect to political rights and relations of symbolic hegemony and whether they can reach well-endowed socio-geographical contexts.

The effect of globalization on social structure was seen by Wallerstein (1979: 61) who argued that political class contestation is framed by the nation state, but its economic roots can only be understood through an analysis of global capitalism. More recent analyses argue that economic exploitation and global hegemonies of race, gender and citizenship are intricately intertwined (Boatcă 2015). Others find that global capitalism has not abolished older socio-cultures riddled with relations of symbolic hegemony but merely transformed and further stabilized them (Jodhka, Rehbein and Souza 2017). These theories do not agree, but they show one thing: Class and ethno-political relations cannot be analyzed separately, but class – which is seen as resource endowment here – and ethno-political relations – which are seen as socio-spatial autonomy – feed on and compensate for one another. An analysis of the social position of migrants therefore is pivotal for an analysis of world social structure.

References

Arrow, Kenneth J. (1973) 'Higher Education as a Filter', *Journal of Public Economics*, Vol. 2, No. 3: 193–216.

Bauman, Zygmunt (1998) 'On Glocalization: Or Globalization for Some, Localization for Some Others', *Thesis Eleven*, Vol. 54, No. 1: 37–49.

Boatcă, Manuela (2015) *Global Inequalities Beyond Occidentalism*, Aldershot: Ashgate.

Bonacich, Edna (1972) 'A Theory of Ethnic Antagonism: The Split Labor Market', *American Sociological Review*, Vol. 37, No. 5: 547–59.

Bourdieu, Pierre (1986) 'The (Three) Forms of Capital', in J. G. Richardson (ed.) *Handbook of Theory and Research in the Sociology of Education*, New York and London: Greenwood, 241–58.

Carroll, William K. (2009) 'Transnationalists and National Networkers in the Global Corporate Elite', *Transnational Networks*, Vol. 9, No. 3: 289–314.

de Haas, Hein (2011) 'Mediterranean Migration Futures: Patterns, Drivers and Scenarios', *Global Environmental Change*, Vol. 21, Supplement 1, S59–69, DOI: http://dx.doi.org/10.1016/j.gloenvcha.2011.09.003.

Feagin, Joe R. and Clairece Booher Feagin (1986) *Discrimination American Style: Institutional Racism and Sexism*, Malabar, FL: Robert E. Krieger Publishing Company.

Hirschman, Albert O. (1970) *Exit, Voice, and Loyalty; Responses to Decline in Firms, Organizations, and States*, Cambridge, MA: Harvard University Press.

International Organisation for Migration (ed.) (2013) *World Migration Report 2013: Migrant Well-Being and Development*, Geneva: IOM.

Jieh-Min, Wu (2010) 'Rural Migrant Workers and China's Differential Citizenship: A Comparative Institutional Analysis', in M. K. Whyte (ed.) *One Country, Two Societies: Rural-Urban Inequality in Contemporary China*, Cambridge, MA: Harvard University Press, 55–81.

Jodhka, Surinder, Boike Rehbein and Jessé Souza (2017) *Inequality in Capitalist Societies*, Singapore and London: Routledge.

Korzeniewicz, Roberto Patricio and Timothy Patrick Moran (2009) *Unveiling Inequality: A World-Historical Perspective*, New York: Russell Sage Foundation Publications.

Levitt, Peggy and Nina Glick Schiller (2007) 'Conceptualizing Simultaneity: A Transnational Social Field Perspective on Society', in A. Portes and J. DeWind (eds.) *Rethinking Migration: New Theoretical and Empirical Perspectives*, New York, Oxford: Berghahn Books, 181–218.

Massey, Douglas S. (1990) 'Social Structure, Household Strategies, and the Cumulative Causation of Migration', *Population Index*, Vol. 56, No. 1: 3–26, DOI:10.2307/3644186.

Nieswand, Boris (2011) *Theorising Transnational Migration: The Status Paradox of Migration*, New York and London: Routledge, Taylor & Francis.

Nohl, Arnd-Michael, Karin Schittenhelm, Oliver Schmidtke and Anja Weiß (2014) *Work in Transition: Cultural Capital and Highly Skilled Migrants' Passages Into the Labour Market*, Toronto: Toronto University Press.

Parreñas, Rhacel Salazar (2001) *Servants of Globalization: Women, Migration, and Domestic Work*, Stanford, CA: Stanford University Press.

Portes, Alejandro and Julia Sensenbrenner (1993) 'Embeddedness and Immigration: Notes on the Social Determinants of Economic Action', *American Journal of Sociology*, Vol. 98, No. 6: 1320–50.

Shamir, Ronen (2005) 'Without Borders? Notes on Globalization as a Mobility Regime', *Sociological Theory*, Vol. 23, No. 2: 197–217.

Spence, Michael A. (1973) 'Job Market Signaling', *Quarterly Journal of Economics*, Vol. 87, No. 3: 355–74.

Wallerstein, Immanuel (1979) *The Capitalist World-Economy*, Cambridge: Cambridge University Press.

Weiß, Anja (2005) 'The Transnationalization of Social Inequality: Conceptualizing Social Positions on a World Scale', *Current Sociology*, Vol. 53, No. 4: 707–28.

Weiß, Anja (2010) 'Racist Symbolic Capital: A Bourdieuian Approach to the Analysis of Racism', in W. D. Hund, J. Krikler and D. Roediger (eds.) *Wages of Whiteness & Racist Symbolic Capital*, Münster: LIT Verlag, 37–56.

Weiß, Anja (2016) 'Understanding Physicians' Professional Knowledge and Practice in Research on Skilled Migration', *Ethnicity & Health*, Vol. 21, No. 4: 397–409, DOI:10.1080/13557858.2015.1061100.

Weiß, Anja (2017) *Soziologie Globaler Ungleichheiten*, Berlin: Suhrkamp.

Weiß, Anja (in print) 'Contextualizing Global Inequalities: A Sociological Approach', in R. P. Korzeniewicz and I. Wallerstein (eds.) *The World-System as a Unit of Analysis: Past Contributions and Future Advances*, New York: Routledge.

Zhou, M. (1997) 'Segmented Assimilation: Issues, Controversies, and Recent Research on the New Second Generation', *International Migration Review*, Vol. 31, No. 4: 975–1008.

9   Inequality, ethnicity and caste

Surinder S. Jodhka

Introduction

In much of the social science writings, as also in the popular imagination, inequalities of caste are commonly viewed as a peculiar case of social differentiation practiced by the Hindus of India. Caste has also been seen as being fundamentally a religious value. By implication, its underlying structures and normative codifications are presumably present in the Hindu religious texts and traditions, spelt out most explicitly in *Manusmriti*, a classic text authored by Manu in the ancient time. As this formulation would suggest, following the textual dictum, a neatly segregated system of social divisions evolved in the South Asian region whereby social groups were assigned occupational monopolies in an order of hierarchy. This order of hierarchy was largely based on an assigned degree of purity to a given occupation. This dialectic of purity and its opposite, pollution, produced a unique system of inequality, which was inherently legitimate, imbedded in local culture and remained unchanged. Given that the everyday practice of caste was reproduced through a neat hierarchy of occupations and a mutually exclusive division of social groups, the mundane materiality of occupational (economic) life was reducible to religious belief. Notions of *karma* (worldly action) and *dharma* (ethical duty) implied an otherworldly orientation of human mind. In this classic construct, the reducibility of the 'economic' to the 'ritual' also produced a separation of the 'social' from the 'political' in the everyday life of the Hindus. Louis Dumont, the most popular proponent of this view, thus argued that in the traditional India, status encompassed power (Dumont 1971).

Against this popular view of caste that sees it as being unique to India, ethnic differences are believed to be present everywhere. Almost every society/nation-state in the contemporary world has social groups that are different from the 'mainstream' culture(s) of a given country. As a generic category, ethnicity refers to culturally bound social groups, often in numeric minorities, living with other dominant groups. Differences of ethnicity could be based on presumed racial origins, national/regional/linguistic identity or simply religious belief. Ethnic differences and diversities are not always horizontal. They often parallel social inequalities, which are generally the outcome of unequal power relations among groups. Such inequalities invariably persist because of prevalence of widespread prejudice and discrimination practiced by the dominant or majority group(s) against the minority group(s) (cf. Hutchinson and Smith 1996).

Thus caste and ethnicity are presumed to be two different kinds of social realities (cf. Brass 1996). Against this popular common sense, I would like to argue that when we look at the two from a critical and relational perspective and ask questions about persistent inequalities that correspond with group identity, and the mechanisms of their reproduction in the present day societies of the capitalist world, the two appear to be very similar in nature and effect.

Even though the primary focus of this chapter is to explore the dynamics of caste and its reproduction in contemporary times in the Indian context, its objective is also to attempt a broader comparison between the two sets of inequalities and mechanisms of their reproduction. Such a comparison could also show how an engagement with caste and its reproduction in the contemporary Indian context could provide us with a useful model for understanding group or community-based ascriptive hierarchies across cultures and countries.

Caste in India

As mentioned above, the dominant view of caste continues to approach it from a position of Indian exceptionalism, a social arrangement unique to the Hindus of India. As a system of social hierarchy, the traditional caste system operated through the categories of *varna* and *jati*. While *varna* provided a normative model, jatis were concrete social or empirical groupings. The idea of *varna* as spelt out in the *Manusmriti* divided the Hindus into four mutually exclusive categories, the Brahmin (priest), the Kshatriya (warrior), the Vaishya (trader) and the Shudra (peasant/artisan/labourer). Beyond the four *varnas* is the *achhoot* (the untouchable). These four or five categories occupied different positions in the status hierarchy, with the Brahmins at the top, followed by the other three *varnas* in the same order as mentioned above, with the *achhoots* occupying a position at the very bottom. The Jatis were groupings of kinship communities that maintained their symbolic border by strictly following rules of exogamy and endogamy in marriage practices. They were further divided into subgroups, which had localized names and systems of classifications. Unlike the four- or five-fold model of *varnas, jatis* and their sub-units number in the hundreds in every linguistic region and in thousands across the entire subcontinent.

However, according to the popular and dominant view, even when the details and names of *jatis* varied across regions and time, the structure of hierarchy remained intact for centuries. Even religious conversions, such as to Islam or Christianity, made little difference to the hierarchical mind of the Indians. Local movements that articulated critiques of the hierarchal system and offered alternative views on transcendence similarly failed to erase the value of hierarchy from the lay minds of the local communities. It was only during the British colonial rule, when modern ideas were infused into Indian life through the introduction of Western-style secular education, modern technology and urban life, that the reality of caste began to loosen its grip. Caste, in this perspective, was to further weaken with the progress of modernization and eventually disappear from the mental and social landscapes of the Indians.

Any attempt at approaching caste as a dimension of social inequality must begin with a critical assessment and a rejection of this dominant viewpoint. Some of this has already been done by the recent and not so recent anthropological and historical scholarship on caste and the broader subject of Hinduism, orientalism, and colonial knowledge systems.

A wide range of critical scholarship has quite convincingly shown that this popular view of caste and Hinduism is founded on several untenable assumptions (Frykenberg 1989; Smith 1998; Fuller 1977; Thapar 1989; Oberoi 1994). First of all, it constructs caste as singular pan-Indian reality and Hinduism as a cohesive faith system with a unified theological structure and without any variations in its social organization and normative belief systems across geographical regions and vertical hierarchies. By implication, Hinduism is presented as a monotheistic faith system, comparable to other religious systems, such as Christianity and Islam, which are similarly presumed to be monotheistic in their ideological moorings. Second, it views caste purely as a religious value, the structural logic of which lies almost exclusively in Hindu religious philosophy and ritual practice, which alone shaped the Indian mind and everyday social/economic life. While it is true that, quite like many other social institutions, such as marriage and family, caste too has an ideational dimension, and does find its articulation in Hindu religious philosophy, the diverse realities of caste could not be entirely reduced to religion and ritual practice (Jodhka 2015). Third, such a view of India, Hinduism or caste system and village life allows no agency to the Indian people and negates any possibility of change through internal processes and critiques (cf. Inden 1990; Cohn 1996).

As mentioned above, this view of caste and the Hindu social order would attribute all changes in the system solely to its encounter with Western modernity during the colonial period. The postcolonial state through its policies of development has been trying to further accelerate this process of modernization, albeit with several shifts and 'compromises.'

How did this influential view of caste evolve, and what explains the hegemonic acceptance of this view by virtually everyone in the popular and political life of India? The next section of this chapter provides a brief overview of how this view came to be formed and accepted and what could be the alternative ways of approaching the contemporary realities of caste. I hope to do this by bringing the evidence on the intersection of caste in contemporary time and manners in which it actively articulates with processes of social, economic and political change and hence reproduces hierarchies of status and opportunities.

Making of the dominant view

The origin of present day social science conceptualizations of caste could be traced to early writings on India by the Western travelers and colonizers.

Though the source of their interest varied, they all tended to look at social and cultural life of the region as being very different from that of Europe. Over the years, India and rest of the 'Eastern' world came to be viewed in the dominant Western discourses as the 'other' to the West European societies. Scholars like Edward Said (1985) and Ronald Inden (1990) have described this as orientalism, a discourse that tries to present oriental culture as being inferior to that of the West. Caste appeared as a good example of an institution of the 'peculiar Orient'.

Given that these writings also became a source of knowing about India for the early social science scholarship in Western Europe, they tended to produce similar kinds of imaginations and arguments about the social and cultural life in the region. Examples of this could be found in writings of scholars like Marx and Weber. Marx, for example, wrote on the positive effects of colonial rule in India because it could break the traditional village community structured around caste (Marx 1853). The orientalist imagination had also presented caste as a rigid and static institution of Hindu religion, which had been around without any significant internal change in the Indian society for centuries. Even though his theoretical orientation was very different from that of Marx and the orientalists, Max Weber too produced a static view of Hinduism, describing it as an otherworldly religious system based on the ideas of karma and rebirth. Caste, for Weber, was also a good example of what he described as 'status groups'. They were like ethnic communities, completely closed to outsiders. Recruitment to a caste group, like an ethnic group, was based exclusively on birth. However, unlike other ethnic communities, castes were also hierarchical and the order of hierarchy was acceptable to those lower down in the hierarchy (Weber 1946). While Weber accepted the 'orientalist' view on the rigid and unchanging nature of caste, he did not think that the presence of caste-like status groups was peculiar to India or the Hindus.

Looking more closely on the subject in the same mould, Louis Dumont, a French scholar, reworked the orientalist view on caste in his well-known book *Homo Hierarchicus: The Caste System and its Implications* (first published in French 1966. The English edition appeared in 1970). Drawn mostly from the classical Hindu scriptures, he constructed a well-integrated theory of the caste system. As was the case with much of the classical orientalist writings, Dumont conceptualized caste as emanating from the Hindu religious system. According to him the structural logic of caste lay in the 'Hindu mind', as an ideological construct, which divided and hierarchized social groups on the basis of ritual purity or impurity of their occupations. Dumont's thesis on caste was, in many ways, an extension of the argument put forward by another French scholar, Celestin Bougle.

In an essay first published in 1908, Bougle had argued against those who looked at caste merely as a system of occupational specialization. He defined caste as a system consisting of hierarchically arranged hereditary groups, separated from each other in certain respects (caste endogamy, restrictions on eating together and on physical contact), but interdependent in others (traditional

division of labour). The word 'caste', he emphasized, not only involved hereditary specialization of occupational groups but also differential rights. Different
occupations were arranged in a hierarchical order that made their members
socially unequal. Inequality was an essential feature of the caste system. Along
with inequality, he also underlined the element of pollution as an important
feature of caste. Different groups, in a caste society, tended to 'repel each other
rather than attract, each retired within itself, isolated itself, and made every
effort to prevent its members from contracting alliances or even from entering
into relation with neighboring groups' (Bougle 1971: 65). Thus Bougle identified three core features of caste system, viz., hereditary occupation, hierarchy
and mutual repulsion.

While Dumont agreed with Bougle's identification of core features of the
system, he however argued that for a proper theoretical explanation of caste,
it was important to identify one common element, 'a single true principle'
to which the three features of the caste system suggested by Bougle could be
reduced. Such a principle, Dumont argued, was 'the opposition of the pure and
the impure'.

> This opposition underlies hierarchy, which is the superiority of the pure to
> the impure, underlies separation because the pure and the impure must be
> kept separate, and underlies the division of labour because pure and impure
> occupations must likewise be kept separate. The whole is founded on the
> necessary and hierarchical coexistence of the two opposites.
>
> (Dumont 1971: 43)

Another important and extremely contentious aspect of his theory was his
assertion about the superiority of the Brahmin over the king. India was different from the West because in India the status was not determined by the logic
of political economy, as was the case with the West. In caste society, status as
a principle of social organization was superior to power. Status encompassed
power, as Dumont would assert.

While Dumont's theory of caste has been very influential, it has also been
widely criticized. He has been accused of presenting an ideologically biased
view, an account that looked at it from upside down, as the Brahmins would
wish to present it. Given that his sources were mostly textual, and that these
texts were all written and retained by the upper-caste Brahmins, he constructed
a theory that presented a Brahmanical perspective on the subject; an uncriti-
cal celebration of tradition. He has also been accused of ignoring the available
empirical accounts of its functioning on the ground, produced by professional
social anthropologists in the form of village studies and monographs (Gupta
1991: 114). Some have accused him of also being selective in the choice of
textual sources (Das and Uberoi 1971).

In his defense Dumont would argue that he only tried to construct an ideal
type of caste that theorized the underlying structure of the system and not the
way caste was practiced in everyday life. However, as Berreman pointed out,

caste did not exist except empirically, in the lives of people as they interacted with each other. The lived experience of caste was very different from what Dumont seems to suggest. 'The human meaning of caste for those who lived it was power and vulnerability, privilege and oppression, honor and denigration, plenty and want, reward and deprivation, security and anxiety. As an anthropological document, a description of caste, which failed to convey this was a travesty in the world today' (Berreman 1991: 87–8; also cf. Gupta 1984). Similarly, Joan Mencher, who conducted her field-work among the lower castes in a South India village, reported that 'from the point of view of people at the lowest end of the scale, caste had functioned and continued to function as a very effective system of economic exploitation' (Mencher 1978). Fuller makes a related point in his criticism of Dumont's theory. It is not only the relations of power that his theory undervalues; such a notion of caste also undermines the obvious facts about the inequalities in material life and the role caste played in their reproduction. In his study of the redistributive system prevailing in pre-colonial India Fuller shows how the village level system of caste relations was integrated into a larger political authority, beyond the village (Fuller 1977).

Another point of contention in Dumont's theory has been his argument that constructs Indian and the Western societies as binaries where India is presented through categories of holism and hierarchy and the West with individualism and equality (Beteille 1986). Such a construct also tends to ignore the internal differences within societies and regions. The actually existing realities have never been so simple, in the West or in India. We can also find echoes of this argument in the historical scholarship on caste. As Bernard Cohn argues, the textual view of caste constructed through orientalist categories is fundamentally flawed because it constructs a picture of Indian society as

> Being static, timeless and space-less. Statements about customs, which derived from third century A.D. texts and observations from the late eighteenth century, were equally good evidence for determining the nature of society and culture in India. In this view of Indian society there was no regional variation and no questioning of the relationship between prescriptive normative statement derived from the texts and the actual behavior of individuals and groups. Indian society was seen as a set of rules, which every Hindu followed
>
> (Cohn 1968: 7–8).

Following the works of Bernard Cohn, some other historians of modern India have also done important work on the subject. Perhaps the most important and influential of this scholarship has been the work of Nicholas Dirks. In his well-known book, *Castes of Mind*, Dirks convincingly shows how the colonial rulers through a process of enumeration and ethnographic surveys raised the consciousness about caste. They also produced social and intellectual conditions where 'caste became the single term capable of expressing, organizing, and above all "synthesizing" India's diverse forms of social identity, community and organization' (Dirks 2001: 5). Dumont's theory of caste is a restatement of the same colonial and orientalist formulation.

Fallacy of this orientalist view of caste is also evident from the fieldwork-based writings on the Indian village. The field studies of the Indian village tend to present a much more diverse picture of caste. Many of these studies question the superiority of Brahmins and place the landowning caste at the centre of village social life. While some emphasized reciprocity and interdependence (Wiser 1936; Dube 1955; Srinivas 1955), some others point to the coercive nature of power in caste society. F.G. Bailey, for example, questioned even the idea of interdependence in caste society:

> The system works the way it does because the coercive sanctions are all in the hands of a dominant caste. There is a tie of reciprocity, but it is not a sanction of which the dependent castes can make easy use.
>
> (Bailey 1960: 258)

Similarly Beidelman pointed to the exploitative nature of the relationship between the landowning and politically dominant *jajmans*, and those who provided them services of various kinds, those belonging to landless caste groups called *kamins* (Beidelman 1959). Some of these writings also raised wider theoretical questions regarding the relationship between status and power and validity of the claims made by Dumont on the encompassment of power by status. Gloria Goodwin Raheja, for example, argues that:

> The relationship between a hierarchical order of castes, with its focus on the superior position of the Brahman, on the one hand, and a conception of sovereignty focused on the Hindu king or the royal functions of the dominant caste at the level of the village, on the other, has been a central reverberating issue in the anthropological and historical study of South Asian society. . . . Virtually all of the major contributions to the anthropological, indological and historical study of Hindu South Asian have been concerned in some fashion with this relationship, and have seen it to be constitutive of the fundamental aspects of social life, polity, and religion.
>
> (Raheja 1988: 497)

Based on her study of villages in northern India, Raheja (1988: 79) offered an alternative theory of caste and ritual practices, a theory that places 'dominant caste' at the centre of the caste system. She also questions the dominant 'Western view of Hindu society', which sees hierarchy as 'the sole ideology defining relations among castes' and reduces the role of the king and the dominant caste to a residual level. Instead, she argues that

> There are several contextually shifting ideologies of inter-caste relationships apparent in everyday village social life. Meanings and values are foregrounded differently from context to context, and they implicate varying

configurations of castes ... data on presentation patterns and language use from ... north Indian village ... indicate that aspects of inter-caste relations that ... I call 'centrality' and 'mutuality', are distinguishable from the ranked aspect that is usually called 'hierarchy' ... Among these configurations of caste, both the ritual centrality of the dominant caste ... and the mutuality among the castes of the village prove to be of more significance in social intercourse than the hierarchical pre-eminence of priestly Brahmans.

(Raheja 1989: 81)

These wide ranging contestations of the popular Western view of caste point to the diversities that have been part of social and cultural life in the subcontinent. They also represent the diverse ways in which an institution like caste can be approached.

Institutionalization of caste

Besides the crafting of its conceptual framework and theoretical formulations that enabled caste to fit in the grand theories/narrative of social transformations evolving in the Western societies around the same time, the British colonial administrators also began to deploy caste in their administrative narratives, particularly after the introduction of the Colonial Census in the late nineteenth century. This had far-reaching implications (cf. Cohn 1996; Dirks 2001). Perhaps the most important of these was the process of classification of caste communities into an all India schema. For example, they clubbed together the so-called untouchable communities into an administrative category, initially as 'depressed classes', and later listed them as Scheduled Caste (SC) in the Government of India Act of 1935. The post-independence Indian state continued with the same category but has over the years expanded the list of communities and scope of state action for their welfare and development. Though SC communities are identified at the state level, they are listed in the Constitution of the Indian Union with the authorization of the President of India. This classification became an important medium for the post-colonial Indian state in its administrative strategies of transforming the institutionalized hierarchies of caste into an open social and economic order with a level playing field.

The post-colonial state also legally abolished the practice of untouchability and initiated several other administrative measures for development and inclusion of the historically marginalized caste communities. The first and the most important of these measures was the quota system, reservations of seats in government-run educational institutions and for employment in government or state sector jobs. Second, the central and state governments also introduced various development schemes/programmes enabling the SCs to actively participate in the emerging economy and new avenues of employment. Third, the Indian Constitution also made provisions for the reservations of seats for Scheduled Castes (along with Scheduled Tribes) in legislative bodies and other representational institutions as per their proportions in the total population.

Notwithstanding these proactive measures initiated by the Indian state, the middle class that inherited power from the British colonial rulers shared the view that caste was essentially a mode of traditional life and would gradually decline and eventually disappear on its own as India moved on the path of development and modernization. The engine of progress was to be the process of economic growth: industrialization, modern technology and urbanization.

Changing caste

As any other aspect of social life, the institution of caste would have always been undergoing change with changes in the larger social structure, economic life and political regimes. However, the nature and extent of change has perhaps been much more rapid over the past four or five decades. The changes in the social order of caste have come about due to a variety of efforts and processes from 'below', from 'above' and from the 'side'.

Persistent mobilizations and organized movements of the traditionally marginalized who were at the receiving end in the 'traditional hierarchies' have been an important source of change in the caste system. It was during the colonial period that certain 'disadvantaged' communities, such the non-Brahmins in South India and untouchables in western India mobilized against the prevailing structures of caste-based domination and exclusions (Pandian 2006; Omvedt 1976; O'Hanlon 1985). Since the early 1980s such mobilizations from the margins of Indian society have only grown and some have described them as a source of a 'silent revolution' (Jaffrelot 2003). Notwithstanding diversities and divergences, growing politicization of the '"backwards' and increasing Dalit assertions have fundamentally altered the grammar of Indian social and political life.

State policies and other initiatives from 'above' have also changed caste. The constitutional provisions in the form of reservation policy have not only enabled a process of social and economic mobility among the ex-untouchable castes but have also been instrumental in producing a modern leadership from within these communities.

Caste has also changed with social, economic and political transformations taking place on the 'side'. For example, the agrarian transformation ushered in by the success of the green revolution technology in some parts of the country and the development of industry in urban centres have made many of the traditional caste occupations redundant. At the same time, they have also provided new opportunities for employment outside the older economic order (Jodhka 2002).

James Manor, who has closely observed Indian politics and society for nearly five decades, has recently argued that among the most important changes to occur in India since Independence, two things stand out: the emergence of a democracy with deep roots in society; and the decline in the power of caste hierarchies across most of rural India. The latter change is not as widely recognized as it should be, but abundant evidence from diverse regions plainly indicates that it has been occurring – unevenly, but widely enough to be a national trend (Manor 2012: 14). Manor is only echoing what many other scholars doing field studies have been reporting from their regions for some time now. Historically, the process of disintegration of *jajmani* ties in some regions had begun during the colonial period.

Independence from colonial rule was an important turning point for the local agrarian economy and its social organization, the institution of caste. State investments in rural development and agricultural growth provided positive impetus to the process of change on the ground. Social anthropologists studying rural social and economic life began to report about declining traditional hierarchies and old structures of dependency, including the traditional structures of caste hierarchy, sometime in the early 1970s (see Breman 1974; Beteille 1971; Thorner 1982). By the early 1980s and 1990s these changes became quite visible and started to reflect even in the democratic or electoral political processes.

For example, on the basis of his fieldwork in Rajasthan villages in the 1980s, Oliver Mendelsohn reported that the idea of the 'dominant caste', as proposed by M.N. Srinivas in the 1950s after his fieldwork in a South India village (Srinivas 1959), no longer made sense in rural Rajasthan. The 'low caste and even untouchable villagers were now less beholden to their economic and ritual superiors than was suggested in older accounts' (Mendelsohn 1993: 808). Interestingly, he also argued that 'land and authority had been de-linked in village India and this amounted to an historic, if non-revolutionary transformation' (ibid: 807). By the turn of the century Srinivas himself argued in a paper, which he titled "An Obituary on Caste as a System", that the "systemic" features of caste were soon disappearing from the rural society in different parts of the country (Srinivas 2003). We can notice similar claims emerging from the writings of many other scholars who have been closely observing the dynamics of caste in contemporary India (Beteille 1997; Gupta 2000, 2004; Jodhka 2002; Karanth 1996; Charsley and Karanth 1998; Krishna 2003; Kapoor et al. 2010).

Declining hierarchy, persisting inequality

Perhaps the most surprising thing about caste in contemporary India is that when all social science evidence points towards a rapid decline of the old *jajmani* relations and erosion of its ideological hold over the minds of those located lower down in the traditional hierarchies, caste seems to be becoming politically more visible and socially more complex. The caste question today presents itself in newer and more complicated forms. Understandably, thus, the academic and popular interest in caste continues to grow.

What makes caste persist?

Social science scholarship has only just begun to engage with this question. One possible factor that makes the reality of caste continue to matter is the fact that even when socially and ideologically the traditional forms of relationships begin to disintegrate, material realities do not change much. For example, economic inequalities across caste groups continue to persist or, in some cases, even witness an escalation.

With its ideological decline, the social and political experience of caste becomes more intense for those at the lower end of traditional hierarchies. As the decline of their dependence on the agrarian economy and the locally dominant caste groups enables them to formally participate in the democratic political process as equal citizens, their entitlements over the local resources remain circumscribed by caste and the 'position' they have occupied in the old system of hierarchy, as the dominant groups view it. However, they no longer accept it as an inevitable reality or a part of their fate. They make claims over 'common' resources of the village, which had hitherto been under the exclusive control of the dominant caste communities. These assertions are not easily entertained by the dominant groups, and often result in different forms of violence against Dalits.

This is not simply a matter of perception. Resistance and caste-related atrocities manifest a clear trend. A broad range of scholars concede to the fact that while the traditional ideological façade of caste or even its institutional hold has weakened, including the decline of untouchability, the violence committed on Dalits appears to be increasing, particularly over the past two or three decades (Beteille 2000; Shah 2000; Teltumbde 2010; Gorringe 2012; Mohanty 2007). However, some recent studies also point to the fact that these growing strains in caste relations, even when they manifest themselves in bloody violence, result in renegotiations of power relations across caste communities (cf. Pandian 2013).

The experience of mobility for those located at the lower end of the traditional caste hierarchy, viz. their moving out of village and agrarian economy, is also not an easy process. Even those who are able to acquire technical and higher education (generally because of the quotas) find it hard to get into the higher echelons of power in the private sector.

A growing redundancy of old caste-based occupations and their dislike for traditional arrangements makes those from the ex-untouchable caste communities (the Dalits) try to move to urban areas for alternative sources of livelihood. However, they find it very hard to make headway beyond the margins of the emerging urban economy. Caste matters in the urban markets in many different ways for Dalits trying to establish themselves in business. Urban markets have never been as open as they are made out to be in the textbooks of economics and sociology. In the Indian context, caste and kinship-based (and sometimes, religion-based) communities actively try to preserve their 'monopolies' in a given trade. Kinship networks play a very critical role in the urban business economy. Apart from working as gatekeepers, they matter in mobilizing capital, through banks and otherwise, the most critical requirement for businesses anywhere in the world. Given their past economic background, those from the historically deprived communities also do not own collaterals, such as agricultural lands or urban properties. The lack of 'social capital' and economic resources is further compounded by the presence of active "prejudice" that manifests itself in many different ways in their everyday business life and aids in the reproduction of both, social/economic inequalities and caste identity among the Dalits, a sense of being different and unequal (cf. Jodhka 2015; Iyer, Khanna and Varshney 2013; Hoff and Pandey 2004).

It is thus a widely recognized fact that caste matters in India's vast informal economy. Based on her study of a South Indian town Barbara Harriss-White concludes:

> Caste . . . provides networks necessary for contracts, for subcontracting and for labour recruitment within the informal economy . . . liberalisation makes these caste-based relationships more important because it places a new premium on the advancement of interests . . . caste is ultimately connected with all the other organizations of civil society that comprehensively regulate economic and social life.
>
> (2003: 178–9)

We see this script repeating itself even in the more advanced corporate sector and its hiring practices. My interviews (Jodhka and Newman 2007) with hiring managers in big private companies in Delhi clearly showed that even when the hiring managers actively deny any consideration of caste and community in the process of recruitment, they openly showed preference for candidates with specific social and cultural skills. Given that the candidates they interview for these relatively high-end jobs are mostly screened, internally or by the hiring agencies, and they are all educated and qualified to be called for the interview, the interviews are meant to judge more than their technical skills and the quality of formal education. They look for the 'suitability' of the candidate, the social and cultural aspects of their personality. Who is a suitable candidate and how do they judge the merit of those who are selected for the upper-end jobs in private sector?

Almost every respondent hiring manager interviewed agreed that one of the most important questions they ask the prospective candidates during the interviews is about their 'family background'. Family background, for them, is an important factor in determining the suitability of a candidate for the culture of the company. An equally important factor for hiring at the senior level is the linguistic skills of the candidate, their ability to speak and communicate in English fluently. In other words, the critical qualification for higher end corporate jobs are as much the "soft skills", the nature and quality of 'cultural capital' (Bourdieu 1986) acquired through one's caste and class habitus which, even according to the hiring managers, was largely a determinant of one's social background and place of residence (rural-urban). The hiring manager we interviewed admitted to the fact that the response to the question about the family background also gave them an idea about their 'social origins'. Caste background of the candidates was not difficult to guess, most of them admitted. This knowledge of 'social background' of the candidate directly impacted their decisions on hiring.

When we followed up with them with questions on 'quotas' and their opinions on reservations for the Scheduled Castes in the government jobs and educational institutions, nearly every one of them had a negative view on the subject. They all wanted 'merit' to be the sole criteria of judging candidates for recruitment, even when they all admitted that qualities other than merit tended to matter more in the selection process. This attitude also emanated from the fact that corporate houses in India are almost exclusively owned and managed by those from upper caste backgrounds. A recent study based on a sample of 1000 companies reported that as many as 92.6 percent of the board members of Indian Corporate houses were from the upper castes (44.6 percent Brahmins and 46.0 percent from various Vaishya castes; their proportion in the total population of India is around 10 to 15 percent). In contrast, those belonging to the traditionally marginal communities (Scheduled Castes, Scheduled Tribes [STs] and Other Backward Classes [OBCs]) who make for more than 70 percent of India's population were only 7.3 percent of the sample (Ajit and Saxena 2012). It will be hard to view it as an outcome of a random process working on the basis of merit. The authors rightly conclude that the upper end of the Indian corporate sector 'is a small and closed world' where social networking plays an important role.

Still Indian corporate boards belong to the "old boys club" based on caste affiliation rather than on other considerations (like merit or experience). It is difficult to fathom the argument that lack of merit is the cause for under-representation. Caste is an important factor in networking. The small world of corporate India has interaction only within their caste kinship (Ajit and Saxena 2012: 42).

Several other studies looking at social mobility in India reinforce the point that caste indeed works to block those located at the lower end of caste hierarchy (Kumar, Heath and Heath 2002; Thorat and Attewal 2007; Thorat and Newman 2010; Vaid and Heath 2010). Even when the cultural or ideological hold of caste disappears; the real possibility of vertical social and economic mobility remains rather limited. Much of the mobility appears to be merely horizontal, from traditional caste occupations or agricultural labour in the village to insecure jobs at the lower end of India's vast informal economy. In the dynamic of change, 'the upper castes' are no longer 'cushioned from the forces of downward mobility', but more importantly, it is hard for those located at the lower end of "traditional" hierarchy to move up (Vaid 2012: 420). In other words, the social mobility scenario in India presents a case of "continuity rather than change" (Kumar, Heath and Heath 2002: 4096).

Conclusions

I have tried to argue in this chapter that quite like ethnicity or race-based inequalities, caste reproduces itself in contemporary India through active process of 'prejudice' and 'discrimination'. It is in this context that I propose to initiate a conceptualization of caste within the framework of prejudice and discrimination as a sociological process, which enables and sustains reproduction of caste

in contemporary times. Such a framework of discrimination has to be comparative in nature that approaches caste as a category of 'status' and 'power', quite
like 'race', or in some other contexts, ethnicity. A comparative understanding of
caste in the framework of status, power and discrimination would thus enable
us to comprehend complex processes of the reproduction of caste and not be
trapped in, what is sometimes described as, the Indian exceptionalism.

At a more practical level, such a perspective on caste would underline the
critical need for interventions, if we wish to create a level playing field in India
and to deal with the question of social inequality by finding ways of block-
ing its reproduction. These interventions could be from above, in the form of
state policies of affirmative action, some of which are already in place in India.
They could also be from below, as social movements for change. To assume and
expect that caste inequalities would disappear on their own with the decline of
traditional social orders, such as the idea of ritual hierarchy or the Hindu *jajmani*
system, under the pressure of capitalist development and neo-liberal economic
reforms, would be quite misleading. Individualization of labour markets only
makes structures like caste 'invisible' (Rehbein and Souza 2014). It does not
make it irrelevant, particularly where it matters, namely, the distribution of the
valued goods in society.

References

Ajit, Han Donker and Ravi Saxena (2012) 'Corporate Boards in India: Blocked By Caste',
  Economic and Political Weekly, Vol. 47, No. 31: 39–43.
Bailey, Frederick G. (1960) *Tribe, Caste and Nation*, Bombay: Oxford University Press.
Beidelman, Thomas O. (1959) *A Comparative Analysis of the Jajmani System*, New York: Asso-
  ciation for Asian Studies, Monograph Series VIII.
Berreman, Gerald (1991) 'The Brahamanical View of Caste', in Dipankar Gupta (ed.) *Social
  Stratification*, New Delhi: Oxford University Press, 84–92.
Beteille, André ([1971] 1996) *Caste Class and Power: Changing Patterns of Stratification in Tanjore
  Village*, New Delhi: Oxford University Press.
Beteille, André (1986) 'Individualism and Equality', *Current Anthropology*, Vol. 27, No. 2:
  121–34.
Beteille, André (1997) 'Caste in Contemporary India', in C. J. Fuller (ed.) *Caste Today*, New
  Delhi: Oxford India Paperback, 150–79.
Beteille, André (2000) 'The Scheduled Castes: An Inter-Regional Perspective', *Journal of
  Indian School of Political Economy*, Vol. 12, No. 3–4: 367–80.
Bougle, Celestin (1971) *Essays on the Caste System*, Cambridge: Cambridge University
  Press.
Bourdieu, Pierre (1986) 'The Forms of Capital', in John G. Richardson (ed.) *Handbook of
  Theory and Research for the Sociology of Education*, New York: Greenwood Press, 241–258.
Brass, Paul R. (1996) 'Ethnic Groups and Ethnic Identity Formation', in John Hutchinson
  and Anthony D. Smith (eds.) *Ethnicity: Oxford Readers*, Oxford: Oxford University Press,
  85–90.
Breman, Jan (1974) Patronage and Exploitation: Changing Agrarian Relations in South
  Gujarat India, Berkley, CA: University of California Press.
Charsley, Simon R. and G. K. Karanth (eds.) (1998) *Challenging Untouchability: Dalit Initiative
  and Experience from Karnataka*, New Delhi: Sage Publications.

Cohn, Bernard S. (1968) 'Notes on the History of the Study of Indian Society and Culture', in Milton Singer and Bernard S. Cohn (eds.) *Structure and Change in Indian Society*, New York: Aldine Publishing Company, 3–28.

Cohn, Bernard S. (1996) *Colonialism and Its Forms of Knowledge: The British in India*, Princeton, NJ: Princeton University Press.

Das, Veena and J. P. Singh Uberoi (1971) 'The Elementary Structures of Caste', *Contributions to Indian Sociology*, Vol. 5, No. 1: 33–43.

Dirks, Nicholas B. (2001) *Castes of Mind: Colonialism and the Making of Modern India*, Princeton, NJ: Princeton University Press.

Dube, S. C. (1955) *Indian Village*, London: Routledge and Kegan Paul.

Dumont, Louis (1971) *Homo Hierarchicus: The Caste System and Its Implications*, New Delhi: Oxford India Paperbacks.

Frykenberg, Robert E. (1989) 'The Emergence of Modern "Hinduism" as a Concept and as an Institution: A Reappraisal With Special Reference to South India', in Gunther Sontheimer and Hermann Kulke (eds.) *Hinduism Reconsidered*, New Delhi: Manohar, 29–49.

Fuller, C. Johnston (1977) 'British India or Traditional India? An Anthropological Problem', *Ethnos*, Vol. 42, No. 3–4: 95–121.

Gorringe, Hugo (2012) 'Caste and Politics in Tamil Nadu', *Seminar*, No. 633: 38–42.

Gupta, Dipankar (1984) 'Continuous Hierarchies and Discrete Castes', *Economic and Political Weekly*, Vol. 19, No. 46: 1955–2053.

Gupta, Dipankar (ed.) (1991) *Social Stratification*, New Delhi: Oxford University Press.

Gupta, Dipankar (ed.) (2004) *Caste in Question: Identity or Hierarchy*, New Delhi: Sage Publications.

Gupta, Dipankar (2000) *Interrogating Caste: Understanding Hierarchy and Difference in Indian Society*, New Delhi: Penguin Books.

Harriss-White, Barbara (2003) *India Working: Essays on Society and Economy*, Cambridge: Cambridge University Press.

Hoff, Karla and Priyanka Pandey (2004) 'Belief Systems and Durable Inequalities: An Experimental Investigation of Indian Caste', Washington, DC: World Bank, Policy Research Working Paper 3351.

Hutchinson, John and Anthony D. Smith (eds.) (1996) *Ethnicity: Oxford Readers*, Oxford: Oxford University Press.

Inden, Ronald (1990) *Imagining India*, Oxford: Blackwell.

Iyer, Lakshmi, Tarun Khanna and Ashutosh Varshney (2013) 'Caste and Entrepreneurship in India', *Economic and Political Weekly*, Vol. 48, No. 6: 52–60.

Jaffrelot, Christophe (2003) *India's Silent Revolution: The Rise of Low Castes in North Indian Politics*, New Delhi: Permanent Block.

Jodhka, Surinder S. (2002) 'Caste and Untouchability in Rural Punjab', *Economic and Political Weekly*, Vol. 37, No. 19: 1813–23.

Jodhka, Surinder S. (2012) *Caste: Oxford India Short Introductions*, New Delhi: Oxford University Press.

Jodhka, Surinder S. (2015) *Caste in Contemporary India*, New Delhi: Routledge.

Jodhka, Surinder S. and Katherine Newman (2007) 'In the Name of Globalisation: Meritocracy, Productivity and the Hidden Language of Caste', *Economic and Political Weekly*, Vol. 42, No. 41: 4125–32.

Kapoor, Devesh, Chandra Bhan Prasad, Lant Pritchett and D. Shyam Babu (2010) 'Rethinking Inequality: Dalits in Uttar Pradesh in the Market Reform Era', *Economic and Political Weekly*, Vol. XLV, No. 35: 39–49.

Karanth, G. K. (1996) 'Caste in Contemporary Rural India', in M. N. Srinivas (ed.) *Caste: Its Twentieth Century Avatar*, New Delhi: Penguin.

Krishna, Anirudh (2003) 'What Is Happening to Caste? A View From Some North Indian Villages', *The Journal of Asian Studies*, Vol. 62, No. 4: 1171–93.

Kumar, Sanjay, Anthony Heath and Oliver Heath (2002) 'Determinants of Social Mobility in India', *Economic and Political Weekly*, Vol. 37, No. 29: 2983–7.

Manor, James (2012) 'Accommodation and Conflict', *Seminar*, No. 633: 4–18.

Marx, Karl (1853) 'The British Rule in India', New-York Daily Tribune, June 25, available at www.marxists.org/archive/marx/works/1853/06/25.htm (12.02.2013).

Mencher, Joan P. (1978) *Agriculture and Social Structure in Tamil Nadu: Past Origins, Present Transformations and Future Prospects*, New Delhi: Allied Publications.

Mendelsohn, Oliver (1993) 'The Transformation of Authority in Rural India', *Modern Asian Studies*, Vol. 15, No. 4: 805–42.

Mohanty, Manoranjan (2007) 'Kilvenmani, Karamchedu to Khairlanji: Why Atrocities on Dalits Persist?', available at www.Boell-India.Org/Download_En/Mohanty_Amrita_Corrected.Pdf (09.11.2009).

O'Hanlon, Rosalind (1985) *Caste, Conflict and Ideology: Mahatma Jotirao Phule and Low-Caste Protest in 19th Century Maharashtra*, Cambridge: Cambridge University Press.

Oberoi, Harjot (1994) *The Construction of Religious Boundaries: Culture, Identity and Diversity in the Sikh Tradition*, New Delhi: Oxford University Press.

Omvedt, Gail (1976) Cultural Revolt in a Colonial Society: The Non-Brahman Movement in Western India: 1873 to 1930, Bombay: Scientific Socialist Education Trust.

Pandian, M. S. S. (2006) *Brahmin and Non-Brahmin: Genealogies of the Tamil Political Present*, New Delhi: Permanent Black.

Pandian, M. S. S. (2013) 'Caste in Tamil Nadu (II): Slipping Hegemony of Intermediate Castes', *Economic and Political Weekly*, Vol. 48, No. 4: 13–15.

Raheja, Gloria G. (1988) 'Caste, Kingship, and Dominance Reconsidered', *Annual Review of Anthropology*, Vol. 17: 497–522.

Raheja, Gloria G. (1989) 'Centrality, Mutuality and Hierarchy: Shifting Aspects of Inter-Caste Relationships in North India', *Contributions to Indian Sociology*, Vol. 23, No. 1: 79–101.

Rehbein, Boike and Jessé Souza (2014) 'Inequality in Capitalist Societies', *Transcience*, Vol. 5, No. 1: 16–27.

Said, Edward (1985) *Orientalism*, Harmondsworth: Penguin.

Shah, Ghanshyam (2000) 'Hope and Despair: A Study of Untouchability and Atrocities in Gujarat', *Journal of Indian School of Political Economy*, Vol. 12, No. 3&4: 459–72.

Smith, Brian K. (1998) *Reflections on Resemblance, Ritual and Religion*, New Delhi: Motilal Banarsidass.

Srinivas, M. N. (ed.) (1955) *India's Villages*, London: Asia Publishing House.

Srinivas, M. N. (1959) 'The Dominant Caste in Rampura', *American Anthropologist*, Vol. 61: 1–16.

Srinivas, M. N. (2003) 'An Obituary on Caste as a System', *Economic and Political Weekly*, Vol. 38, No. 5: 455–9.

Teltumbde, Anand (2010) *The Persistence of Caste*, New Delhi: Navayana.

Thapar, Romila (1989) 'Imagined Religious Communities? Ancient History and the Modern Search for a Hindu Identity', *Modern Asian Studies*, Vol. 23, No. 2: 209–31.

Thorat, Sukhadeo and Paul Attewell (2007) 'The Legacy of Social Exclusion: A Correspondence Study of Job Discrimination in India', *Economic and Political Weekly*, Vol. 31: 4141–5.

Thorat, Sukhadeo and Katherine S. Newman (eds.) (2010) *Blocked by Caste: Economic Discrimination and Social Exclusion in Modern India*, New Delhi: Oxford University Press.

Thorner, Alice (1982) 'Semi-Feudalism or Capitalism? Contemporary Debate on Classes and Modes of Production in India', *Economic and Political Weekly*, Vol. 17, No. 49: 993–9.

Vaid, Divya (2012) 'Caste-Class Association in India: An Empirical Analysis', *Asian Survey*, Vol. 52, No. 2: 395–422.

Vaid, Divya and Anthony Heath (2010) 'Unequal Opportunities: Class, Caste, and Social Mobility', in Anthony Heath and Roger Jeffery (eds.) *Diversity and Change in Contemporary India*, Oxford: Oxford University Press, 129–64.

Weber, Max (1946) 'Essays in Sociology', in H. H. Gerth and C. Wright Mills (eds.) *From Max Weber: Essays in Sociology*, Oxford: Oxford University Press.

Wiser, William H. (1936) *The Hindu Jajmani System*, Lucknow: Lucknow Publishing House.

10 Inequality and race

Gerhard Maré

Introduction – what is the problem?

The need to include the word "race" in discussing inequality seems obvious: a larger proportion of people classified "black" than other such race collectivities find themselves at the lower end of the inequality spectrum – in its various forms, in various countries, using various measures. The issue explored, then, is the status of the link that is drawn. Where does "race" fit in explaining inequality?[1] The status given "race" has practical implications, directly affecting ways in which inequality is addressed, whether in research and analysis, or through subsequent policy and practice. "Inequality" too, needs questioning. My argument, presented below and drawing on various sources, is that inequality – in an expanded approach – inter-relates with race in particular ways, which I will refer to as articulation. This occurs not in direct causal form but in a complex range of uneven ways affecting outcomes – such as in distribution of positions and material rewards, and also of human dignity and life chances. The essence of inequality, and the additional introduction and maintenance of race (as racialism and racism), is to be found in exploring exploitation in historical forms of capitalism, whether as slavery, colonialism, or contemporary forms of global capitalism. Through employing the term articulation I, first, draw attention to an inevitable hierarchy of power and benefit in such interactions – they are never innocuous. Such articulation of race in forms of social structures and social interaction leaves an ongoing complexity that demands expansion of the field of enquiry: the notion of inequality has to be extended beyond just material conditions, the content given to racialism and racism changes depending on the when and the where of application, and an historical and globally comparative approach is an imperative.

In order to introduce this approach to race and inequality, the complexity of the task, the approach, and tools I employ are first presented. Second, I suggest how those tools aid in investigating the various fields of inequality where the social construct "race" has ancillary or primary effects. Finally, I draw attention to the implications of attributing causal effects to race, and therefore specific solutions that do not solve the issue of inequality, instead, whether deliberately or unintentionally, hiding effective solutions; confirming as acceptable massively unequal existing power relations; and detracting from the urgent attention that needs to be paid to the role that racialism and racism (and related categories) do play in distorting social relations.

Confronting complexity

Kenan Malik captures the difficulties when he questions frequent, apparently inclusive, historical commitments to "equality of all", while gross inequality, confirmed through comparisons between life chances of "races", continues largely undisturbed. He ascribes this to inequality as social right, "created through human endeavor", hence

> Determined by the nature of particular societies. It is the social nature of equality, and the dilemmas this often creates, that lies at the heart of the ambiguous attitude of Western [or Westernized] society towards the notion of "race".
>
> (1996: 39)[2]

Malik draws on the USA, while Saul Dubow points in the same direction in the context of South Africa: "conceptions of 'race' are almost invariably related to social issues in some way" (1995: 10). Amongst scholars at least, "race" is today overwhelmingly accepted as a social construct, even if social acceptance remains bio-cultural. But this is only the start of the exploration – "If there is nothing natural about 'races', the question arises *why society feels it necessary* to categorize people according to race", Malik asks. Construction takes place at specific historical moments. At issue here, the "social issue" that Dubow mentions, is inequality, where categorization of humans brings race into the same problematic – "Attributing inequality to race does not solve the *conundrum of equality* because races themselves are social constructions, the creation of which has to be explained" (Malik 1996: 39, emphasis added; Thompson 2006). What social conditions required the creation (or "signification" as Miles [1989: 75] called the process) of race – and introduced the connection with inequality?

Concepts and terms

Articulation is the concept that is utilized as explanatory mechanism.[3] I use it to refer to *processes* of interaction, with reciprocal effects, between two or more elements within a shared system, with one in dominance in shaping the forms and ultimate outcomes of such interaction – rejecting either/or thinking. My use owes much to debates in South Africa in the 1970s on articulation of, or within, modes of production (e.g. Foster-Carter 1978; Wolpe 1980; Resch 1992). Such discussions overlapped, for obvious reasons, with the "class-race debate" during the struggle against apartheid, grappling with the relationship between these factors as related to exploitation, discrimination, inequality, and domination (Posel 1983). Articulation is employed to explore the link between race and inequality, where the complexity of bringing processes and concepts together is similar to demands posed in earlier uses of the notion.

Inequality most often refers to comparison of material conditions – the distribution of income and wealth in society. Here the Gini coefficient – based as it is on measuring primarily net income – is the most frequently used measure. It allows national as well as international comparisons to be made.[4] However, introducing race as group identification – ideological creation, foundation of policy, and social identity – immediately requires a wider approach, one that acknowledges comparisons and effects extending beyond unequal material conditions. Göran Therborn provides such additional fields, drawing on a global-historical overview, in *The Killing Fields of Inequality*:

> Inequality is a violation of human dignity; . . . a denial of the possibility for everybody's human capabilities to develop. It takes many forms, and it has many effects: . . . Inequality, then, is not just about the size of wallets. It is a socio-cultural order, which (for most of us) reduces our capabilities to function as human beings, our health, our self-respect, our sense of self, as well as our resources to act and participate in the world.
>
> (2013: 1, also 2006; on capabilities Therborn refers to
> Martha Nussbaum 2011 and Amartya Sen 2009)

He develops three kinds of inequality, based on the "basic dimensions of human life": human beings as "organisms" ("vital inequality"), as "persons" (field of "existential inequality"), and as "actors" (the more familiar "resource inequality") (Therborn 2013: 48–9). Such an expanded notion of inequality recognizes "race" as a social category, affecting multiple dimensions of human existence – not just those measured through income and wealth but also the consequences on the body and the dignity of the person.

What then is *race*, the other element in Malik's conundrum? Kwame Anthony Appiah writes that "For anyone who shares this project [in his case to 'struggle against racism'], an adequate understanding of racism, *and of the conception of race it presupposes*, is fundamental" (1989: 38, emphasis added). Racisms rely on "racialisms" or "race thinking", what Fields and Fields (2012: 18–19) call "racecraft", the "rational irrationality" as Gilroy calls it (2000: 69). Racialism refers to the manner in which notions of the existence of races serve as important, if not the most important, elements in everyday social cognition, and hence behavior, in many societies (Appiah 1989: 44; Gilroy 2000: 12). Racialism permeates at micro- and macro levels. It can, and does, serve as the "template" for state legislation, policy formulation, implementation and measurement (such as through census-taking) (Alexander 2007: 93); part of what Bowker and Star calls the "built information landscape" (2000: 320). In this way racialism is effectively institutionalized, requiring complicity from all citizens in various ways. It is so everyday that it serves as the basis of social life, through such as relationships, public discourse, through multiple descriptions: media, profiling, census data and analysis (Nobles 2000), through legislation and policies (Maré 2014). Karen Fields and Barbara

Fields call the effect of such saturation "sumptuary codes", or "rules" which "produce a regular supply of circumstantial evidence about what the world is made of and who belongs where within it" (2012: 37, 33). I therefore refer to *race* when it indicates the end-product of processes "where social relations between people have been structured in such a way as to define and construct differentiated social collectivities" (Miles 1989: 75). The "characteristics signified [to human collectivities] vary historically and, although they have usually been visible somatic features, other non-visible (alleged and real) biological features have also been signified" (Miles 1989: 75). It is believed that races can be recognized, but the categories are attributed with "additional, negatively evaluated characteristics", "and/or must be represented as inducing negative consequences for others" (Miles 1989: 79), and attributed with essential cultures. Once races have been constructed "race relations" serves, through its common-sense banality, to obfuscate or prevent other ways of understanding society.

Contexts

Such an introductory focus on terminology is necessary because very little is, or ever can be, certain about the specific historical content of these terms.[5] "Race" is a slippery notion, metamorphosing constantly, waxing and waning, over time and place, and held by both oppressors and the oppressed. What is of concern here is what causal, or ancillary, weight to give to race in understanding inequality and effectively acting towards more equal societies and world? It is essential too, to take into account changes in the social context within which articulation occurs; and the changes in the elements themselves through the process of articulation and through factors beyond the direct links.[6]

To return to Malik's conundrum – how could revolutionary Enlightenment thinking, of the equality of all humans against a hierarchical old order, be suspended or subverted to allow effective acceptance of gross inequalities, at the heart of modern slavery, of industrial and of colonial capitalism? Race, in the constructed forms that it came to exist in articulation with inequality, had not always existed – why and with what effect did it come to exist? Argues Malik:

> Capitalism destroyed the parochialism of feudal society, but it created divisions anew; divisions, moreover, which seemed as permanent as the old feudal ones. As social divisions persisted and acquired the status of permanence, so these differences presented themselves as if they were natural. The conviction grew that inequality, whether within Western society or between the West and the non-Western world, was in the natural order of things.
> *The tendency to view social differences as natural became rationalised through the discourse of race.* The concept of race emerged, therefore, as a means of reconciling the conflict between the ideology of equality and the persistence of inequality. *Race accounted for social inequalities by attributing them to nature.*
> (Malik 1996: 6, emphases added)

Ian Hacking, too, raises the issue of race as justification: "Perhaps we tend to think of races as essentially different just because we want to excuse or to justify the domination of one race by another" (2005: 102). He adds, "You do not have to treat people equally, if they are sufficiently different" (2005: 104). In the colonizing and settler projects "race" overlapped with such differentiating notions as "civilized", "Christian", "cleanliness", and their opposites – all of them already naturalized attributes amongst those in power, created by humans towards deliberate ends. The process, the power, and the agents to ensure pervasive acceptance of the common-sense validity of racialism, take different forms. Similar questions applied and applies to constructed gender inequality and discrimination, existing in variable ways across time and place.

In the USA, was slavery the result of racism or was the notion of race introduced to allow or even justify slavery? In South Africa, who were and are the beneficiaries of racialism (and racism), created and confirmed through classification and separation – physically and in the mind? Cause and justification are related, but not the same. Kenan Malik states it bluntly: "My key argument is that inequality is not the product of racial differences, but rather that the perception of racial difference arises out of the persistence of social inequality" (1996: 7). He adds, in summary:

> The modern discourse of race developed through the racialisation of social and class differences, through the *attribution of racial inferiority to the lower orders of society* – the "dangerous classes" . . . . The racial categories developed in relation to differences *within* European societies were subsequently transposed to the non-European world.
>
> (1996: 225, emphases added; also Bundy 2016: 47)

As Ian Hacking put it, "Classification and judgment are seldom separable. Racial classification *is* evaluation" (2005: 109). He adds later,

> Despite all their differences, the Canadian, French, and American racial obsessions have a single historical source: Empire. Conquest and control – whether of North Africans, West Africans, or the first nations of North America. . . . Empires have a penchant for classifying their subjects. Doubtless there are administrative reasons: . . . there seems to be an imperative to classify subject peoples almost as an end in itself. Or rather, the end is to magnify the exploits, glory, and power of the ruler. Classification, as an imperial imperative, invites stereotyping.
>
> (2005: 113)

In relation to the USA, Karen Fields and Barbara Fields address the conundrum Malik identified and argue that the ideology of race meant that during the American Revolution both supporters and opponents of slavery "collaborated in identifying the racial incapacity of Afro-Americans as the explanation for enslavement. . . . Those holding liberty to be inalienable, and holding

Afro-Americans as slaves, were bound to end by holding race to be a self-evident truth. Thus, we ought to begin by restoring to race – that is, the American version of race – its proper history" (2012: 121).

On another continent, in the mid-seventeenth century, initial clashes at the Cape of Good Hope were over two incompatible notions of relationship to land: the seasonal movement of the existing population of Khoi pastoralists around Table Mountain, and the notion of property ownership demanding fixed borders. This came with the Dutch East-India Company and the re-supply post its officials had been instructed to create at the foot of the same mountain. As settlers moved east and north in the sub-continent, they were to confront further non-capitalist relationships to land. When incursions were made into Xhosa and later Zulu polities, in the nineteenth century, both pastoralist and agricultural groups resisted strongly. The contestation and conquest were variously described as religious (the introduction of Christianity played an ever-increasing part in domination, and conversion, of the heathen) and as civilizational, but everywhere it introduced private ownership and increasing demand for labor in forms ranging from slave to waged. Such racially categorized labor components came to dominate in the expansion of capitalism: sugar plantations in Natal colony from the early 1860s (built through indentured labor from India, and to this day retaining a category called "Indian") (Terreblanche 2002: 210); diamond discovery in the same decade (where migrant waged labor drawn from the remnants of African/black kingdoms and chiefdoms served under settler/white concession holders) (Terreblanche 2002: 9); and then the discovery of gold in commercially-viable quantities in the 1880s (continuing, but on a much expanded scale, with the patterns of migrant and compound dwelling labor established on the diamond mines) (Terreblanche 2002: 12).

What had been African kingdoms and chiefdoms were designated "reserves" when the Union of South Africa was established in 1910, in effect increasingly becoming sites of African labor under dominated pre-capitalist forms of production and authority. The articulation of modes of production took a spatial and racial form as justification for separation. Apartheid policies formalized the already well-established race template, and extended the spatial consequences for the dominated and exploited, to serve mining and industrial expansion through migrant labor, ostensibly of single males. The crudities of nineteenth century scientific racism were somewhat adapted in forms of categorization to suit the post-World War II world – ethnic "nations" added – but the racialized essence and purpose remained the same – facilitating and justifying labor exploitation and political exclusion.

Cause or effect?

In societies where racialism and racism have historical grip, especially during or through conquest, settlement, imperialism, and colonialism, it is clear that there is a firm link to a variety of indicators of "violation of human

dignity and prevention of realizing capabilities", as Therborn defined inequality. Whether through slavery or capitalist relations, those laboring at the
lowest levels were labeled in race terms. Does that then answer, in the affirmative, the question whether race allocation *causes* inequality affecting "humans
as actors"? I have answered that in the negative above. However, does race
articulate in the additional fields identified by Therborn in the same way, a
point to which I return?

Race has played, and still plays in some instances, a role in *justifying and
explaining* resource inequality. I have referred specifically to slavery and capitalism. The latter system again not fixed in its forms, but remaining core to
global resource inequality, and consequently with dramatic effect on vital and
also existential inequality. In addition to work (or unemployment) race *provides
categories for allocation* of resources and of roles, but does not form the most
important source of inequality. Even if not a causal relationship in terms of core
aspects of such exploitative systems as slavery, colonialism, and capitalism, race
nevertheless is central – why and what are the correlations race and resource
inequality, what is being justified?

Seekings and Nattrass, in their study of inequality in South Africa, also note
that "[t]he correlation between race and relative income in a society built on
racial discrimination *is often deemed sufficient as an explanation of inequality*". They
argue that "in the absence of explicit and systematic racial discrimination, race
alone cannot be a sufficient explanation. . . [and that] by the end of apartheid
vast inequalities existed in the distribution of income within racial groups"
(2006: 197, emphasis added). Such intra-racial inequality has increased since
1994, while inter-racial inequality has decreased. Bundy writes that an African
National Congress (ANC) government has managed to make "a modest dent
in income *poverty*". But South Africa is more unequal now than it was in 1994:

> Between 1994 and 2008, *inequality* increased measurably. The Gini coef-
> ficient rose from 0.66 in 1993 to 0.70 in 2008. Two factors, in particular,
> caused inequality to deepen. First, income was increasingly concentrated at
> the upper end of the scale. In 1993, the wealthiest 10% of the population
> accounted for 54% of the country's income; but by 2008 their share had
> risen to over 58%. Over the same period, the share of . . . the poorer 50% of
> the population . . . dropped from 8.3% in 1993 to 7.8% in 2008.
> Secondly, by 2008 about half of the wealthiest 10% of the population
> was African. They shared in a post-apartheid tsunami of consumerism.
> (2016: 138–9, emphases added)

This is because of a deliberate policy of "deracializing capitalism", effectively
aimed at achieving racial proportionality of the rich and, by implication, of the
poor (Maré 2014: 103–5).

Seekings and Nattrass (2006: 4) refer to an inclusive concept of "distributional regimes", which they test through extensive data. Therborn uses the
term "distributive action", defined as "any social action, individual as well as

collective, with direct distributive consequences, be they actions of systemic advance or retardation, or of allocation/ redistribution", to extend explanation of inequality (2013: 55). This is where "affirmative action" and (in South Africa) also "black economic empowerment" policies operate.

These distributional regimes or actions can relate directly to the economic structure, to class exploitation, through the racialized (or gendered) "allocation" of agents to their roles as producers (workers) or appropriators (capitalists) of benefits in various forms, wages being the most important – "but that is simply one of variable aspects employed in allocation within structures, and cannot be the determinant of the structure itself".[7] And, as argued, it is in the structure that the understanding of resource inequality lies in the first, explanatory, place. Slavery as system, capitalism as structure – both exist independently of the labels attached to those allocated to serve or benefit. Distributional regimes, however, are relevant beyond the dominant economic structure in such as forms of poverty relief, or provision of housing and education, in the allocation of dignity or stigma, and the realization or limiting of capabilities.

Here labels do count. Which explains why, as Bundy noted, poverty can be reduced, while inequality increases: "That tackling inequality is more complicated and politically contentious than tackling poverty, as the former implies a 'rearrangement' of the positions of the poor *and* the rich ... whereas the latter only involves the socio-economic conditions of the poor" (Bundy 2016: 139, emphasis original).

Moncrieffe (2007: 2–3) draws us back to the first step in the introduction of race as justification for, and supplementary factor in maintaining and distributing inequality. She writes that labeling, or classification, "*involve relations of power*, in which more powerful actors ... use frames and labels to influence how particular issues and categories of people are regarded and treated. ... [*T*]*here are diverse motivations for labeling* and *labeling processes produce varied, including unanticipated, outcomes.* . . .". Labeling, through its "framing" effect, "refers to how we understand something to be a problem, which may reflect how issues are represented (or not represented) in policy debates and discourse" (2007: 2). Individuals falling within the labeled categories are mere "specimens" of what applies to all, even though the result may simply be what Joy Moncrieffe called "unanticipated consequences" in the process of labeling (2007: 3, see Bauman's illuminating discussion of categorization 2000: 227). Race ideology created categories *within* the elements crucial to the structure, but do not change the structure.

If inequality, then, is not "caused" by race, but through embedding this social construct as one form of discriminatory distributive action, it means that correlations do change – while the underlying structures and practices remain. Both the changes over time and the actual meaning of "correlation" and its equivalents at any one moment need exploration, such as that undertaken by Seekings and Nattrass (2006). Such investigation will no doubt find changes in the relative power displayed in societies – for example the strengthening of trade unions, or changes in political parties holding power.

In discussing correlations I shall do no more than draw attention to Ian Hacking's article seriously asking "why race still matters", in which he challenges easy interpretations of extensive correlations. Statistical overlap is displayed when a number of quantitative measures are employed in comparative research on lives of already race-described collectivities. He explores the issue of statistical overlap, but cautions: "We need some new concepts: I will use the words 'significant', 'meaningful', and 'useful'. All three go with the dread word 'statistical'" (2005: 105). A *significant* correlation is technically useful; but "the idea of being statistically *meaningful* is a hand-waving concept that points at the idea of an explanation or a cause" – but it comes with a warning:

> Imprecise hand-waving concepts are dangerous when they are given fancy names. They can be put to wholly evil ends. But *if* we do not give them phony names and are well aware of their imperfections, they *can be useful* when we need them.
>
> (2005: 105, emphases added)

He asks, "When, if ever, is it useful to speak in terms of the category of race, on the grounds that the races in some contexts are not only statistically significant but also statistically useful classes?" (205:108). Hacking gives examples where such "hand-waving" can be medically useful, but others where they are misused to "evil ends". Any use to confirm "race" as biological fact falls under that misuse.

Race, whether deliberately, or having unintended consequences, through its powerful presence, is linked to all dimensions in Therborn's expanded notion of inequality (2013: 83–6). What are the articulations other than justifying exploitation of human categories or discriminatory distributional regimes? It is obvious, first, that racism, during all periods where the race construction is at work, serves as a direct, and even deliberate, cause of existential inequality ("humans as persons"). It is at the heart of such inequality, with extensive social and psychological damage. Racialism attributes a hierarchy of variable values specific to race collectivities. It defines capabilities. As ideology, it fills the lives and perspectives of the elites and of those suffering the effects. The effects of existential inequality are *real*, even if the construct – that relies on the false claim of biological fact – is not. Race removes human dignity in multiple ways. It allocates, and subsequently it allows no escape while it functions. Escape demands rejection, not only the institutionalization but the whole system of inescapable belonging on which it is constructed. The seed-bed of racism is something apparently innocuous, namely racialism, or the thinking that accepts race as natural, as everyday.

There is, however, a complexity within the field of existential inequality. What if specimens within a race category, or at least some of them, wish to draw existential worth through accepting the label, operating from within it; even attempting to turn that social identity against the classifier, against power (see, for example, Dubow 1995: 290). It then both confirms the basis of race-based existential inequality, and finds race-solidarity from which to resist. In

South Africa debates before 1994 regularly arose around this issue, and remain unresolved today: a constitutional commitment to "non-racialism" but policy and legislation that relies on race classification, forcing all to actively participate.

These complexities have implications, beyond intellectual debate, for addressing resource inequality: through obfuscation of meaningful reasons for inequality, by focusing on distribution regimes, based on race. Fields and Fields deal with this issue head-on:

> Racecraft operates like a railroad switch, diverting a train from one track to another. . . . By crowding inequality off the public agenda, racecraft has stranded this country [the USA] again and again over its history. It may do so again, permitting an economic sickness that arose from inequality to be treated homeopathically by further doses of inequality, which may eventually provoke rage that will sweep away respect for democratic politics and for the rule of law.
>
> (2012: 298–90)

To forestall "that calamity" (one that applies elsewhere too) is to "observe racecraft in action, study its moves, listen to its language, and root it out". Only then "will we be prepared for the still harder work of tackling inequality" (2012: 290).

Such claims to maintaining racialism also reinforce race ideology – Appiah confronts African-American struggles against racism through retaining the "conceptual economy of 'race'" (1989: 40), with the words:

> I am enough of a scholar to think that the truth is worth telling and enough of a political animal to recognize that there are places where the truth does more harm than good. But, so far as the United States is concerned, I can see no reason to believe that racism is advanced by denying the existence of race.
>
> (1989: 40)

Race is also part of vital inequality ("humans as organisms"). Here the inequality resulting from economic structures primarily, both locations within – such as through employment – and the effects of such as unemployment, is unevenly distributed, at the top and the bottom of the racialized pyramid that results. The consequences can be measured against a myriad of possible dimensions of vitality, unevenly to be found, but unsurprisingly in terms of the argument here correlating also with race categories. Further complexity is introduced when the interactions between vital and existential inequality is explored, along with resource hierarchies.

How then?

A major question remains: how are we to address inequality in its multiple fields, and in this case in its articulation with race? "Deracializing capitalism", one of the pillars in South African policy to address resource inequality, is a classic case of shunting the train to a side line, as mentioned above. Will confirming race, by acting on its crude discriminatory and exclusionary consequences, through race-based measures – affirmative action, distributive action, and census measurement – achieve the existential utopia that apartheid also aimed at? Is vital inequality, the health and lifespan of its citizens, not to be addressed through measures that any state owes its citizens, or should this be approached in racialized terms? And, most important in terms of the approach argued for, does the racial distribution of positions within the structure, to achieve racial proportionality within the same system, alleviate inequality? Statistics answer in an emphatic negative.

I have argued strongly against such maintenance of the race construct, for the main reasons that essentialized racialism cannot be rescued from its functions: it hides more accurately directed actions to overcome such as resource and vital inequality, and it remains temptingly available for populist and murderous racisms (Maré 2014). Correlations of real inequalities with race categories have to serve as hand-waving, as Hacking argued, signs that flag for attention, and not for acceptance as independent causes, to be explored in articulation with other factors. They could well serve as indicators of where redress should take place, but in effective and non-harmful ways, addressed as mentioned already as obligations to citizens not races.

Conclusion

To summarize the essence of the argument: yes, race, in its forms of racialism and racism, relates directly and in most cases essentially with inequality and its causes; no, racialism does not cause inequality, but reflects already-existing practices that become over-laid and informed by race and its memories of meanings – various forms of articulation take place. Thus, race can justify, and explain through ideological practice, slavery, and apartheid, the effects of discrimination and exploitation; it can, and does, result in discriminations and in effect determine the distribution of goods and services; it can, and does, shape state and personal templates of essential difference and inter-personal behavior and values, both positive and degradingly negative. So, while race does not direct attention to the essence of inequality, it has to be factored into any of the contexts in which it is relevant – relevant in the sense that historical constructions of the notion of race have played themselves out in relation to the relations of exploitation and discrimination; race continues to articulate with structures of exploitation and the politics of discriminatory distribution, and forms of vital and existential inequality.

Race remains a central factor in many societies, in some cases increasingly so. There are real and perceived benefits in maintaining it by both beneficiaries and in resistance to its effects – most effective as a step in combating existential inequality. Aggravated by its own articulation with contemporary threatening conditions of migrancy, religious intolerance, and new politics of exclusion and hatred in the developed world, race is there for the taking in populist and essentialist identity mobilization (whether as culture, nation, civilization, religion, or other forms).

I have presented arguments on where power resides, what motivations inform construction, and maintenance, of a race frame, and how such ideological and structural "framing" removes other interpretations of consequences from debate and action. Race classification, whether formal in the templates maintained by the state, or in social common sense, becomes invisible in its obviousness, its banality. As Bowker and Star note, "Everyday categories are precisely those that have disappeared into infrastructure, into habit, into the taken for granted" (2000: 319).

To return to the question asked in the introduction, and to its expected initial answer – yes, race is directly related to inequality, except now integrated into Therborn's *plurality of inequalities*. And then to what flows from that, and the subsequent discussion of why that should be the case, what to do about it. Two directions are indicated: first, to take steps to undermine the taken for granted of race framing, and to remove its inextricable link to notions of inferiority in its multiple forms, and thus to demand the "equality of all" in ways that actually make a difference; second, to confirm race, and to create equality between races, but do very little other than to benefit a small minority with access to power.

The first is fraught with difficulties (maybe even impossibilities) explained above, unless a careful and slow process of delegitimation is undertaken by the state. Such a process has to deal with the common sense of race, with the confirmation that is the general rule, with the benefits to the powerful to maintain it. Existential value is claimed for racialism – unfortunately for both "white" and "black", to both of the poles of inequality. Race is always plural – confirmation of one, confirms the other; one might be resistance solidarity, the other in embedded privilege and the racism that created and justified it, but both confirm race.

The structures of capitalism, and slavery that preceded it, have over centuries created extreme inequality. Shuffling the occupants by race does not change either system. Both race and capitalist inequality seem the natural order. But the effects are such that they create demands for change outside of the structures and order that maintain them. *Global* flows of people as refugees and migrants because of wars and oppression and global inequality, and the unpredictable consequences of *global* warming, will distribute the effects towards the poor and marginalized, the dangerous classes. Race is, and will remain, one label to be attached to such victims of inequality, by those who benefit, a label that will increasingly serve to exclude and demand barricades.

Notes

1 How people explain inequality: www.bbc.com/news/magazine-33613246. Also Sachweh 2014.
2 'How can racism and egalitarianism coexist? Because equality is among those who are essentially the same. If races are essentially different, they need not be treated alike' (Hacking 2005: 111).

3 'Articulate' (*adj* or *v*) refers both to speech, and to join in interaction (as in 'articulated lorry').
4 Gini index: A measurement of the income distribution of a country's residents. This number, which ranges between 0 and 1 and is based on residents' net income, helps define the gap between the rich and the poor, with 0 representing perfect equality and 1 representing perfect inequality: www.investopedia.com/terms/g/gini-index.asp
5 Let me note, too, that I am writing and you are reading in English, the language of British imperialism affecting vast areas of the modern world, the language in which these terms – and the practices reliant on or justified by them – came largely to be used. In addition I am writing from South Africa, drawing on that particular history of racialism and racism. Fascinating would be a comparative study of terms, their meanings, and their historical origin and location in different languages – multiple versions of Raymond Williams' 'keywords' (1984).
6 I can refer to the enormous influx of refugees into the EU, and the presidency of Donald Trump, that have already and will continue to affect all forms of inequality, through categorizations of people and because of the structural impact on the world.
7 I wish to thank Glenn Moss – personal communication (November 2016) – for this formulation.

References

Alexander, Neville (2007) 'Affirmative Action and the Perpetuation of Racial Identities in Post-Apartheid South Africa', *Transformation*, Vol. 63: 92–108.

Appiah, Kwame Anthony (1989) 'The Conservation of "Race"', *Black American Literature Forum*, Vol. 23, No. 1: 37–60.

Bauman, Zygmunt (2000) *Modernity and the Holocaust*, Ithaca, NY and New York: Cornell University Press.

Bowker, Geoffrey C. and Susan Leigh Star (2000) *Sorting Things Out: Classification and Its Consequences*, Cambridge, MA: MIT Press.

Bundy, Colin (2016) *Poverty in South Africa: Past and Present*, Auckland Park: Jacana.

Dubow, Saul (1995) *Scientific Racism in Modern South Africa*, Cambridge: Cambridge University Press.

Fields, Karen E. and Barbara J. Fields (2012) *Racecraft: The Soul of Inequality in American Life*, London and New York: Verso.

Foster-Carter, Aidan (1978) 'The Modes of Production Controversy', *New Left Review*, Vol. 107, No. I: 47–77.

Gilroy, Paul (2000) *Against Race: Imagining Political Culture Beyond the Color Line*, Cambridge, MA: The Belknap Press.

Hacking, Ian (2005) 'Why Race Still Matters', *Daedalus*, Vol. 134, No. 1: 102–16.

Malik, Kenan (1996) *The Meaning of Race: Race, History and Culture in Western Society*, London: Macmillan.

Maré, Gerhard (2014) *Declassified: Moving Beyond the Dead End of Race in South Africa*, Auckland Park: Jacana.

Miles, Robert (1989) *Racism*, London: Routledge.

Moncrieffe, Joy (2007) 'Labelling, Power and Accountability: How and Why "Our" Categories Matter', in Joy Moncrieffe and Rosalind Eyben (eds.) *The Power of Labelling: How People Are Categorized and Why It Matters*, London and Sterling VA: Earthscan.

Nobles, Melissa (2000) *Shades of Citizenship: Race and the Census in Modern Politics*, Stanford, CA: Stanford University Press.

Nussbaum, Martha (2011) *Creating Capabilities*, Cambridge, MA: The Belknap Press.

Posel, Deborah (1983) 'Rethinking the "Race-Class Debate" in South African Historiography", *Social Dynamics*, Vol. 9, No. 1: 50–66.

Resch, Robert Paul (1992) *Althusser and the Renewal of Marxist Social Theory*, Berkeley, CA: University of California Press.

Sachweh, Patrick (2014) 'Unequal by Origin or by Necessity? Popular Explanations of Inequality and Their Legitimatory Implications', *European Journal of Cultural and Political Sociology*, Vol. 1, No. 4: 323–46.

Seekings, Jeremy and Nicoli Nattrass (2006) *Class, Race and Inequality in South Africa*, Pietermaritzburg: UKZN Press.

Sen, Amartya (2009) *The Idea of Justice*, London: Allen Lane.

Terreblanche, Sampie (2002) *A History of Inequality in South Africa 1652–2002*, Scottsville: University of Natal Press; Sandton: KMM Review.

Therborn, Göran (2006) 'Introduction', in Göran Therborn (ed.) *Inequalities of the World: New Theoretical Frameworks, Multiple Empirical Approaches*, London and New York: Verso.

Therborn, Göran (2013) *The Killing Fields of Inequality*, London: Verso.

Thompson, Eric C. (2006) 'The Problem of "Race as a Social Construct"', *Anthropology News*, Vol. 47, No. 2: 6–7.

Williams, Raymond (1984) *Keywords: A Vocabulary of Culture and Society*, New York: Oxford University Press.

Wolpe, Harold (ed.) (1980) *The Articulation of Modes of Production: Essays From Economy and Society*, London, Boston, MA and Henley: Routledge, Kegan Paul.

11 Rural–urban inequality and poverty

Anirudh Krishna

More than 80 percent of the population in Ethiopia, Kenya, Malawi, Niger, and Sri Lanka lives in rural areas – and more than 60 percent of the population in Bangladesh, India, Madagascar, Pakistan, Uzbekistan, and Vietnam. In other developing countries, too, the share of the rural population is large, consisting of at least 40 percent of the population in countries far apart, including China, Georgia, Ghana, Guatemala, Indonesia, and Nicaragua. Overall, more than half the world's people live in developing countries that have a largely agrarian population. Each country has, to varying degrees, opened its borders to cross-national flows of goods, services, investments, lifestyles, and ideas. But how globalization will affect the rural population of these countries remains under-appreciated.

The transformation of the population from mostly rural to largely urban that occurred within countries that industrialized earlier serves poorly as guide for the transformations that developing countries are experiencing and will experience. To expect that Kenya will be transformed in a relatively short period of time from what it is presently – more than 70 percent rural and less than 30 percent urban – to a largely urban country, *and* to expect that these transformations, like those of the United States or Japan, will be beneficial for the largest number of individuals, is to blind oneself to important changes in the demographic situation, in the nature of global interconnectedness, and in the technologies of production.

New ways of addressing an old problem are required for dealing with the problems faced by rural people of largely agrarian developing countries. Unless these ways are pioneered, ever-rising inequality will become the defining feature of globalization in these countries.

Persistent under-provisioning

The spread of lifestyles has widened across a swathe of countries. Within countries, inequalities between the rural and the urban parts of the population have grown measurably wider (Brulhart and Sbergami 2009). China's remarkable economic growth, for example, is

> a result of only a handful of urban centers such as Shanghai, Shenzhen, and Beijing ... each of which is a world apart from its vast impoverished rural

areas. In 2006, average household incomes in urban China were two and a half times those in rural areas . . . The prospects for bridging these gaps are weak . . . But all that pales in comparison with the growing pains felt by India's poor. India's growing economic spikes – city regions such as Bangalore, Hyderabad, Mumbai, and parts of New Delhi – are also pulling away from the rest of that crowded country.

(Florida 2008: 35–6)[1]

In other countries, too, including Vietnam, Peru, and parts of Sub-Saharan Africa, evidence has been uncovered of growing urban-rural differences in wealth and income.[2] Investigations of trends in 58 developing and transitional countries found unequivocally that such "spatial inequalities are high and rising" (Kanbur and Venables 2007: 211). Another examination, of 47 countries for the period from 1990 to 2007, found "a positive and statistically significant association between economic globalization and the magnitude of regional income disparities" (Ezcurra and Rodrigues-Pose 2013: 92).

The gap between urban and rural areas was not created by greater global integration. A wide urban-rural gap existed long before the current era of globalization. Biases in policies favoring a country's big cities played a large part in structuring colonial governments, many of which had only a thin presence beyond district towns and provincial capitals (Boone 2003; Davidson 1992; Mamdani 1996). The post-independence states' extended dalliance with state-led industrialization exacerbated these differences, producing a greater concentration of public services, infrastructure, and government offices within big cities (Bates 1981). Remoter villages, far from cities and highways and far from sight of government officials, were underprovided in terms of projects and personnel (Lipton 1977; Chambers 1997). Urban-rural differences kept getting higher in these years of urban bias.

When global firms alighted upon these countries, arriving mostly in the 1990s and 2000s, it was only natural that they would select to locate in big cities. Those were the only places where the minimally necessary bundle of services and facilities existed: communications and banking, universities and research centers – and the kinds of schools and colleges, bookshops, sporting arenas, theater, restaurants, and shopping malls that are necessary for attracting the managers and technologists who staff global companies. The agglomerations that existed in Western cities had become the early hubs of globalization (Moretti 2012; Sassen 2001). Eager to offer up similar agglomerations in their own countries, developing country elites invested heavily in their biggest cities.

These investments resulted in transforming the earlier urban bias into a "metropolitan bias." The quality and availability of services is greatest "in the largest cities – precisely those where governments, the middle-classes, opinion-makers and airports are disproportionately located" (Ferré, Ferreira and Lanjouw 2012: 353–4). Meanwhile, rural areas were under-provisioned with services and infrastructure. The differences that have arisen are stark. Gated communities in Bangalore and Lima, Nairobi and Kampala, private-island resorts near Manila – all have First-World amenities. But deep into the countryside, Third World pockets persist, people living in much the same ways and using much the same technologies as they did a hundred years earlier.

Poverty levels are much lower in cities compared to rural areas. In Malawi, 17 percent of the urban population lives below the poverty line – but more than three times as many, 57 percent, of the rural population. The corresponding proportions are 11 and 39 percent in Ghana; 28 and 78 percent in Zambia; 16 and 49 percent in Ecuador; 9 and 24 percent in Cambodia; and 5 and 22 percent in Vietnam. In each case, the rural poverty ratio is three times that of urban areas.[3]

If you're poor, the chances are high that you are rural. And if you are rural, the chances are high that you are poorly served by electricity, roads, education, health care, and much else – information, communications, water supply, sanitation – that goes into the making of a secure livelihood and a chance for upward mobility.

The examples are many; the following figures are illustrative. More than 95 percent of the urban population of Ethiopia has access to improved drinking water sources, but less than half that share (42 percent) of the rural population; more than 60 percent of city residents in India have improved sanitation facilities, but only 25 percent of village residents.

Chronic under-provisioning has had dire consequences for people from rural areas. The average rural adult has fewer years of education compared to the average urban adult, and there are very significant differences in the quality of education. Fewer and poorer-quality schools serve rural areas, resulting in a large gap in educational achievement. More than 60 percent of the urban population in Pakistan completes secondary school – but only 30 percent of rural residents.[4]

Without completing secondary school, the chances of getting a well-paid job in the formal sector are severely diminished, particularly in this era of globalization, when "technologies like big data and analytics, high-speed communications, and rapid prototyping have decreased the demand for less skilled labor while increasing the demand for highly skilled labor" (Brynjolffsson and McAfee 2014: 135). A single computer can take over the jobs of dozens of people (Cage 2014). "Technology has created a growing reservoir of less-skilled labor," a report in the *Economist* notes, "while simultaneously expanding the range of tasks that can be automated."[5] Measured as the difference in average earning between people with a college degree and others with only a few years of education, the college premium increased over the 1980s and 1990s within each of seven developing countries: Argentina, Brazil, Chile, Colombia, Hong Kong, India, and Mexico. "The evidence has provided little support for the conventional wisdom that trade openness in developing countries would favor the less fortunate" (Goldberg and Pavcnik 2007: 77). The share of labor in national incomes has declined across a range of countries – and the share of the least educated has fallen the furthest (Karabarbounis and Neiman 2013). Software engineers in India quadrupled their average take-home pay in the 1990s. But simultaneously the gap in earnings between people with zero years and ten years of education was reduced to a sliver.[6]

But how is a young person growing up in a remote village to acquire the necessary high level of education? Few schools existed in the villages of most largely agrarian countries at the time of national independence. High schools and colleges are still dozens of miles from most village residents. The roads in remote rural areas aren't as good, and there are fewer public buses than in cities. Schools in rural areas are of a poorer quality, and the teachers are often missing (Chaudhury et al. 2006).

All of this diminishes the life chances of rural youth, no matter how capable and how hardworking. Their prospects for upward mobility are severely limited. I saw some effects in rural communities of India, Peru, Uganda, Bangladesh, and Kenya, where I went to study poverty and social mobility. In the nearly 400 communities that I visited, I saw many signs of poverty but little evidence of substantial upward mobility. Hardly anyone from these communities has become an engineer or a doctor, an investment banker, sports star, or media personality. The vast majority of people from remoter rural areas, both the more and the less educated, have found positions within the informal sector, getting the most insecure jobs and the least well-remunerated.[7] The conditions of life are precarious for these people; many have fallen into persistent poverty (Krishna 2009).

There are no ready-made remedies for these situations. The prospects from people from rural areas will not automatically improve on account of growth, globalization, urbanization, technology, or education. I will illustrate these propositions with the help of data and examples drawn from a larger study of India.[8]

The effects in India

More than two thirds of India's population lives in its rural areas, a total of 833 million people in 2011. Instead of falling, this number has kept increasing, rising by 80 million over the decade between 2001 and 2011. Urbanization has gathered pace, and much more than before, rural people are traveling to cities. Still, the decadal rate of decline in the rural share of the population has been of the order of 2 to 3 percent, implying that "it will be another 50 years before urbanization reaches even 50 percent" (Panagariya 2011: 159).

Planners in India consider its cities, however, as this country's "reservoirs of skills, capital and knowledge ... the centers of innovation and creativity ... the generators of resources for national and state exchequers ... [and] the hopes of millions" (GOI 2010). The government's policies have been "heavily oriented toward urban areas, and new public investments have privileged mostly urban areas as well as more prosperous regions."[9] Private investments have also been concentrated close to major cities (Ghani, Kerr and O'Connell 2013; Lall and Chakravorty 2005; World Bank 2011).

Regional differences in income and wealth have increased as a result (Deaton and Dreze 2002, 2009; Dev and Ravi 2007; Sen and Himanshu 2004a; Sen and Himanshu 2004b; World Bank 2006). Compared to urban areas, incomes in rural areas are much lower.

Consider the spread of incomes in the second decade of the new millennium. Table 11.1 shows the percentage of individuals who lived below different levels of monthly per-capita income.[10]

More than 17 percent of rural individuals are in the lowest income bracket, less than 500 rupees monthly, but only 4.6 percent of urban individuals. In the next higher income bracket, too, there is a greater proportion of rural compared to urban individuals. The three highest income brackets are, however, disproportionately constituted by urban individuals.

Nearly half of all rural individuals have incomes below 1,000 rupees monthly (which in PPP terms equates to roughly $1.50 per day)[11] – the minimum level required to achieve a bare existence. Poverty rates are lowest in the largest cities and highest in rural areas (Kundu and Sarangi 2007).

The sliver of the population that has a monthly per-capita income of more than 5,000 rupees constitutes 1.7 percent of the rural population and 5.7 percent of the urban population. These are the individuals who are more likely to own durable assets and other markers of international middle-class status. As illustrated by Table 11.2, a far greater share of urban, compared to rural, households possess each type of asset.

Globalization and growth have benefited rural and urban people very unequally. The rich in urban areas are richer than the rich in rural areas. The poor in rural areas are much poorer than the poor people of cities. The average income of people living in city slums in 2012 was 1,816 rupees, but the average

Table 11.1 Monthly per-capita income in 2011–12

	Percentage share	
Monthly per-capita income (2012 rupees)	*Rural*	*Urban*
Below 500	17.4	4.6
500–1,000	29.4	14.3
1,000–2,000	19.9	33.7
2,000–5,000	4.8	22.9
5,000–10,000	1.5	4.9
Above 10,000	0.2	0.8

Data: India Human Development Survey, 2012

Table 11.2 Urban–rural differences in asset possession

	Share of households possessing assets in 2011–12 (%)				
	Television	*Refrigerator*	*Scooter or motorcycle*	*Computer*	*Car*
Urban	88	49	42	15	9
Rural	54	17	22	3	3

Data: India Human Development Survey, 2011–12

incomes of the poorer half in villages more than 5 kilometers from the nearest city was only 664 rupees.[12]

On multiple dimensions – in terms of education, health care, and infrastructure availability – villages have fared worse than cities. The situation is worse in villages located more than 5 km from the nearest city (Table 11.3).

Higher education is necessary for an individual to get ahead in a globalizing economy. The threshold at which education makes a large economic difference has risen in India, as in other countries (Chamarbagwala 2006; Sarkar and Mehta 2010). At least a high school diploma, and more often, a college degree is necessary for being within the zone of consideration for secure and higher-paying positions.

But many young people in rural areas are not able to avail themselves of a higher, or a higher-quality, education. The share of individuals 15 years old and older who had a college degree was only 3.7 percent in rural areas (NSSO 2008). Colleges are at great distances from remote villages, and only the children of the richest can afford to get a college education. Public and private assistance has helped some children of poorer parents, but higher education continues to be the domain of higher class (and upper caste) males; women students are fewer (Azam and Blom 2008).

The share of poorer rural people who are going to college has been increasing. However, low attendance numbers are not the only problem. What is worse is the low quality of education in schools attended by children of poorer villagers. Tests of learning ability carried out among schoolchildren aged 8–11 years by the India Human Development Survey of 2011–12 showed that while 61 percent of urban children had the requisite computational abilities (they could do basic addition and subtraction), the corresponding share in rural areas was below 40 percent. The share in urban areas of those with basic English-language abilities was 22 percent, falling to 5 percent in rural areas. The percentages of schoolchildren achieving basic competence levels was even lower in beyond-5km villages. After attending school for the same number of years, village children learned comparatively little.

Table 11.3 Greater distance and lower provision

	Within 5 km	*Beyond 5 km*
Percentage of all villages	*32*	*68*
Distance in (kilometers) from:		
Middle school	2.7	4.6
Secondary school	3.8	7.8
Basic health care (sub-centre/PHC/private clinic)	4.3	8.6
Bank	4.6	11.4
Percentage of households with electricity connection	64.6	55.8
Percentage of villages with canal irrigation	15.8	12.6
Percentage of villages with bank branches	24.8	12.8

Data: DLHS-3 data (2007–08)

Healthcare, too, is poorer in rural areas, becoming worse in villages deep into the interior. Malnutrition is more prevalent in beyond-5km villages – and the gap between cities and beyond-5km villages, instead of becoming narrower, is growing (Baru et al. 2010). Compared to beyond-5km villages, villages located closer to towns are three times as likely to have a hospital (government or a private), and more than twice as likely to have a basic care facility, like a primary health center or government dispensary (Hammer, Aiyar and Samji 2006).

Seeking better opportunities, millions of individuals have been moving from rural areas into cities, but very few among the migrants who entered the city in a lower economic bracket were able to achieve significant upward mobility. The number of people living in slums has burgeoned (UN-Habitat 2010). Many families have lived in slums for multiple generations. "Most of the slum communities saw little or no increase in their real income or in improved job opportunities. Longer urban experience did not necessarily ensure access to better opportunities. Children tended to ply, by and large, the same trades and occupations as their parents" (Bapat 2009: 19).[13]

Their prospects stymied by generations of under-provisioning, young people in villages have gravitated toward low-paying menial positions. Where it was once derived from tilling the land, the greatest share of the income of the poorer 50 percent is now obtained from agricultural and non-agricultural labor. The grandsons of peasant farmers have become *mazdoors* (daily laborers) in the tens of millions.

Looking for better policies

Large differences in the lifestyles of the urban rich and the rural majority bode poorly for civic harmony and shared sense of social justice (Atkinson 2015; Barnes and Hall 2013). But no solutions to the problems created by widening urban-rural differences have been handed down by richer countries. Western societies were transformed in an earlier age from largely rural to mostly urban. The lessons that matter today will not be derived from these countries' economic histories.

Solutions that hold promise do not exist; they will need to be demonstrated. Nations will mount their own projects, guided by their politics and their own dominant beliefs about rural-urban differences and inequalities.

Growing inequalities impose diverse burdens upon a society (Berg and Ostry 2011; Wilkinson and Pickett 2009). Nations desirous of preventing inequalities from growing to a point where the burden becomes too large for society will do well to invest in developing the required policies.

Three principles should guide the quest for better policies:

- a minimum living standard;
- equality of opportunity; and
- democracy near one's doorstep.

The first principle requires setting and enforcing a minimum living standard. Some societies, for example, Scandinavian ones, are comparatively generous in defining their minimum standards, while others, such as the United States, have constructed their social safety nets differently. Developing countries, too, should work toward installing legal rights and institutionalizing social assistance programs that will help unite their people in a shared national undertaking. Each citizen must have enough to give her family a nutritious diet, a firm roof above her head, clothes that she's not ashamed to wear in public, and affordable and useful education and health care for her children. Providing affordable and reliable health care is an important part of what it will take to reduce vulnerability. Countries that have low poverty rates do not commonly have a high average income; what they do have is reliable universal health care.

The second principle upholds the need for a level playing field: everyone's son or daughter should have an equal shot at upward mobility. A bright and hardworking individual, no matter where she is born, should be able to rise to a level commensurate with her dedication and capability. Building bridges between opportunity and talent is important for a just society. It is important, as well, for nurturing a wider base of talent, which helps countries compete successfully in the global economy.

Raising the capacities of poorer rural people to compete for better jobs and newer opportunities is essential as well for greater social cohesion and for promoting a greater sense of oneness with the nation. Bringing a larger share of the talent pool to bear upon the task of building economic growth will also help propel national economies faster. For a variety of reasons, therefore, it is important to invest in national projects of social mobility.

The third principle has to do with the need for a functioning democracy, not just at the highest levels of government but all across the country. No matter where she lives, in a big town or in a remote rural area, a citizen must have low-cost venues where she can express her discontent, be listened to patiently, and be able to obtain redress with assurance. It is not simply a matter of being able to elect and dismiss a country's leaders. The protections, opportunities, and benefits of democracy must be easy to access by all manner of people.[14]

The widening inequalities of opportunity will not go away of their own accord. Policies will be needed to take action against these inequalities. The largely agrarian countries of the developing world will learn from each other's follies and innovations.

Notes

1 See also Wang, Piesse and Weaver (2011) and Zhang and Zhang (2003).
2 See, for instance, Chomitz, Buys and Thomas (2005); Forster, Jesuit and Smeeding (2005); Jensen and Tarp (2005); Escobal and Torrero (2005) and Christiaensen, Demery and Paternostro (2005).
3 See Population Reference Bureau (2015) for these percentages in these and many other countries.

4   These figures were obtained from Population Reference Bureau (2015) and World Bank (2013).

5   *Economist*, October 4, 2014.

6   See Azam (2012); Azam and Blom (2008); Cain et al. (2010); Chamarbagwala (2006); Sarkar and Mehta (2010).

7   The informal sector is the largest and fastest growing employer in many countries. Fewer than 10 percent of rural households in India have formal jobs, the types that come with regular salaries, employment benefits, and legal protections. The situation in many other countries is equally depressing. More than 70 percent of all non-agricultural employment is provided in the informal sector in, for instance, Indonesia, the Philippines, Vietnam, Bolivia, and Peru (ILO 2012)

8   For a detailed exposition of the results see the author's larger study (Krishna 2017).

9   Fan, Chan-Kang and Mukherjee (2005: 14).

10 Data for this table were taken from a large national survey – the India Human Development Survey (IHDS) – undertaken between 2011 and 2012 by the National Council for Applied Economic Research (NCAER), a well-known applied economics research institution in India, in collaboration with the University of Maryland. See http://ihds.info/ for more details. A different analysis, using data on monthly expenditures (instead of incomes), produced a very similar percentage distribution. Using NSSO data of 2009–10 for monthly per-capita expenditure (MPCE), we found, for instance, that 22 percent in urban areas and 43 percent in rural areas had MPCEs below 1,000 rupees. I thank Devendra Bajpai for help with this examination of data.

11 A level of $2.10 per day has suggested by the World Bank as a measure of acute poverty. The government of India has set its national poverty line below this level.

12 Author calculations using data from India Human Development Survey, 2011–12. I thank Devendra Bajpai for research assistance.

13 Few among the individuals who came into cities were able to put down roots. Circular – or short-term or itinerant – migrants constitute the largest number, as revealed by a survey undertaken between 2009 and 2011, which found a variety of migrants who had spent different lengths of time living in a city. Only 18 percent of migrants had been in a city for a year or longer; 22 percent had stayed in the city for more than four months but less than a year; 9 percent had gone into cities for only a few weeks, spending the rest of the year in their native villages; and another 7 percent, whose villages were located closer, commuted daily to earn a livelihood in a nearby city (Mazumdar, Neetha and Agnihotri 2013). Other investigations show that up to 40 percent of the labor force in cities is composed of a floating population, with more than 100 million coming annually as itinerant immigrants (Deshingkar and Akter 2009).

14 Similar arguments are advanced by Jayal (2013) and Kohli (2012).

References

Atkinson, Anthony B. (2015) *Inequality: What Can Be Done?* Cambridge, MA: Harvard University Press.

Azam, Mehtabul (2012) 'Changes in Wage Structure in Urban India, 1983–2004: A Quantile Regression Decomposition', *World Development*, Vol. 40, No. 6: 1135–50.

Azam, Mehtabul and Andreas Blom (2008) 'Progress in Participation in Tertiary Education in India From 1983 to 2004', World Bank Policy Research Working Paper Series, No. 4793.

Bapat, Meera (2009) 'Poverty Lines and Lives of the Poor: Under-Estimation of Urban Poverty – the Case of India', London, UK: International Institute of Environment and Development, Working Paper.

Barnes, Lucy and Peter A. Hall (2013) 'Neoliberalism and Social Resilience in the Developed Democracies', in Peter A. Hall and Michele Lamont (eds.) *Social Resilience in the Neoliberal Era*, New York: Cambridge University Press, 209–38.

Baru, Rama, Arnab Acharya, Sanghmitra Acharya, A. K. Shivakumar and K. Nagaraj (2010) 'Inequities in Access to Health Services in India: Caste, Class and Region', *Economic and Political Weekly*, Vol. 45, No. 38: 49–58.

Bates, Robert (1981) *Markets and States in Tropical Africa: The Political Basis of Agricultural Policies*, Berkeley, CA: University of California Press.

Berg, Andrew and Jonathan Ostry (2011) 'Inequality and Unsustainable Growth: Two Sides of the Same Coin?', IMF Staff Discussion Note SDN/11/08, available at www.imf.org/external/pubs/ft/sdn/2011/sdn1108.pdf (15.05.2015).

Boone, Catherine (2003) *Political Topographies of the African State: Territorial Authority and Institutional Choice*, New York: Cambridge University Press.

Brulhart, Marius and Federica Sbergami (2009) 'Agglomeration and Growth: Cross-Country Evidence', *Journal of Urban Economics*, Vol. 65: 48–63.

Brynjolffson, Erik and Andrew McAfee (2014) *Second Machine Age: Work, Progress, and Prosperity in a Time of Brilliant Technologies*, New York: W.W. Norton.

Cage, Nicholas (2014) *Glass Cage: Automation and Us*, New York: Norton.

Cain, J. Salcedo, Rana Hasan, Rhoda Magsombol, and Ajay Tandon (2010). 'Accounting for Inequality in India: Evidence from Household Expenditures', *World Development*, Vol. 38, No. 3: 282–97.

Chamarbagwala, Rubiana (2006) 'Economic Liberalization and Wage Inequality in India', *World Development*, Vol. 34, No. 12: 1997–2015.

Chambers, Robert (1997) *Whose Reality Counts? Putting the First Last*, London: Intermediary Technology Publications.

Chaudhury, Nazmul, Jeffrey Hammer, Michael Kremer, Karthik Muralidharan and F. Halsey Rogers (2006) 'Missing in Action: Teacher and Health Worker Absence in Developing Countries', *Journal of Economic Perspectives*, Vol. 20, No. 1: 91–116.

Chomitz, Kenneth M., Piet Buys and Timothy S. Thomas (2005) 'Quantifying the Rural-Urban Gradient in Latin America and the Caribbean', World Bank Policy Research Working Paper Series, No. 3634.

Christiaensen, Luc, Lionel Demery and Stefano Paternostro (2005) 'Reforms, Remoteness, and Risk in Africa: Understanding Inequality and Poverty During the 1990s', in Ravi Kanbur and Anthony J. Venables (eds.) *Spatial Inequality and Development*, Oxford: Oxford University Press, 209–36.

Davidson, Basil (1992) *Black Man's Burden*, New York: Random House.

Deaton, Angus and Jean Dreze (2009) 'Food and Nutrition in India, Facts and Interpretation', *Economic and Political Weekly*, Vol. 44, No. 7: 42–65.

Deaton, Angus and Jean Dreze (2002) 'Poverty and Inequality in India; A Re-Examination.' *Economic and Political Weekly*, September 7: 3729–48.Deshingkar, Priya and Shaheen Akter (2009) 'Migration and Human Development in India', United Nations Development Programme Human Development Research Paper, No. 2009/13.

Dev, S. Mahendra and C. Ravi (2007) 'Poverty and Inequality: All-India and States, 1983–2005', *Economic and Political Weekly*, Vol. 42, No. 6: 509–21.

Escobal, Javier and Maximo Torrero (2005) 'Adverse Geography and Differences in Welfare in Peru', in Ravi Kanbur and Anthony J. Venables (eds.) *Spatial Inequality and Development*, Oxford: Oxford University Press, 77–122.

Ezcurra, Roberto and Andres Rodrigues-Pose (2013) 'Does Economic Globalization Affect Regional Inequality? A Cross-Country Analysis', *World Development*, Vol. 52: 92–103.

Fan, Shenggen, Connie Chan-Kang and Anit Mukherjee (2005) 'Rural and Urban Dynamics and Poverty: Evidence From China and India', Washington, DC: International Food Policy Research Institute, FCND Discussion Paper, No. 196.

Ferré, Celine, Francisco H. G. Ferreira and Peter Lanjouw (2012) 'Is There a Metropolitan Bias? The Relationship Between Poverty and City Size in a Selection of Developing Countries', *World Bank Economic Review*, Vol. 26, No. 3: 351–82.

Florida, Richard (2008) *Who's Your City: How the Creative Economy Is Making Where to Live the Most Important Decision in Your Life*, New York: Basic Books.

Forster, Michael, David Jesuit and Timothy Smeeding (2005) 'Regional Poverty and Income Inequality in Central and Eastern Europe: Evidence From the Luxembourg Income Study', in Ravi Kanbur and Anthony J. Venables (eds.) *Spatial Inequality and Development*, Oxford: Oxford University Press, 311–47.

Ghani, Ejaz, William R. Kerr and Stephen D. O'Connell (2013) 'Input Usage and Productivity in Indian Manufacturing Plants', Washington, DC: World Bank, PREM Policy Research Working Paper, No. 6656.

GOI (2010) *Report of the Committee on Slum Statistics/Census*, New Delhi: Government of India, Ministry of Housing and Urban Poverty Alleviation, available at http://mhupa.gov. in/W_new/Slum_Report_NBO.pdf.

Goldberg, Pinelopi K. and Nina Pavcnik (2007) 'Distributional Effects of Globalization in Developing Countries', *Journal of Economic Literature*, Vol. 45: 39–82.

Hammer, Jeffrey, Yamini Aiyar and Salimah Samji (2006) 'Bottom's Up: To the Role of Panchayati Raj Institutions in Health and Health Services', Washington DC: World Bank, Social Development Papers: South Asia Series, No. 98.

ILO (2012) 'Statistical Update on Employment in the Informal Economy', available at labor-sta.ilo.org/informal_economy_E.html (01.11.2015).

Jayal, Niraja Gopal (2013) *Citizenship and Its Discontents: An Indian History*, New Delhi: Permanent Black.

Jensen, Henning and Finn Tarp (2005) 'Trade Liberalization and Spatial Inequality: A Methodological Innovation in a Vietnamese Perspective', *Review of Development Economics*, Vol. 9, No. 1: 69–86.

Kanbur, Ravi and Anthony J. Venables (2007) 'Spatial Disparities and Economic Development', in David Held and Ayse Kaya (eds.) *Global Inequality: Patterns and Explanations*, Cambridge: Polity Press, 204–15.

Karabarbounis, Loukas and Brent Neiman (2013) 'The Global Decline of the Labor Share', National Bureau of Economic Research Working Paper, No. 19136, available at www. nber.org/papers/w19136 (06.05.2014).

Kohli, Atul. (2012) *Poverty Amid Plenty in the New India*, New York: Cambridge University Press.

Krishna, Anirudh (2009) 'Are More People Becoming Vulnerable to Poverty? Evidence From Grassroots Investigations in Five Countries', in Boike Rehbein and Jan Nederveen Pieterse (eds.) *Globalization and Emerging Societies*, New York: Palgrave Macmillan.

Krishna, Anirudh (2017) *The Broken Ladder: The Paradox and Potential of India's One-Billion*, Cambridge: Cambridge University Press and Penguin India.

Kundu, Amitabh and Niranjan Sarangi (2007) 'Migration, Employment Status and Poverty: An Analysis across Urban Centres', *Economic and Political Weekly*, Vol. 42, No. 4: 299–307.

Lall, Somik Vinay and Sanjoy Chakravorty (2005) 'Industrial Location and Spatial Inequality: Theory and Evidence From India', *Review of Development Economics*, Vol. 9, No. 1: 47–68.

Lipton, Michael (1977) *Why Poor People Stay Poor: Urban Bias in World Development*, Cambridge, MA: Harvard University Press.

Mamdani, Mahmood (1996) Citizen and Subject: Contemporary Africa and the Legacy of Late Colonialism, Princeton, NJ: Princeton University Press.

Mazumdar, Indrani, N. Neetha and Indu Agnihotri (2013) 'Migration and Gender in India', *Economic and Political Weekly*, Vol. 48, No. 10: 54–64.

Moretti, Enrico (2012) *New Geography of Jobs*, New York: Houghton, Mifflin, Harcourt.

NSSO (2008) 'Education in Indai: 2007–08. Participation and Expenditure', Government of India: National Sample Survey Organization.

Panagariya, Arvind (2011) 'Avoiding Lopsided Spatial Transformation', in Ejaz Ghani (ed.) *Reshaping Tomorrow: Is South Asia Ready for the Big Leap?* New Delhi: Oxford University Press, 143–67.

Population Research Bureau (2015) 'The Urban-Rural Divide in Health and Development: Data Sheet', Population Reference Bureau, available at www.prb.org/pdf15/urban-rural-datasheet.pdf (31.05.2016).

Sarkar, Sandip and Balwant Singh Mehta (2010) 'Income Inequality in India: Pre- and Post-Reform Periods', *Economic and Political Weekly*, Vol. 45, No. 37: 45–55.

Sassen, Sasskia (2001) *The Global City*, Princeton, NJ: Princeton University Press.

Sen, Abhijit and Himanshu (2004a) 'Poverty and Inequality in India – I', *Economic and Political Weekly*, Vol. 39, No. 38: 4247–63.

Sen, Abhijit and Himanshu (2004b) 'Poverty and Inequality in India – II', *Economic and Political Weekly*, Vol. 39, No. 39: 4361–75.

UN-Habitat (2010) *State of the World's Cities 2010/2011: Bridging the Urban Divide*, London: Earthscan.

Wang, Xiaobing, Jenifer Piesse and Nick Weaver (2011) 'Mind the Gaps: A Political Economy of the Multiple Dimensions of China's Rural-Urban Divide', Manchester, UK: Brooks World Poverty Institute, BWPI Working Paper 152.

Wilkinson, Richard and Kate Pickett (2009) *The Spirit Level: Why Greater Equality Makes Societies Stronger*, New York: Bloomsbury Press.

World Bank (2006) *Inclusive Growth and Service Delivery: Building on India's Success*, World Bank Development Policy Review, Washington, DC: World Bank.

World Bank (2011) *Perspectives on Poverty in India: Stylized Facts From Survey Data*, Washington, DC: World Bank.

World Bank (2013) *Global Monitoring Report 2013*, Washington, DC: World Bank.

Zhang, Xiaobo and Kevin H. Zhang (2003) 'How Does Globalization Affect Regional Inequality Within a Developing Country? Evidence From China', *Journal of Development Studies*, Vol. 39, No. 4: 47–67.

12 Inequality, education and skills

Michael Kinville and Giulio Pedrini

The aftermath of the latest global financial crisis has seemingly rallied the social sciences behind a common theme: inequality. There is, however, a significant divide between how the problems associated with rising inequality are imagined by, for example, economists and sociologists. The point of this article is to draw attention to this divide with regard to educational inequality. In the broadest of senses, economic studies of educational inequality focus on whether productivity has grown and how income is distributed once pupils graduate and join the labor force. Sociological studies of educational inequality concentrate on the informal and formal processes which reward certain types of capital or skills by lending their bearers prime and highly functional positions in the social division of labor. Both disciplines have dealt with the interpretation of the notion of equality of opportunities, which may range from non-discrimination to egalitarianism, and is usually advocated as one of the main justifications for public intervention in this area.

While it has become fashionable to focus on the increasing concentration of wealth amongst the world's top centile (a strict distributional perspective), this article addresses the broader relationship between skill density, human capital and income inequality. This is not to say, of course, that the rapidly increasing concentration of wealth in the hands of a few is somehow superfluous to the unequal distribution of incomes and skills. Instead of simply repeating a common tautology – that concentrations of wealth are bad because they lead to further concentrations of wealth – the objective here is to understand how skill-biased technical change and human capital commingle to advance or diminish inequality from the perspectives of economics and sociology.

This chapter consists of five short sections. The first two sections present the issue of education and skill inequality in sociology and economics. This will be followed by a brief explanation of skill-biased technical change (SBTC) and human capital externalities in urban areas where educational-related inequality is a major issue and is usually associated with other socio-economic problems. Next, educational assessment, comparison and the STEM (science, technology, engineering and mathematics) subjects as cultivators of the "right" kinds of skills will be discussed in terms of their abilities to decrease educational inequalities from the perspectives of sociology and economics. In other words, the first two sections will present problems, while the third and fourth sections will focus on specific topics and illustrate tentative solutions. Finally, the last section will bring together the ideas presented in the first four.

Education and skill inequality in sociology

If it is true that "knowledge and skill diffusion" is the key to increasing productivity and reducing inequality (Piketty 2014: 21), it is necessary to begin by signposting the conceptual connection between education and the economy. For the most part, national education systems have their institutional origins in the ideas of nineteenth century Europe. Emile Durkheim (1858–1917) suggested that "diversified and specialized" education provided a rational link between individuals and the functional division of labor in society (Durkheim 1956: 71). The logic behind this skill specialization was not overly complicated. After all, those pupils who were to become bankers required a different education than those who were to become tailors. In the end, the functional division of labor, supported by education, would lead to what Durkheim called "organic solidarity", the gravity of which would increase over time, leading to the best possible version of society. In the classical sociological imagination, the relationship between the education system and the economic and social system was first and foremost harmoniously symbiotic. That education systems have been slow to adapt to changes in economic systems and their requisite demands, to say the least, suggests the relationship has not always been harmonious.

The concept of human capital, cultivated and transmitted through schooling for the benefit of the economy at large, provides a link connecting Durkheim to Piketty. Human capital as understood by Gary S. Becker (1975) refers to the stock of skills and aptitudes an individual can operationalize in order to help create profit – or increase productivity – within the economy or society's functional division of labor. The concept opened the door to the analysis of education in economic terms, namely with respect to "the amounts invested in and the rates of return on education in both rich and poor countries" (Becker 1975: viii). Accordingly, it could be concluded that the challenges presented by technical change could be met by more prudential investments in human capital, an argument which most certainly has not gone away.

Theories and empirical studies in the sociology of education, however, have shown that the cultivation of human capital is perhaps too complicated an affair to be addressed solely by more rationalized educational investment strategies. According to Pierre Bourdieu (1979), capital in a broader sense refers not merely to the capabilities – skills – that one has at his or her disposal but also to an individual's ways of seeing the world and being seen by it. The transmission of material goods from one generation to the next is economic capital; the transmission of mannerisms and habits, cultural capital; and the transmission and codification of social values and hierarchies, symbolic capital. That the latter two forms of capital are somewhat difficult to substantiate empirically does not diminish their importance.

Amartya Sen's (2003) "capabilities and functionings" approach is particularly useful for describing the problem in more economic terms. Capabilities can refer to the skills a person develops during his or her schooling, and functionings can be understood as how that person's accumulated skills are received in the labor market. Unequal levels of cultural and symbolic capital – skills that are more difficult to measure – frustrate the translation of capabilities into functionings. The task of matching skills to occupations, or turning skills into occupations, would be comparatively simple absent the filters governing their translation. Bourdieu (1979) called these filters symbolic power (83); Clifford Geertz (1973) referred to them as culture (52). For simplicity's sake, we can call them society. What is more, society can help explain why an ethic of frustration related to the seeming intransigence of social reproduction has obtained in the sociology of education (cf. Esping-Andersen 2005: 32), meaning skills, capabilities, educational attainment and achievement have largely come to be viewed as heritable, biological traits, a fact for which purely economic studies seemingly do not account.

The dissonance becomes clear when one considers the extent to which formal schooling in "liberal" societies pays lip service to egalitarian and inclusive educational principles. Rehbein and Souza (2014) referred to this generalized phenomenon as "symbolic liberalism". Critical sociologists of education, however, are much less ambiguous in their systemic critiques. Bourdieu and Passeron (2013), for example, interpreted the mechanisms at work in the French education system as symbolic violence geared toward what they referred to as the "cultural arbitrary" (5). Every act of formal teaching and learning is a symbolically violent imposition on the pupil, an imposition necessary to achieve the desired "subjective transformation" (Bourdieu 1989: 112). It follows, then, that those pupils with reserves of capital (economic, cultural and symbolic) already in line with the cultural arbitrary undergo less severe and less violent subjective transformations. The relative ease or difficulty with which the cultural arbitrary is absorbed by the pupil is the primary arbiter of educational reproduction.

While Bourdieu and Passeron (2013) were writing about schools in France, their ideas can be adjusted slightly and tentatively applied to different cultural or national contexts. Germany, for example, has a tripartite secondary school system, whereby pupils are, with some regional exceptions, "sorted" onto one of three different school paths after the fourth grade in order that they can learn the right skills for their future careers. This is a prime example of a formal process of educational reproduction. Unsurprisingly, levels of parental education have direct and indirect effects on the school achievement and attainment of pupils (cf. Schneider and Tieben 2011: 22). These formal and systematic sorting mechanisms combine with informal social sorting processes to reproduce educational inequality.

In the United States, however, with its professed adherence to the educational progressivism of John Dewey (1859–1952), the reproduction of social inequalities through education is significantly less formalized. In principle, each pupil has equal access to educational opportunities through secondary school, with the major exception being private education. Informal mechanisms related to how schools are funded and the reputations well-funded schools enjoy result in pronounced interregional and even intraregional differences in school quality. In other words, there is no formal difference between a high school in suburban Boston and one in rural East Texas. In the end, the same kinds of educational inequalities are reproduced as in Germany. Even though much of the reproduction unfolds along informal lines, its obstinance is difficult to deny.

Those pupils whose ways of being in the world are aligned with the respective cultural arbitrary are rewarded, while those pupils who are forced to undergo a more intense subjective transformation are disciplined or, to borrow a term from subaltern studies, rendered "voiceless" (Spivak 2010). The cultural arbitrary – which professes egalitarianism yet practices meritocracy unreflectingly – ultimately sets the parameters for reproduction over generations.

Questions of intergenerational educational reproduction, the cultural arbitrary and society aside, even if the point of a given modern education system was simply to allocate positions in the division of labor, the very task of allocation would be no easy feat. The most well-meaning, forward-thinking and technocratic reform endeavors in education have, for perhaps obvious reasons, been unable to respond quickly enough to transformations in the division of labor. The shelf-life of a given skill has become perilously short, as the skill's locus either shifts geographically or becomes obsolete via technical change. Somewhat optimistically, and as will be discussed in the next section, this can be offset by the adaptability of some skills.

Education and skill inequality in economics

In economics, the issue of inequality in education and skills refers to the distribution of schooling achievements and skill levels among the adult population. This distribution is then analyzed in relation to productivity growth and income distribution, which taken together form the most important and common measure of economic inequality. Any call for a more equal distribution of human capital should be discussed in this respect; otherwise, it may appear as meaningless. In economics, the distribution of educational attainments, as forged by market forces as well as institutions and public policies, is a major driver of inequality dynamics. Indeed, the mechanisms behind unequal incomes "include the supply of and demand for different skills, the state of the educational systems" (Piketty, Saez and Stantcheva 2014). Actually, taken in isolation, the evolution of educational and skill inequality would not raise many concerns. After all, the hierarchical dispersion of schooling among the adult population and employed workers has shown a constant diminishing trend since the early 1970s (Wolff 2006). In parallel, however, the relevance of the quality of education, rather than its quantity, in shaping income distribution has been stressed (Hanushek and Woesmann 2008). Moreover, Piketty (2014) has remarkably shown how inequalities in family income and labor earnings have risen across the same period in lockstep with rising returns of education, arguing that current disparities in income and wealth are driven by long-term trends in the supply and demand of skills. Thus, the smaller dispersion of educational attainment, in general, and workers' educational attainment, in particular, has not resulted in a reduced level of earnings inequality.

There is, to be sure, a small share of very wealthy people who do not have to perform labor and therefore do not "need" skills and for whom income mainly arises from savings and investment behavior. For the rest of the population, income inequality is mainly driven by labor earnings dynamics. In turn, as long as the demand for high-skilled jobs increases relative to the demand for low-skilled jobs, the actual reduction in educational inequality can be insufficient to reduce wage inequality in labor markets and, eventually, income inequality in the overall society. This is what Atkinson (2008) calls "the race" between education and technology: in order to reduce inequality, the supply of suitable skills (and the share of skilled workers) should increase at a higher rate than the needs of those technologies that affect the dynamics of productivity and labor demand. Accordingly, countries affected by the same change in demand – those exposed to the same influences wrought by globalization and technical change – may end up with heterogeneous levels of inequality because of their different speeds of adjustment to skill supply. In parallel, according to the balance between efficiency and fairness that an institutional model endorses, educational systems may or may not fully compensate for exogenous circumstances that affect individual attainment and reward innate abilities and individual effort, typically by posing monetary and/or meritocratic barriers to access to higher education, thus leading to divergent distributional outcomes. For instance, in the United States, the widening of wage inequality that started in the 1980s has been attributed to the combination of a relative slowdown in the growth of the supply of more educated workers with a greater dispersion of cognitive test scores (Blau and Kahn 2005), on the one hand, and to a more rapid increase in the demand for skills driven by technological change (Goldin and Katz 2001), on the other hand. In contrast, Nordic countries, which have more responsive and accessible education and training systems, show a relatively smaller rise in income inequality in the long run (Nickell 2004).

This basic idea can be further scrutinized by looking at the economic forces that have changed the relationship between skills and productivity throughout the last decades. It is important to note that the evolution of inequality varies not only between countries but also between regions and cities. The relationship between education and wage dynamics can therefore be affected by other institutional and space-based factors: industrial relations, industrial policies, sectoral compositions of economic systems and the presence of amenities. Overall, the residual effect of skills and education inequality on income distribution can be strengthened by a heterogeneous set of factors: a) skill-biased technical change; b) international trade; c) the shift of employment to services; d) declining unionization; and e) human capital externalities in local labor markets. Additionally, the most recent financial crisis has reduced the convergence trend that had previously been observed in terms of educational attainment. Within this framework, we focus on the relationship between skill-biased technical change and human capital externalities in the generation of educational divergence and income inequality in urban areas. The rationale for this choice is twofold. On the one hand, in urban areas, education and skills play a stronger role in stimulating local productivity through knowledge spillovers and flows of ideas that stimulate innovation across sectors, leading to the creation of new goods and services in the long run. On the other hand, the issue of inequality is particularly worrying in urban areas where social conflicts, poverty and social unrest are usually concentrated. Not surprisingly, it has been argued that this second problem associated with inequality has become a hindrance to further economic growth and development (Partridge and Weinstein 2013).

Skill-biased technical change and human capital externalities: the issue of skill inequality in urban areas

Skill-biased technical change (SBTC) represents one of the main explanations provided by the economic literature dealing with the wage inequality and job polarization that have been observed in developed countries since the 1970s. The diffusion of new technologies places a high premium on college-educated and skilled labor while reducing the demand for semiskilled and unskilled workers (Acemoglu 1998). This biases income distribution by making it more skewed than in the case of Hicks–neutral technical change, which equally affects all production factors, primarily labor and capital. SBTC may, however, also penalize skilled workers if either the new techniques do not complement the skills that they hold or if they simply make the skills obsolete. In a more nuanced version of this theory, the prediction is that it will result in an asymmetric job polarization, whereby technological change may also lead to growth in demand for low-skilled workers relative to medium-skilled ones (Autor, Levy and Murnane 2003). In this case, the impact on inequality seems ambiguous. Despite the relative increase in demand for low-skilled jobs, the simultaneous growth of complex tasks at the top end of the distribution would generate higher wage gaps between high-skilled workers and the rest of the labor force. Moreover, job "polarization" does not merely reflect a change in the composition of skills available in the labor market; it also signifies a change in the allocation of skill groups across occupations, with a consequent increase in the explanatory power of tasks and occupations in the generation of wage differences, while assuming that tasks' boundaries are endogenous and will respond to changes in skill supplies and technology (Acemoglu and Autor 2011). Although this advancement of SBTC theory has relaxed the implicit equivalence between skills and tasks and has emphasized the importance of a task-based rather than a skill-based approach to study and understand the dynamic interaction between employment trends and technical change (Autor 2013), the workers' assignments to task-based occupations and the consequent structure of employment and wages still eventually depend on their endowment of skills. Accordingly, when assessing whether a job can be considered as high-skill or low-skill, the cognitive content associated with the constituent tasks of that job is the main discriminant (Asheim and Hansen 2009).

This scheme of analysis has been applied to the topical issue of occupational developments and wage inequalities across urban areas, in particular in the United States. Highly educated individuals, in fact, interact chiefly with each other, thereby increasing their own levels of knowledge and skills (Lucas 1988). An initial advantage in the localization of human capital is thus expected to produce positive effects over time in terms of productivity, income and economic growth. Reference can be made to direct effects through the exploitation of positive externalities arising from agglomerations such as technological spillovers, be they intra-sectoral or inter-sectoral. The concentration of high-skilled people promotes the accumulation and production of knowledge, increases the speed of learning capacities of workers and enables better interactions between physical and human capital (Acemoglu 1996). Agglomeration forces are thus at work in strengthening the complementarity between physical and human capital and the connectivity of different tasks, especially among those that demand higher levels of skill (Glaeser and Resseger 2010). The dominant field of knowledge (or domain) of each location thus becomes a place-based characteristic that affects the locational choices of firms and workers. By expanding the frontier of technological possibilities, such complementarity incessantly produces new knowledge and organizational routines. This causes a substantial change in the return of certain types of skills and a shift in the assignment of skills to tasks. As a result, the organizational knowledge and skills held by some groups of workers, in particular those workers who are less likely to upgrade their skills or specialize in other areas of production, will become obsolete. Technical change can thus generate a level of knowledge and skill obsolescence sufficient to "crowd out" low-skilled and low-qualified workers. Overall, this raises further questions about the existence of inequalities between workers that are not merely due to different levels of education or locational choice. In a job polarization framework, however, the positive effects of human capital concentration are not limited to "smart" people. High-skilled workers are highly dependent on an underclass of service occupations performed by low-skilled workers, who in turn experience declining real earnings (Peck 2005; McCann 2007).

Economic theory has thus called for a greater scrutiny of human capital externalities in urban areas and the questioning of their effects on education and skills inequality. Moretti (2012) highlights the multiplier effect that moves along with human capital: the creation of a job post in the high-tech industries in the so-called innovation hubs (such as Seattle, San Francisco-San Jose, or Austin) will create the conditions for employing five people in other sectors that are not necessarily innovative but are still sheltered from international competition, such as personal care services. The presence of educated people also favors cities' quality of life through the growth of consumption amenities (such as green areas) and reductions in crime and pollution. Quality of life, in turn, stimulates employment growth of both skilled and unskilled workers through the pull factors of these amenities. According to this model, the level of education, qualification and skill becomes the crucial factor for spatial divergence and income inequality. The great divergence between increasingly dynamic and increasingly depressed metropolitan areas can thus be explained by referring to the so-called brain-gap, a peculiar path-dependent phenomenon first described by Glaeser and Berry (2006). Throughout the years, cities with an initial small advantage in terms of high-skilled workers have been able to expand this gap with increasing speed, exploiting the complementarities between productivity and the urban dimension. The more urban areas react positively to the presence of highly skilled workers by increasing the quality of life through expanding the number and quality of amenities and local services, the more this human capital accumulation process will depend on the initial conditions. For instance, in the US there are cities in which more than 40 percent of the workforce is highly skilled, while the same category holds for only 10 to 12 percent of the workforce in cities with the lowest skilled workforce (Kok and Weel 2014). However, the rise in wage inequality associated with educational attainment diminishes after accounting for the higher living costs that well-remunerated, college-educated workers have to bear in metropolitan areas. Still, if high housing prices reflect the quality of amenities offered by an area, these higher prices are not a pure cost. In general, it is difficult to distinguish between negative and positive externalities attached to urban areas since many high education cities feature high environmental and housing costs and locational amenities. Moreover, such features are differentially valued by workers (see Black, Kolesnikova and Taylor 2009).

According to this theoretical framework and the associated evidence, the level of education, qualification and skill becomes the crucial arbiter of spatial divergence and income inequality. Interestingly, since the very beginning the concept has been applied to urban areas in a multidimensional way by looking at technological and economic aspects together with those related to the quality of life. Special attention has been paid to social interactions and cooperation among firms, with a particular focus on relational capital and ecological factors along with the complementarity between physical and human capital. Thriving ecosystems based on innovative businesses are therefore the result of a plurality of forces of attraction (Marlet and Woerkens 2007) which determine the spatial pattern of economic phenomena. In this respect, migration between urban areas can be viewed as empirical confirmation of the effect of the wage divergence generated by these economies. Mobile workers not only enjoy wage increases due to the higher productivity of the firms located there; they also benefit from the increase in individual productivity engendered by their own accumulation of knowledge generated through mobility. In particular, the newer approach that focuses on consumption and quality of life and the preferences of consumers and workers can be related to the smart city concept through the common feature of the citizens' standpoint (Glaeser, Kolko and Siaz 2001).

Interesting specificities could arise from the concentration of the so-called knowledge-intensive business services (KIBS) in urban areas. Although there is little consensus on their exact boundaries, KIBS are understood to rely on professional knowledge and are based on labor qualifications and the quality of human capital (Muller and Doloreux 2009). Firms operating in KIBS industries leverage the complementarities between skills and technologies to the maximum extent, limiting Baumol's classical argument that the demand for labor from services might be greater because they experience slower technical advances and productivity increases. In these sectors, knowledge is not only a key production factor for the firms but is also the good they sell after packaging it as an in-depth interaction and cumulative learning process between supplier and user (Strambach 2008). Accordingly, the combination of spatial proximity and human capital density favors the diffusion of KIBS as opposed to physical production or consumption. In KIBS industries, both agglomeration economies and related varieties are in place. In particular, among the reasons for the increased density of KIBS in urban areas, we find the local division of labor and labor pool (Overman and Puga 2010), knowledge and experiences that they "inherit" from their founders' and core employees' prior places of employment (Campell et al. 2012), suitable matching in the markets of production factors and better learning opportunities. Evidence suggests that human capital is positively related to a given city's resilience in the event of an adverse economic shock and that cities with high adaptability have the highest rate of employees in KIBS (Eriksson and Hane-Weijman 2015). The ability of an urban area to respond to a negative exogenous shock, such as the financial crisis of 2007–2009, depends on its human capital endowment. Educational attainment may also have a strong influence on worker turnover. The presence of educated workers is likely to increase the number of resignations since their skills are adaptable to various tasks. In turn, since resignations lead to replacement hiring, the turnover rate of plants or factories with educated workers should be higher than plants or factories with less educated ones. When looking at job flow data across different sectors in European cities, it is important to note that net employment change (NEC) is, on average, higher in KIBS industries. This finding is in line with the hypothesis that these industries greatly benefit from urban agglomeration. What is more, it suggests that human capital is positively related to a city's level of resilience in the event of an adverse economic shock and is in line with the previous findings that cities with high adaptability have the highest rate of employees in KIBS.

Assessment and SBTC-friendly STEM education

Education and skill inequality in economics deals with the relationship between education, technology and demand for skills. Broadly speaking, demand is increasing in two polar directions: on the one hand, in the direction of STEM and skilled-biased technical change and on the other, toward semi-skilled and unskilled, services-based employment. In other words, the nascent division of labor is composed of the STEMs and the services. Educational investment in STEM subjects makes perfect sense from a human capital perspective insofar as it translates into the filling of socially valued and economically necessary positions, at least for the foreseeable future. As discussed above, the filling of these

STEM positions can, in turn, create demand for service employees. The question of how future service employees should be educated is seldom addressed.

Between-country comparisons in education grab the headlines every so often and can even lead to soul-searching on the part of policymakers (cf. Martens and Niemann 2013; Maguire 2010). The heretofore dominant comparative platform, the Programme for International Student Assessment (PISA), has been criticized for its cultural biases, flawed procedures and unreliable results (cf. Dohn 2007). The Trends in Mathematics and Science Study (TIMSS) exams, established in 1995, have seemingly been able to sidestep similar criticisms by focusing on the "international language" of STEM. These results more faithfully reflect the returns on educational investment in those fields which matter. The non-STEM skills are not exactly rendered insignificant; rather, they are viewed as superfluous to the functional division of labor. To put it differently, knowledge of Shakespeare's works neither contributes to nor detracts from a hotel worker's or caterer's ability to perform his or her job (this might be different in the field of KIBS). Knowledge of geometry and calculus, however, are central to an engineer's function in a division of labor framed by SBTC.

It is no small wonder that discussions about STEM education have come to carry so much weight. Policymakers cannot expect a measurable return on investment by championing literary studies. The situation is apparently different with regard to the STEM subjects, especially when it comes to interdisciplinary approaches to teaching the four subjects. The argument is that an understanding of the relationship between the subjects will lend itself to a highly useful and adaptable skillset, at least as far as future employment is concerned (Asghar et al. 2012: 86).

As explored above, certain urban areas have benefitted enormously from implicitly prioritizing SBTC-friendly STEM subjects in industry and education. The ancillary benefits to the division of labor are evident, at least insofar as the STEMs create demand for semi-skilled and unskilled service jobs, display a spillover effect of skills, foster knowledge-intensive business services (KIBS), lead to a better quality of life and increase overall productivity. This division of labor between the STEMs and services is on full display within certain urban conglomerations, albeit with mixed results. Whether or not the lessons of this division can stand up in the face of increasing labor market and trade flexibility (along with the other factors enumerated in the first subsection) and can be extended to semi-urban areas and urban areas within the global South are important points of discussion.

Alternative educational models for more faithfully responding to skill demand certainly do exist. In Germany, for example, the dual vocational training system, whereby pupils split their time between the classroom and the (private) workplace, has been tentatively upheld as a model for marrying public education to the skill requirements of private industry (Euler 2013). This system focuses on the transmission of skills at the end of a pupil's educational career. In the US, SBTC-sensitive educational models have emphasized STEM education in the primary years, as evidenced by the rise of charter and magnet schools with an explicit emphasis on STEM. It is too early to tell whether this approach has had or will have a positive effect on educational attainment and long-term employability (Judson 2014). These models, however, are only concerned with one aspect of inequality – namely skill inequality – and the question of whether they will be able to foster positive human capital externalities related to society, culture or symbolic capital must be answered. In other words, the broader dispersion of capabilities is likely not coterminous with a more equitable distribution of social functionings.

Can dramatic increases in local and regional investments in SBTC-sensitive STEM education make up for the so-called brain gap which have provided the now dynamic metropolitan areas with the initial comparative advantages they needed in order to become and remain dynamic? Economic policymakers no longer possess the tools of the trade, including import substitute industrialization, which might have allowed their forebears to successfully incubate high-skill industries. If a given society were able to increase and democratize its overall technical skill level and decrease the brain gap, would this lead to decreases in economic and social inequality? Although we like to think of the labor market as being rational and predicated first and foremost on the laws of supply and demand, societies seem to march to the tune of a different drummer with a much different rhythm. To be sure, increasing the social stock of the "right" kinds of skills and thereby decreasing wage inequality *could* contribute to the reduction of other kinds of inequality, although it is difficult to imagine how this could happen given formal education's furtive role in reproducing social inequalities.

Discussion

In this chapter, we have addressed the issue of education and skill inequality by focusing on two interrelated topics that have been studied in economics and sociology.

On the one hand, a large stream of literature has shown that the effects of different educational attainments on income inequality are magnified in urban areas through knowledge spillovers that stimulate local productivity. In cities that benefit the most from dynamic agglomeration economies, innovation can foster interaction between physical and human capital by creating new jobs for educated workers at the expense of less educated workers (who would actually face a destruction of jobs due to the advancing bias in favor of technical skills), thus giving rise to a high reallocation of work. Under some circumstances, however, innovative sectors increase not only the size of the pool of highly skilled workers but also the level of demand for low-skilled workers. This reallocation, however, depends on whether the growth of an economic system relies on traditional manufacturing sectors or on KIBS.

At risk of overstating the implications of SBTC, if the structural change in labor demand causes an increase at the lower end of the income distribution, a mix of people holding different education and income levels, i.e. local inequality, generates more benefits for the less skilled (Mazzolari and Ragusa 2013; Glaeser 2000) than would be the case if people were segregated into homogenous communities, which is indeed less desirable. Egalitarians can simultaneously hope for policies that would ensure fair educational opportunities at the national level, such as increasing the schooling levels for the least fortunate, while opposing policies that would superficially reduce localized income inequality by sequestering rich people from poor people. Policy initiatives can help bolster the ability of economic systems and institutions to provide both equal access to education and to combat the negative effects of wage and spatial inequality on economic development.

On the other hand, it has been noted that SBTC models should not equate skills with generic schooling to explain recent trends in inequality, but to refer to skills in multidimensional terms, as various types of skills are not perfect substitutes for one another (Liu and Grusky 2013). In this regard, a reconfiguration of school education, with a more intense and universal focus on the cultivation of skills that are adaptable to SBTC and labor market flexibility, could spike productivity across the board. This would at least close the gap between skill supply and labor market demand, although the inequality-inducing filters that negotiate between supply and demand − society, culture, symbolic power − would be left unaddressed. To be sure, the knowledge spillovers and flows of ideas highlighted above are positive trends, provided they are not exclusive features of those urban economies that have benefitted from the brain gap.

In reality, universal education of the technical variety is not a panacea to wage and spatial inequality. One should also not forget additional issues related to the role of higher education in society, such as whether it is to be considered as an individual capability per se or as a form of investment for generating economic and social returns later in life. Universalizing access to SBTC-sensitive education, however, may lead to a more desirable matching of skills to tasks, or of "capabilities to functionings", allow local technical industries to flourish by increasing the general social stock of technical knowledge, engender more extensive flows of ideas and allow for faster speeds of adjustment to skill supply. If concentrations of "smart" people, the hallmark of dynamic urban areas, can result in both skilled and unskilled workers rapidly increasing their knowledge, skills and productivity through processes of mutual learning, a primary goal could be to cultivate more smart people with the right kinds of skills. Increases in the stock and quality of human capital would bolster physical capital, which in turn would foster additional increases in the stock and quality of human capital. This all sounds very good. We should not be surprised, however, if society gets in the way.

References

Acemoglu, Daron (1996) 'A Microfoundation for Social Increasing Returns in Human Capital Accumulation', *The Quarterly Journal of Economics*, Vol. 111, No. 3: 779–804.

Acemoglu, Daron (1998) 'Why Do New Technologies Complement Skills? Directed Technical Change and Wage Inequality', *The Quarterly Journal of Economics*, Vol. 113, No. 4: 1055–89.

Acemoglu, Daron and David H. Autor (2011) 'Tasks and Technologies: Implications for Employment and Earnings', in David Card and Orley Ashenfelter (eds.) *Handbook of Labor Economics*, New York: North Holland, Vol. 4 (B), 1043–171.

Asghar, Anila, Roni Ellington, Eric Rice, Francine Johnson and Glenda M. Prime (2012) 'Supporting STEM Education in Secondary Science Contexts', *Interdisciplinary Journal of Problem-Based Learning*, Vol. 6, No. 2: 85–12.

Asheim, Bjorn T. and Hogni K. Hansen (2009) 'Knowledge Bases, Talents, and Contexts: On the Usefulness of the Creative Class Approach in Sweden', *Economic Geography*, Vol. 85, No. 4: 425–42.

Atkinson, Anthony B. (2008) *The Changing Distribution of Earnings in OECD Countries*, Oxford: Oxford University Press.

Autor, David H. (2013) 'The Task Approach to Labor Markets: An Overview', National Bureau of Economic Research, Working Paper No. 18711.

Autor, David H., Frank Levy and Richard Murnane (2003) 'The Skill Content of Recent Technological Change: An Empirical Exploration', *The Quarterly Journal of Economics*, Vol. 116, No. 4: 1279–333.

Becker, Gary S. (1975; second edition) *Human Capital: A Theoretical and Empirical Analysis, With Special Reference to Education*, New York: National Bureau of Economic Research.

Black, Dan, Natalia Kolesnikova and Lowell Taylor (2009) 'Local Price Variation and Labor Supply Behavior', *Federal Reserve Bank of St. Louis Review*, Vol. 91, No. 6: 613–25.

Blau, Francine D. and Lawrence M. Kahn (2005) 'Do cognitive test scores explain higher US wage inequality?', *Review of Economics and Statistics*, Vol. 87, No. 1: 184–93.

Bourdieu, Pierre (1979) 'Symbolic Power', *Critique of Anthropology*, Vol. 4: 77–85.

Bourdieu, Pierre (1989) *The State Nobility: Elite Schools in the Field of Power*, Stanford: Stanford University Press.

Bourdieu, Pierre and Jean-Claude Passeron (2013; second edition) *Reproduction in Education, Society and Culture*, London: Sage.

Campell, Benjamin A., Martin Ganco, April Franco and Rajshree Agarwal (2012) 'Who Leaves Where to and Why Worry? Employer Mobility, Entrepreneurship and Effects on Source Firm Performance', *Strategic Management Journal*, Vol. 33, No. 1: 65–87.

Dohn, Nina Bonderup (2007) 'Knowledge and Skills for Pisa—Assessing the Assessment', *Journal of Philosophy of Education*, Vol. 41, No. 1: 1–16.

Durkheim, Emile (1956) *Education and Sociology*, New York: The Free Press.

Eriksson, Rikard H. and Emelie Hane-Weijman (2015) 'How Do Regional Economies Respond to Crises? The Geography of Job Creation and Destruction in Sweden (1990–2010)', *European Urban and Regional Studies*, Vol. 24, No. 1: 87–103.

Esping-Andersen, Gosta (2005) 'Inequality of Incomes and Opportunities', in Anthony Giddens and Patrick Diamond (eds.) *The New Egalitarianism*, Cambridge: Polity Press, 8–38.

Euler, Dieter (2013) *Germany's Dual Vocational Training System: A Model of Other Countries?* Gütersloh: Bertelsmann Stiftung.

Geertz, Clifford (1973) *The Interpretation of Cultures*, New York: Basic Books.

Glaeser, Edward L. (2000) 'The New Economics of Urban and Regional Growth', in Gordon L. Clark, M. P. Feldman and M. S. Gertler (eds.) *The Oxford Handbook of Economic Geography*, Oxford: Oxford University Press.

Glaeser Edward L. and Christopher R. Berry (2006) 'Why Are Smart Places Getting Smarter?', Rappaport Institute/Taubman Center Policy Brief 2.

Glaeser Edward L., Jed Kolko and Albert Saiz (2001) 'Consumer City', *Journal of Economic Geography*, Vol. 1, No. 1: 27–50.

Glaeser, Edward L. and Matthew G. Resseger (2010) 'The Complementarity Between Cities and Skills', *Journal of Regional Science*, Vol. 50, No. 1: 221–44.

Goldin, Claudia and Lawrence F. Katz (2001) 'The Legacy of U.S. Educational Leadership: Notes on Distribution and Economic Growth in the 20th Century', *American Economic Review*, Vol. 91, No. 2: 18–23.

Hanushek, Eric A. and Ludger Woessmann (2008) 'The Role of Cognitive Skills in Economic Development'. *Journal of Economic Literature*, Vol. 46, No. 3: 607–68.

Judson, Eugene (2014) 'Effects of Transferring to STEM-Focused Charter and Magnet Schools on Student Achievement', *The Journal of Educational Research*, Vol. 107: 255–66.

Kok, Suzanne and Bas ter Weel (2014) 'Cities, Tasks, and Skills', *Journal of Regional Science*, Vol. 54, No. 3: 856–92.

Liu, Yujia and David B. Grusky (2013) 'The Payoff to Skill in the Third Industrial Revolution', *American Journal of Sociology*, Vol. 118, No. 5: 1330–74.

Lucas, Robert E. (1988) 'On the Mechanics of Economic Development', *Journal of Monetary Economics*, Vol. 22, No. 1: 3–32.

Maguire, Meg (2010) 'Toward a Sociology of the Global Teacher', in Michael Apple, Stephen J. Ball and Luis Armando Gandin (eds) *The Routledge International Handbook of the Sociology of Education*, New York: Routledge, 59–68.

Marlet, Gerard and Clemens Van Woerkens (2007) 'The Dutch Creative Class and How It Fosters Urban Employment Growth', *Urban Studies*, Vol. 44, No. 13: 2605–26.

Martens, Kerstin and Dennis Niemann (2013) 'When Do Numbers Count? The Differential Impact of the PISA Rating and Ranking on Education Policy in Germany and the US', *German Politics*, Vol. 22, No. 3: 314–32.

Mazzolari, Francesca and Giuseppe Ragusa (2013) 'Spillover from high-skill consumption to low-skill labor markets', *Review of Economics and Statistics*, Vol. 95, No. 1: 74–86.

McCann, Eugene J. (2007) 'Inequality and Politics in the Creative City-Region: Questions of Livability and State Strategy', *International Journal of Urban and Regional Research*, Vol. 31, No. 1: 188–96.

Moretti, Enrico (2012) *The New Geography of Jobs*, New York: Houghton Mifflin Harcourt.

Muller, Emmanuel and David Doloreux (2009) 'What We Should Know About Knowledge Intensive Business Services', *Technology and Society*, Vol. 31, No. 1: 64–72.

Nickell, Stephen (2004) 'Poverty and worklessness in Britain', *Economic Journal*, Vol. 114: C1–25

Overman, Henry G. and Diego Puga (2010) 'Labour Pooling as a Source of Agglomeration: An Empirical Investigation', in Edward L. Glaeser (eds.) *Agglomeration Economics*, Chicago: University of Chicago Press.

Partridge, Mark D. and Amanda D. Weinstein (2013) 'Rising Inequality in an Era of Austerity: The Case of US', *European Planning Studies*, Vol. 21, No. 3: 388–410.

Peck, Jamie (2005) 'Struggling With the Creative Class', *International Journal of Urban and Regional Research*, Vol. 29, No. 4: 740–70.

Piketty, Thomas (2014) *Capital in the Twenty-First Century*, London: Belknap.

Piketty, Thomas, Emmanuel Saez and Stefanie Stantcheva (2014) 'Optimal Taxation of Top Labor Incomes: A Tale of Three Elasticities', *American Economic Journal: Economic Policy*, Vol. 6, No. 1: 230–71.

Rehbein, Boike and Jessé Souza (2014) *Ungleichheit in kapitalistischen Gesellschaften*, Weinheim: Beltz Juventa.

Schneider, Silke L. and Nicole Tieben (2011) 'A Healthy Sorting Machine? Social Inequality in the Transition to Upper Secondary Education in Germany', *Oxford Review of Education*, Vol. 37, No. 2: 139–66.

Sen, Amartya (2003) *Inequality Reexamined*, New York: Russell Sage Foundation.

Spivak, Gayatri Chakravorty (2010) '"Can the Subaltern Speak?" Revised Edition, From "The History Chapter" of Critique of Postcolonial Reason', in Rosalind Morris (ed.) *Can the Subaltern Speak? Reflections on the History of India*, New York: Columbia University Press, 21–80.

Strambach, Simone (2008) 'Knowledge-Intensive Business Services (KIBS) as Drivers of Multi-Level Knowledge Dynamics', *International Journal of Services, Technology and Management*, Vol. 10, No. 2–4: 152–74.

Wolff, Edward N. (2006) *Does Education Really Help? Skill, Work, and Inequality*, Oxford: Oxford University Press.

13 Innovation and inequality

Riccardo Leoncini

Introduction

It is since the seminal contribution of Simon Kuznets (1955) that the analysis of the trade-off between growth and inequality has become a central topic in the economic literature. Kuznets highlighted that a diverging path of income inequality could be temporary as it was destined to decrease in the wake of a progressive shift from low-productivity agriculture towards high-productivity industry. Thus, as capitalism progresses through successive phases of development, inequality tends to diminish (after an early increase) as the process of transition from a pre-industrial to a fully advanced industrial stage completes.

At the beginning of the process of development inequality rises as the industrial sectors show wide differences in productivity (and thus in earnings). However, as development progresses, the industrial transformation of the economy causes the inequality to decrease again. As this model was subsequently expanded to also accommodate transition patterns between sectors with different productivity due, for instance, to differential innovative capacity, it rapidly became a very general theory. The famous inverted U-shaped Kuznets curve became thus an integral part of any manual on development economics.

Although Kuznets himself was well aware of the limits of this model ("This is perhaps 5% empirical information and 95% speculation, some of it possibly tainted by wishful thinking" (Kuznets 1955)), his theory had a wide impact on the literature on inequality and growth, becoming the centerpiece of all the policy-oriented debates aimed at empirically assessing this sort of 'natural' association between growth stages and inequality levels. While few early studies found a negative growth-inequality relationship (e.g. Galor and Zeira 1993; Alesina and Rodrik 1994; Persson and Tabellini 1994), more recent studies found a positive one (e.g. Benabou 1996; Galor and Tsiddon 1997; Li and Zou 1998). Forbes (2000) found a positive empirical growth-inequality relationship, arguing that previous results were due to omitted-variable bias and measurements errors.

Despite these controversial results, the relevance of Kuznets's contribution is to be seen in the following series of elements. First, he identified a trade-off between forces acting in favor of and against inequality: the economy does not 'spontaneously' drive towards a more equal distribution. Second, there is a fundamental role in the structure of the economy and in particular in its compositional effects due to sectoral imbalances. Thus, the processes of economic growth and technological change are the fundamental drivers of a demographic transition among industrial sectors, which affects income distribution through compositional effects. Third, compositional effects are so-to-say continuously pushing and pulling the level of inequality of the system, as long as they open up new opportunities for further compositional effects, for instance, through (but not only) technological change. Fourth, institutions play an important role as they impact the outcome of the socio-economic transformations: Kuznets himself explicitly stressed that the structural differences among rural and urban economies determined the result of the compositional effects, causing a decrease in inequality in urban economies. Hence, the distributional results of the transition are shaped by the role of institutions on the new asset of power relations (and therefore on its distributional consequences), and thus on how the system dynamics is continuously recomposed into a set of power relationships that are in turn one of the key determinants of inequality. Finally, Kuznets provided important evidence that inequality regards both income and assets: assets property constitutes a relevant issue at this regard. For instance, García-Peñalosa and Turnovsky (2006, 2007) argue that the growth-inequality relationships are ambiguous as they come to depend on the underlying structural changes: incorporating wealth heterogeneity into an endogenous growth model they show that a positive relationship is again more likely to emerge.

Several reasons can be highlighted to explain the trend in labor income inequality. The following is a surely partial list of the elements that it is necessary to take care of in trying to look for some explanations. First, it is the high unemployment since the global financial crisis that has accounted for very high levels of inequality. Moreover, the last two decades have witnessed a strong decrease in the workers' bargaining power (Lemieux 2008). Another element can be found in productivity divergence across firms (OECD 2011). Thomas Piketty has emphasized the role of the rising income shares at the top (1%) of the distribution (Piketty 2014). The role of globalization and of the increased international connectedness has already been addressed (Milanović 2006). Finally, another element is the skill-biased characteristics of the huge wave of technological change that has characterized the last two decades.

Framing the relationships between innovative activity and inequality

From a purely theoretical perspective, it could be said that technological change has not very much to do with inequality. Innovative activity has in fact long been (especially within the neoclassical account, but not only) considered as the main determinant of economic growth with no regards for its distributive impact. The most acclaimed of these account rests in the book from Joel Mokyr, *The Lever of Riches: Technological Creativity and Economic Progress*, which, since its inception, is quite clear in saying that technological progress is the most powerful engine of economic growth we have seen in the whole history. The innovative activity that results from technological change impacts the society in such a way as to supply it with a "free lunch", that comes from the possibility the technological change gives to firms to produce more with the same amount of inputs (Mokyr 1992: 3). Just to make it even clearer, Frederick Taylor, in his praise of the scientific management he invented, pointed out that it further pushed the frontier of economic efficiency to the point that the division of labor possible under Taylorism could increase "the size of the surplus until this surplus becomes so large that it is unnecessary to quarrel over how it shall be divided" (cited in Pursell 2016: 23–4).

Therefore, as the distributive impact of technological change must be considered in the light of its consequences on economic growth, it should more properly be referred to the policy side dealing with the normative problems arising as an inevitable outcome of the innovative process (though not always, as we have seen). Hence, where markets appear to be unable to produce a Pareto optimality, there is room for public intervention to correct the ensuing market failures. These market failures can derive from the overlapping of two different market failures: one is the positive externalities deriving from the public nature of the innovative discoveries (Arrow 1962) responsible for the systematic underinvestment in R&D (Jones and Williams 1998), and the other derived from the distributive outcomes.

Therefore, in principle we would expect that technology, and the ensuing innovation diffusion, makes people better: customers will benefit from an abundant supply of cheaper and quality-improved goods, firms will increase their profits, and workers will benefit from higher wages and less wearing working conditions. However, although these might be the desirable outcomes of the process of innovation diffusion within the society, less desirable effects have been taking place that deserve keen attention and that must be thoroughly analyzed.

First, it is at least since David Ricardo in 1821 added chapter 31 "On Machinery" to the third edition of his *Principles*, that he "enter[ed] into some enquiry respecting the influence of machinery on the interests of the different classes of society", providing some of the founding thoughts on how the invention and the diffusion of new machinery affects the economic system, and in particular labor. His analysis is thought to be the initiator of the literature on what is now commonly termed technological unemployment. Later on, two effects (the substitution effect of machinery for labor and the compensation effect of a bigger market for less expensive goods) were described as two contrasting forces to determine the effects on unemployment. As we will see below, this has obvious and relevant effects on the level of inequality in a society, affecting both the relationships between laborers affected or not by the technological unemployment and between laborers and profit earners.

Another element to be considered to evaluate the impact of technological change on inequality is related to the necessity of a certain level of the so-called "absorptive capacity". This is necessary to understand, put at work and profit from technological knowledge (Cohen and Levinthal 1989). Without a preexisting knowledge, it is very difficult (or impossible) to understand the knowledge content of a technological advance. Therefore, innovative activity is path-dependent, that is it depends on previous innovative activity. The implications for inequality are evident if one thinks that absorptive capacity is usually a function of previous investments in learning activities and thus on previous income levels. Thus, the worse-offs are due to see a worsening of their positions as innovative activity progresses: two, quite clear and well-known examples of which are the digital divide and the skill-biased technological change. In both cases, the worse-offs are those who could not bring their learning levels up to the point to be positively selected by the new technology, which they are not able to competently manage.

Another important element to consider is that, differently from the previous viewpoints on the theme, if in some cases innovation can have a negative impact on the prices of goods, in some other cases (especially in recent times) technology increases the quality of the goods produced. The increase in quality is likely to be mirrored by increases in their prices. As prices go up, the worse-offs will be increasingly less able to afford them, and thus less able to benefit from the increased level of technology available in the system.

Moreover, several industries are more likely to develop goods for the affluent, as their innovative activities will more likely target rich rather than the poor people. For instance, the pharmaceutical industry is more likely to produce drugs that benefit the well-offs by targeting certain diseases (such as, for instance, obesity or cardiovascular problems) rather than some other diseases that particularly affect the worse-offs (such as, for instance, malaria or tuberculosis). AIDS is another relevant example of how the price of drugs can determine the overall rate of both morbility and morbidity. Another example can be ICT, as it will more likely develop small, expensive global devices rather than basic communication devices for, say, rural populations. As the latest World Development Report of the World Bank states: "When the internet automates many tasks but workers do not possess the skills that technology augments, the outcome will be greater inequality, rather than greater efficiency" (World Bank 2016).

Finally, the worse-offs are more vulnerable to the negative side effects of science and technology, as far as the environmental justice is concerned. And these negative side effects are not only affecting the worse-offs because they are less able to protect themselves in terms of political power, but also in terms of mere (orthodox) economic reasoning. See, for instance the debate following the (in)famous internal memorandum that the then Chief Economist of the World Bank, Lawrence Summers, wrote to some colleagues and that once it was leaked to the public engendered a very heated debate on the relationships between globalization, environment and developing nations. In brief, it stated that a nation should export a good that it can produce more cheaply (for instance because of technology) to other (less efficient) nations in exchange for goods the latter finds costlier to produce. In particular, the 'good' that Summers meant to be traded was pollution, which could be traded to developing nations: "I think the economic logic behind dumping a load of toxic waste in the lowest-wage country is impeccable and we should face up to that" (Summers cited in *The Economist* 1992).

The between countries perspective

When speaking of global inequality, it is preliminarily important to highlight the differences that exist in its different components: inequality between countries and inequality within countries. Lakner and Milanović (2016) and Milanović (2006) distinguish between three types of global inequality, which have important consequences, both theoretically and empirically. The first definition (called unweighted international inequality) regards inequality between countries, that is, inequality in per capita incomes between the various countries of the world. The second definition is the between country inequality weighted by each country population (between-country inequality). This definition measures inequality by inputting the same per capita income to all the inhabitant of a nation. The third definition is about the inequality of individual agents.

Anand and Segal (2008) propose several estimates of different measures of inequality: on average, world inequality, as estimated by the Gini index, is around 70%, and it has fallen in the last twenty years (especially in the period 2003–2008). These values of the world Gini index are on the same level of the most unequal countries (i.e. Lesotho and Namibia, with values of 0.632 and 0.743 respectively). The largest share of inequality is due to differences between countries, although it has diminished in time, while the within-country inequality has increased in the last two decades. As for the regional composition, substantial changes are observed in the last two decades. While China's position was improving, together with India (although more slowly), sub-Saharan African countries have been plummeting into the bottom ranking.

The conventional view about economic inequality (e.g. OECD 2011) is that its recently increasing levels come to depend mainly from a set of not mutually exclusive but reciprocally reinforcing factors that are identified respectively in technological change, globalization and the role of institutions. And while Aghion, Caroli and García-Peñalosa (1999) identify technical change as the main driver of inequality, and Jaumotte, Lall and Papageorgiou (2013) state that "the observed rise in inequality across both developed and developing countries over the past two decades is largely attributable to the impact of technological change", Rodrik (2016) points to the different impacts that technological change and globalization had on advanced and developing countries respectively. While technological progress seems to be largely responsible for employment deindustrialization in the former countries, for the latter countries it seems that trade and globalization played a comparatively bigger role.

Caselli and Coleman (2006) propose an analysis of the cross-country differences in the aggregate production function, considering skilled and unskilled labor as imperfect substitutes. They find a skill-bias in cross-country technology differences. In fact, advanced countries use skilled labor more efficiently than developing countries, and this, by making advanced countries abundant in skilled-labor, leads them to target technologies that are best suited to skilled workers. On the other side, in developing countries technologies more appropriate to unskilled workers are chosen, as in these countries unskilled-labor is more abundant.

Maskin (2015) highlights the differential impact of globalization between the advanced and developing nations in increasing inequality: by advocating to the globalization of the production process, he advocates that the inequality is increasing due to the fact that the skilled workers in the poor countries will be 'matched' with the skilled ones in the rich countries, and so the unskilled. In this way, the gap between skilled and unskilled will be amplified globally.

A more focused approach on the very important differences in technological change between advanced and developing nations deals with the nature itself of the innovative activity. A first approach that was proposed to understand the differential impact of technology on advanced countries with respect to developing ones, was that of the so-called appropriate technology. This term indicates the attempt to shape technologies to best suit the developmental needs, such as low capital cost, local materials, local skills, small scale, etc. Hence, this would not require, for instance, high education levels and skills and intellectual property rights. Together with the implementation of proper development practices, appropriate technologies would also imply less inequality by themselves (safe for the other elements bringing inequality within the society). As an example of this, appropriate technologies found their best environment in small rural communities where the majority of the people were living in conditions of poverty under significant inequality (see Fressoli and Arond 2015 for a recent survey).

A very interesting and promising line of research is pioneered by Cozzens and Thakur (2014), what they call emerging technologies in global inequality. These technologies are research-based with a possible wide impact on both local and global inequality. Moreover, as they are based on research they are both malleable and high-valued. In order to benefit from these emerging technologies many developing countries try to invest in local capabilities to develop enough absorptive capacity to (a) adapt the emerging technology to the local context and (b) to benefit from the newly created competitive advantage.

The empirical analysis of Cozzens and Thakur (2014) covers five technologies (mobile phones, open source, RDNA insulin, GM maize and plant tissue culture) in ten countries from both the global North and the global South. The evidence emerging from the analysis is that the local and the global contexts are crucial to the final outcome. Just to make an example that reverses the 'common' knowledge on such a dynamic, it can be that, on the one side, commercial laboratories can act to spread technologies to also benefit poor people, while, on the other side, public laboratories can develop technologies in such a way as to increase the monopoly power and the global control of multinational corporations.

To understand where the process will head, it is necessary, according to Cozzens and Thakur, to examine the pathway chosen for the commercialization of the emerging technologies. The role of the institutions becomes thus central. A first crucial factor is identified in the way the public authority intervenes to regulate the intellectual property. Indeed, it is the owner of the technology that has (or that has close association with who has) the power over the organization of production, and thus over the division of the benefits from the production process between the various participants. Which means, finally, over the distribution of the incomes and the resulting inequality. The second institutional element regards how the public authorities decide to enforce the competitive environment. Again, counterintuitive results can emerge. The role of public monopolies can be detrimental to a wide and even diffusion, while strong competitive pressure could lead to more even diffusion. Crucial at this regard is the fact that prices are not the only barrier to benefit from the emerging technologies. Also in this case, for instance, public procurement can make expensive technologies available to the public at large. Or make the necessary infrastructure to diffuse a technology available to anybody. These are the reasons why the price of emerging technologies is one, and maybe not the most important, element among many to determine its distributional impact.

This analysis therefore points to structural differences between advanced and developing nations, where in the former the adaptation to emerging technologies follows a path of step-by-step upgrading to gradually absorb the new technology. In the case of developing nations, more actions are needed to benefit from the emerging technologies, and a continuous tune-up of the system has to be planned in order not to leave only the high-income part of the population to access the benefits, so increasing the inequality levels. The absence of a complete framework does not permit a 'smooth' transition path, but continuous investments in the specific capabilities are needed to make the emerging technologies to spread their benefits.

The former analysis brings us to a very important element in the relationships between technological changes and inequality, and is related the role of skilled migration and to the institutional factors behind this phenomenon (it must be noted that it is not this chapter's aim to investigate the topic of migration by itself: in this chapter, the focus in on the relationships between migration and institutional factors related to technology such as IPR protection only. For a thorough analysis of migration and inequality, see the chapter by Weiß in this volume).

A large literature suggested that skilled labor provides invention and the emigration of skilled labor changes the capacity of a country's innovation. Grubel and Scott (1966) used "brain drain" to capture the trend that migration of skilled labor from developing countries may reduce the capacity of innovation of source countries (Commander, Kangasniemi and Winters 2004). In a recent study, Agrawal et al. (2011) found that the emigration of skilled labor weakens local knowledge networks (through the brain drain effect) and yet, it allows for innovators retaining their access to knowledge accumulated abroad (which is called brain bank effect).

Intellectual property rights (IPRs) account for an important institutional element. Indeed, IPR schemes allow for public intervention. The strength of

IPRs impacts on innovation by encouraging the mobility of inventors, which, in turn, leads to the change in wage premium for the skilled labor. For instance, the Office of the US Trade Representative (USTR) releases 'Special 301 Reports' identifying its trading partners' protection and enforcement of IPRs. In the latest 2016 Special 301 list, some emerging countries such as China and India are in the Priority Watch List (PWL), which indicates the poor enforcement of IPR in such countries. Coincidently, these countries are recognized as the main sources of emigration of highly educated labor. There is clear evidence for a growing brain drain from developing countries since the 1970s (Docquier and Rapoport 2008).

Some recent studies (for example Straubhaar 2000; McAusland and Kuhn 2011; Naghavi and Strozzi 2015) have explored the link among IPR protection, skilled labor mobility and innovation. However, almost all the above-mentioned literature focuses on the welfare effect on skilled labor, such as change in skilled labor income, by exploring the direct impact of IPR, or how IPR leads to spill-over of technique and in turn have impact on skilled labor's income. One important issue that remains unsettled is the extent to which IPR regime affects the wage of unskilled labor and the return to capital, and, furthermore, the wage inequality of an economy. Many existing studies have attempted to identify the determinants of skilled-unskilled wage inequality. For example, Zhang (2012), Anwar (2010, 2013), Anwar et al. (2013), Pi and Zhou (2015) argue that international trade and factor mobility can contribute to skilled-unskilled wage inequality. However, none of the existing studies appear to have explicitly considered the link between IPR protection and skilled-unskilled wage inequality.

Putting into perspective of public policy, in particular, in the trade domain for this technology-labor relationship, the strength of IPR regimes across borders can constitute a powerful instrument through which the rate of innovation and the direction of technology development are affected.

There is a vast literature on IPR enforcement and its implications for technological transfer through the channels of foreign direct investments and licensing (see for instance Hoekman, Maskus and Saggi 2005; Mukherjee and Tsai 2013). By improving technological transfer, the innovative capability in a country can be enhanced (Diwan and Rodrik 1991) and, thus, a rising capacity to catch-up with the technological frontier (see, for an example, Franco and Leoncini 2013). Nonetheless, Foredo-Pineda (2006) emphasizes the hazard of the opening-up of the techno-economic system due to structural obstacles, vulnerability of the science and technology system and the limits to cooperation. Consequently, these problems might encourage the substitution of indigenous technologies by cheaper and/or more efficient imported ones. This, in turn, leads to less local technological activities. Cassiolato and Lastres (2000) take a different perspective and argue that it can be more profitable to address imitative effort that could encourage the development of an indigenous technological system while reducing the wage of skilled labor. Public policies might, therefore, influence the relationships between technology and labor and drive towards more equitable results.

The within-country perspective

The rising inequality in wages that most countries have experienced since the late 1970s has spurred extensive discussions. Since the seminal work of Rosen (1981), it has been acknowledged that technology serves as a key driver of changes in wages and income (surveys of which are in Saint-Paul 2008 and Goldin and Katz 2009). Amongst other factors, the role that educated/skilled workers play in facilitating rapid development of the modern technology is well documented (see, for instance, Acemoglu 2002). Skilled workers are favored in countries that engage in diffusion due to rapid technological changes. As a result, wage premium of the skilled workers exceeds that of the unskilled workers and inequality becomes an inevitable outcome. Nonetheless, technological changes cannot be expected to be always skill-biased since the degree of substitutability and complementarity between technology and labor matters (Saint-Paul 2008).

The skill-bias technological change hypothesis has been built starting from the empirical evidence of a positive relationship between the diffusion of technical change (especially, but not only, with reference to computer usage on the job sites) and wage differentials between workers with low and high skills respectively (e.g. Katz and Murphy 1992).

Starting from the seminal work of Krueger (1993), several contributions analyzed the relationships between the skill premium and the impact of technological change. They addressed the role of technological change in shifting the labor demand in favor of skilled workers with respect to the unskilled ones (see Levy and Murnane 1992 for an early survey). The quick rise in the adoption of ICT that started in the 1970s showed the peculiarity of being complementary to the skilled workers and substitute to the unskilled ones (Krueger 1993). Workers that have invested in education to obtain ICT-complementary skills are more likely to gain in their productivity with ICT technologies that are bigger relative to less skilled workers. The increase in productivity implies an increase in relative wages.

Examples abound in the positive relations between the adoption of ICT technologies and the increase in demand for a college-educated workforce. For instance, Krueger (1993) reports estimates during 1984–1989 that the impact of the use of a computer on employees' wage increased the latter from 10% to 15%. Moreover, since higher educated workers are likely to be those using computers, the increase in the rate of return to education ranges in the interval of one third to one half. Even if all the impact is not due to the computer diffusion, the reported impact still appears to be significant.

A more recent stream of literature has emphasized the role of the content of the different job tasks rather than the 'simple' skilled/unskilled dichotomy in explaining inequality patterns in wages (Autor, Levy and Murnane 2003; Acemoglu and Autor 2011; Autor and Dorn 2013; Beaudry, Green and Sand 2014). The rationale is that technology (i.e. computers) is substitute to workers employed in routine/non-cognitive (in relative terms)/simple (not complex) tasks, and is complementary to workers in non-routine/cognitive/ complex tasks. If the two types of tasks cannot readily be substituted among them, then the effect of technological change is to reduce the need for routine-based tasks that can be substituted by 'machine programmed rules'. On the contrary, it will increase non-routine problem-solving in creative and complex tasks. The model proposed explained a large fraction of the shift in demand triggered by decreasing computer prices in the task composition, although with nominally unchanged occupations (Autor, Levy and Murnane 2003: 1321).

Other institutional factors have usually been mainly identified in the labor market, more particularly in the set of mechanisms that contribute to determine the wage levels: minimum wage law, unionization, non-standard employment contracts, etc. (Lemieux 2008). The implications for inequality lie in the decrease in their role in helping the market forces to determine wages. At the beginning of the 1980s several conservative governments were determined to decrease the role of wage-setting institutions, while leaving wages to become more closely aligned with individual productivity. This was possible, for instance, by means of declining unionization and the fall in the real value of the minimum wage. These wage-setting mechanisms worked complementarily to the skill bias technical change (Kristal and Cohen 2015).

Although the skill bias technological change hypothesis has had a significant impact in the literature, several problems linked to this hypothesis remain unsettled (Acemoglu 2002). Objections to this skill-bias hypothesis argue against the observation that was conducted mainly in the US and the UK. This suggests that international trade and institutions ought to be given a greater role while investigating the patterns of wage inequality across the globe. Indeed, as already said, trade explains wage differentials well, since it facilitates not only the exchanges between developing countries and developed ones but also between countries with high endowment of low skill workers (the developing nations) and high skill ones (the developed nations). The latter alone can induce an increase in the demand for high-skilled labor in the developed nations. This would engender pressure on low skill laborers in developed countries and, thus, raise the level of inequality within the developed countries (e.g. Krueger 1993). Several reasons stand, however, against this view since, for example in the US, the skill bias induced by trade is not enough to induce the downward pressure on low skill wages (Acemoglu 2002).

References

Acemoglu, Daron (2002) 'Technical Change, Inequality, and the Labor Market', *Journal of Economic Literature*, Vol. 40, No. 1: 7–72.

Acemoglu, Daron and David H. Autor (2011) 'Skills, Tasks and Technologies: Implications for Employment and Earnings', in *Handbook of Labor Economics*, Vol. 4b, Elsevier.

Aghion, Philippe, Eve Caroli and Cecilia García-Peñalosa (1999) 'Inequality and Economic Growth: The Perspective of the New Growth Theories', *Journal of Economic Literature*, Vol. 37, No. 4: 1615–60.

Agrawal, Ajay, Devesh Kapur, John McHale and Alexander Oettl (2011) 'Brain Drain or Brain Bank? The Impact of Skilled Emigration on Poor-Country Innovation', *Journal of Urban Economics*, Vol. 69, No. 1: 43–55.

Alesina, Alberto and Dani Rodrik (1994) 'Distributive Politics and Economic Growth', *Quarterly Journal of Economics*, Vol. 109, No. 2: 465–90.

Anand, Sudhir and Paul Segal (2008) 'What Do We Know About Global Income Inequality?', *Journal of Economic Literature*, Vol. 46, No. 1: 57–94.

Anwar, Sajid (2010) 'Wage Inequality, Increased Competition, and Trade Liberalization: Short Run vs Long Run', *Review of International Economics*, Vol. 18, No. 3: 574–81.

Anwar, Sajid (2013) 'Outsourcing and the Skilled–Unskilled Wage Gap', *Economics Letters*, Vol. 118, No. 2: 347–50.

Anwar, Sajid, Sizhong Sun and Abbas Valadkhani (2013) 'International Outsourcing of Skill Intensive Tasks and Wage Inequality', *Economic Modelling*, Vol. 31: 590–97.

Arrow, Kenneth (1962) 'Economic Welfare and the Allocation of Resources for Invention', in *The Rate and Direction of Inventive Activity: Economic and Social Factors*, Princeton, NJ: Princeton University Press, 609–26.

Autor, David H. and David Dorn (2013) 'The Growth of Low-Skill Service Jobs and the Polarization of the US Labor Market', *American Economic Review*, Vol. 103, No. 5: 1553–97.

Autor, David H., Frank Levy and Richard J. Murnane (2003) 'The Skill Content of Recent Technological Change: An Empirical Exploration', *Quarterly Journal of Economics*, Vol. 118, No. 4: 1279–333.

Beaudry, Paul, David A. Green and Benjamin M. Sand (2014) 'The Declining Fortunes of the Young Since 2000', *American Economic Review*, Vol. 104, No. 5: 381–6.

Benabou, Roland (1996) 'Heterogeneity, Stratification, and Growth: Macroeconomic Implications of Community Structure and School Finance', *American Economic Review*, Vol. 86: 584–609.

Caselli, Francesco and Wilbur J. Coleman (2006) 'The World Technology Frontier', *American Economic Review*, Vol. 96, No. 3: 499–522.

Cassiolato, José Eduardo and Helena Maria Lastres (2000) 'Local Systems of Innovation in Mercosur Countries', *Industry and Innovation*, Vol. 7, No. 1: 33–53.

Cohen, Wesley M. and Daniel A. Levinthal (1989) 'Innovation and Learning: The Two Faces of R&D', *Economic Journal*, Vol. 99: 569–96.

Commander, Simon, Mari, Kangasniemi and Alan Winters (2004) 'The Brain Drain: Curse or Boon? A Survey of the Literature', in *Challenges to Globalization: Analyzing the Economics*, Chicago: University of Chicago Press, 235–78.

Cozzens, Susan and Dhanarj Thakur (eds.) (2014) *Innovation and Inequality: Emerging Technologies in an Unequal World*, Cheltenham: Edward Elgar.

Diwan, Ishac and Dani Rodrik (1991) 'Patents, Appropriate Technology, and North-South Trade', *Journal of International Economics*, Vol. 30, No. 1: 27–47.

Docquier, Frédéric and Hillel Rapoport (2008) *Skilled Migration: The Perspective of Developing Countries*, Bonn: IZA.

The Economist (1992) 'Let Them Eat Pollution', Issue 7745, February 8: 82.

Forbes, Kristin J. (2000) 'A Reassessment of the Relationship Between Inequality and Growth', *American Economic Review*, Vol. 90, No. 4: 869–87.

Franco, Chiara and Riccardo Leoncini (2013) 'Measuring China's Innovative Capacity: A Stochastic Frontier Exercise', *Economics of Innovation and New Technology*, Vol. 22, No. 2: 199–217.

Forero-Pineda, Clemente (2006) 'The Impact of Stronger Intellectual Property Rights on Science and Technology in Developing Countries', *Research Policy*, Vol. 35, No. 6: 808–24.

Fressoli, Mariano and Elisa Around (2015) 'Technology for Autonomy and Resistance: The Appropriate Technology Movement in South America', Brighton: STEPS Centre, STEPS Working Paper 87.

Galor, Oded and Daniel Tsiddon (1997) 'Technological Progress, Mobility, and Economic Growth', *American Economic Review*, Vol. 87: 363–82.

Galor, Oded and Joseph Zeira (1993) 'Income Distribution and Macroeconomics', *Review of Economic Studies*, Vol. 60, No. 1: 35–52.

García-Peñalosa, Cecilia and Stephen J. Turnovsky (2006) 'Growth and Income Inequality: A Canonical Model', *Economic Theory*, Vol. 28: 25–49.

García-Peñalosa, Cecilia and Stephen J. Turnovsky (2007) 'Growth, Income Inequality, and Fiscal Policy: What Are the Relevant Tradeoffs?', *Journal of Money, Credit and Banking*, Vol. 39: 369–94.

Goldin, Claudia and Lawrence L. Katz (2009) *The Race Between Education and Technology*, Cambridge, MA: The Belknap Press of Harvard University Press.

Grubel, Herbert and Anthony D. Scott (1966) 'The International Flow of Human Capital', *American Economic Review*, Vol. 56, No. 1/2: 268–74.

Hoekman, Bernard, Keith Maskus and Kamal Saggi (2005) 'Transfer of Technology to Developing Countries: Unilateral and Multilateral Policy Options', *World Development*, Vol. 33, No. 10: 1587–1602.

Jaumotte, Florence, Subir Lall and Chris Papageorgiou (2013), 'Rising Income Inequality: Technology, or Trade and Financial Globalization?', *IMF Economic Review*, Vol. 61, No. 2: 271–309.

Jones, Charles I. and John C. Williams (1998) 'Measuring the Social Return to R&D', *Quarterly Journal of Economics*, Vol. 113: 1119–35.

Katz, Lawrence F. and Kevin M. Murphy (1992) 'Changes in Relative Wages, 1963–1987: Supply and Demand Factors', *Quarterly Journal of Economics*, Vol. 107, No. 1: 35–78.

Kristal, Tali and Yinon Cohen (2015) 'What Do Computers Really Do? Computerization, Fading Pay-Setting Institutions and Rising Wage Inequality', *Research in Social Stratification and Mobility*, Vol. 42: 33–47.

Krueger, Alan B. (1993) 'How Computers Have Changed the Wage Structure: Evidence From Microdata', *Quarterly Journal of Economics*, Vol. 108, No. 1: 33–60.

Kuznets, Simon (1955) 'Economic Growth and Income Inequality', *American Economic Review*, Vol. 45, No. 1: 1–28.

Lakner, Christoph and Branko Milanović (2016) 'Global Income Distribution: From the Fall of the Berlin Wall to the Great Recession', *World Bank Economic Review*, Vol. 30, No. 2: 203–32.

Lemieux, Thomas (2008) 'The Changing Nature of Wage Inequality', *Journal of Population Economics*, Vol. 21, No. 1: 21–48.

Levy, Frank and Richard J. Murnane (1992) 'US Earnings Levels and Earnings Inequality: A Review of Recent Trends and Proposed Explanations', *Journal of Economic Literature*, Vol. 30, No. 3: 1333–81.

Li, Hongyi and Heng-fu Zou (1998) 'Income Inequality Is Not Harmful for Growth: Theory and Evidence', *Review of Development Economics*, Vol. 2, No. 3: 318–34.

McAusland, Carol and Peter J. Kuhn (2011) 'Bidding for Brains: Intellectual Property Rights and the International Migration of Knowledge Workers', *Journal of Development Economics*, Vol. 95, No. 1: 77–87.

Maskin, Eric (2015) 'Why Haven't Global Markets Reduced Inequality in Emerging Economies?', *World Bank Economic Review*, Vol. 29, suppl. 1: S48–52.

Milanović, Branko (2006) 'Global Income Inequality: What It Is and Why It Matters?', DESA Working Paper No. 26.

Mokyr, Joel (1992) The Lever of Riches: Technological Creativity and Economic Progress, Oxford: Oxford University Press.

Mukherjee, Arijit and Yingyi Tsai (2013) 'Technology Licensing Under Optimal Tax Policy', *Journal of Economics*, Vol. 108, No. 3: 231–47.

Naghavi, Alireza and Chiara Strozzi (2015) 'Intellectual Property Rights, Diasporas, and Domestic Innovation', *Journal of International Economics*, Vol. 96, No. 1: 150–61.

OECD (2011) 'Divided We Stand – Why Inequality Keeps Rising', Paris: OECD.

Persson, Torsten and Guido Tabellini (1994) 'Is Inequality Harmful for Growth?', *American Economic Review*, Vol. 84: 600–21.

Pi, Jiancai and Yu Zhou (2015) 'International Factor Mobility, Production Cost Components, and Wage Inequality', *The BE Journal of Economic Analysis & Policy*, Vol. 15, No. 2: 503–22.

Piketty, Thomas (2014) *Capital in the 21st Century*, Cambridge, MA: Harvard University Press.

Pursell, Carroll (2016) 'Technology and Social Inequality', *Spontaneous Generations: A Journal for the History and Philosophy of Science*, Vol. 8, No. 1: 22–6.

Rodrik, Dani (2016) 'Premature Deindustrialization', *Journal of Economic Growth*, Vol. 21, No. 1: 1–33.

Rosen, Sherwin (1981) 'The Economics of Superstars', *American Economic Review*, Vol. 71, No. 5: 845–58.

Saint-Paul, Gilles (2008) *Innovation and Inequality: How Does Technical Progress Affect Workers?* Princeton, NJ: Princeton University Press.

Straubhaar, Thomas (2000) 'International Mobility of the Highly Skilled: Brain Gain, Brain Drain or Brain Exchange', HWWA–Inst. für Wirtschaftsforschung.

World Bank (2016) 'World Development Report', Washington, DC: World Bank.

Zhang, Jingjing (2012) 'Inflow of Labour, Producer Services and Wage Inequality', *Economics Letters*, Vol. 117, No. 3: 600–3.

Part IV
Methodology

14 Quantitative methods for inequality measurement

Pinuccia Calia

Introduction

This chapter describes some of the measurement tools that can be used in the quantitative analysis of inequality. Inequality refers to the unequal distribution of socially relevant resources among individuals or groups in society. Therefore, at the base of inequality measurement is the definition of the variable describing the resources. This can be interpreted as an overall indicator of well-being or as a specific attribute. Depending on the problem at hand, it is measured according to a numerical scale or nominal/categorical scale.

Most of the chapter is devoted to the techniques developed for measuring economic inequality, traditionally intended as inequality in income distribution; many of them, however, have important counterparts in sociological and political studies. These methods apply to the measurement of inequality in a single attribute that can be described by a quantitative variable, such as income, wage, wealth, land-ownership, consumption, life expectancy, etc. Such an attribute must be measurable and comparable among different individuals, and we will discuss inequality measurement within the framework of distributional analysis. To make the exposition easier we call it "income", but the same principles extend to the distribution of any other measurable variable.

In addition, we briefly introduce some quantitative methods used to discover and assess inequalities among population groups in multiple dimensions, typically described by categorical variables.

Due to space constraints, this presentation is not exhaustive in either reviewing the approaches for measuring different types of inequalities, or discussing theoretical or empirical issues. For the same reasons, we do not discuss the related issues of poverty, social mobility, and polarization.

Simple measures of inequality

Simple inequality measures originate from the statistical concept of variability of a distribution. All the measures are zero when all incomes are equal and increase with inequality.[1]

The Relative Mean Deviation (RMD) measures the average deviation of an individual's income around the mean relative to total income.[2] Its maximum value is $2(n - 1)/n$, where n is the number of individuals. RMD remains unchanged when multiplying all incomes by a factor α, while it increases or decreases if the same amount is added or subtracted to all incomes.

The variance is the most common index of variability. It is the average of the squared deviations from the mean, therefore it gives more weight to those values which are further away from the mean itself. By multiplying all values by a factor α, the variance increases by a factor α^2, and depends on the measurement unit. This is a very serious shortcoming when comparing different income distributions, for example, among countries or groups. On the contrary, it remains unchanged if we add or subtract the same amount to or from all incomes. The variance depends on the measurement unit; therefore, for the purpose of comparison, we need to transform it into an index free from the measurement unit. The coefficient of variation (CV) is defined as the ratio of the standard deviation (the square root of the variance) and the average level of income. Unlike variance, CV is invariant to multiplication to a scale factor.

Both V and CV are not bounded from above; in particular, CV tends to become larger especially when the mean level of the character is low. We can obtain relative indexes by dividing the variance (or CV) by the variance (CV) that the same distribution could generate if total amounts were concentrated in the hands of only one individual (maximum inequality). We obtain two relative indexes V(I) and C(I) that range from zero to one: zero if all values are equal, one when all values are zero except one.

Lastly, another index of inequality can be defined applying the formula for variance to the logarithms of income values, the Standard Deviation of Logarithms (SDL). When income is the same for all individuals, SDL is zero. Further properties of these indexes are discussed later.

Graphical representations

Different kinds of graphical representation can provide useful insights into income distribution. Income may be thought of as a random variable Y with a distribution from which the incomes of individuals are drawn; the cumulative probability distribution function (CDF) then shows the probability for Y to be smaller or equal to some value y:

$$F(y) = \Pr(Y \leq y)$$

and the probability density function (PDF) summarizes the incomes at exactly y:

$$f(y) = dF(y)/dy$$

The quantile function is the inverse of the CDF:

$$Q(p) = F^{-1}(p)$$

and shows the income value below which a fraction $0 \leq p \leq 1$ of individuals is found; the median is the income splitting the population ranked in income order into two equal-sized groups ($p = 0.5$), the x-th percentile is $Q(x/100)$ (Jenkins and Van Kerm 2012).

Histograms and kernel densities

A histogram (Figure 14.1) is a graph that shows the fraction of the population with an income comprised in specific intervals. The histogram is related to the CDF since the proportion of population with income in the interval $[a,b]$ is $F(b) - F(a)$; also, when $[a,b]$ become so small (tend to zero), the height of the histogram between a and b, divided by $(b - a)$, would equal $f(b)$, the value of PDF at b.

The PDF could be estimated by using a histogram with very narrow income intervals, but some intervals may contain either no or very few observations since the number of sample observations is finite. Typically, the PDF is estimated by a kernel density estimator (see the curve in Figure 14.1), which "smooths" the histogram values over a number of overlapping income intervals.

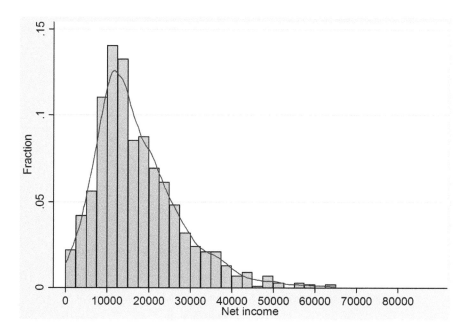

Figure 14.1 Histogram and kernel density curve

Notes: author's elaboration using the Stata Package DASP (Araar and Duclos 2007)

PDFs are useful for identifying the income ranges with high concentrations of incomes, the mode, and the overall location and spread of the distribution (Jenkins and Van Kerm 2012).

Quantile function (Pen's Parade)

Another way of representing a distribution is to plot the curve (Figure 14.2) obtained by showing the proportion p of the population on the horizontal axis and the corresponding income y on the vertical axis (Pen's Parade). The population is arranged in ascending order of income: two points $y_{0.2}$ and $y_{0.8}$ show the income of the person appearing at exactly 20 and 80% of the way along the list of ordered incomes (Parade), respectively. For example, 20% of the population with the lowest incomes have a gross income lower than or equal to 10,000. More details are found in Cowell (2000). This curve is simply the inverse function of the CDF and reports the quantiles corresponding to given shares of the population; it can be used to compare the inequality of distributions.

Lorenz curve

The Lorenz curve is a powerful method of illustrating inequalities in an income distribution. It relates the cumulative proportion of income (income share) to

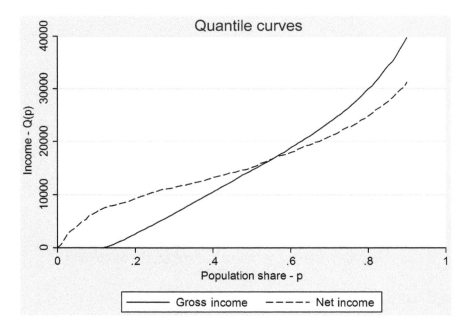

Figure 14.2 Quantile functions

Notes: author's elaboration using the Stata Package DASP (Araar and Duclos 2007)

the cumulative proportion of individuals (population share). Representing the income distribution in a population with n individuals as the list of incomes $\mathbf{y} = (y_1, y_2, \ldots, y_n)$ ordered from the lowest to the highest, the horizontal axis records the cumulative proportion of population ranked by income level. Its range is therefore $(0,1)$. The vertical axis records the income share calculated by taking the cumulated income of a given share of the population, divided by the total income Y, as follows:

$$L(p_i) = q_i = \frac{\sum_{k=1}^{i}(y_k)}{Y} \tag{1}$$

where $i = 1, \ldots, n$ is the position of each individual in the ordered list of incomes, $p_i = i / n$ is the cumulative proportion of population up to the i-th individual (population share), y_k is the income of the k-th individual in the ordered list, and $\sum_{k=1}^{i}(y_k)$ is the cumulated income up to the i-th individual in the ordered list of incomes. $\sum_{k=1}^{i}(y_k) = 0$ if $i=0$ and $\sum_{k=1}^{i}(y_k) = Y$ if $i=n$ so $L(p_i)$ ranges between zero and one.[3]

Figure 14.3 illustrates the shape of a typical Lorenz curve. The curve starts from the origin at $(p_0, q_0) = (0,0)$, as a zero fraction of the population owns a zero fraction of income, and has coordinates $(p_n, q_n) = (1,1)$ at the end point, since the total population owns total income.

If everyone were to have the same income (perfect equality), a given proportion of the population (let's say 20%) would have the same proportion of income (20%). This situation is represented by the line along the 45° ray from the origin. Typically, the 20% share of the population owns less than 20% share of the total income, therefore the Lorenz curve is the convex curve, as in Figure 14.3.

When incomes are not equal and poor individuals own proportionally less income than rich people, the more the Lorenz curve lies below the perfect equality line, the more there is inequality. In the extreme case of a distribution where all individuals but one have zero income, the Lorenz curve is a kinked curve, running on zero until the last individual is reached and then jumping to one: there is the maximum concentration of income as possible.

The shape of the Lorenz curve is therefore a good visual indicator of how much inequality there is in an income distribution.

The Lorenz curve is more than a useful device for describing inequality in a distribution. A key result is that if the Lorenz curves of two distributions $\mathbf{y}$ and $\mathbf{y}\star$ do not cross and $L(p; \mathbf{y}) < L(p; \mathbf{y}\star)$ for any cumulative population shares p, then inequality is higher in distribution $\mathbf{y}$ than in distribution $\mathbf{y}\star$. Distribution $\mathbf{y}\star$ is said to Lorenz-dominate the distribution $\mathbf{y}$.

However, there is no guarantee that, given two income distributions, one Lorenz-dominates the other, because the Lorenz curves may intersect. In this case, by considering only Lorenz curves, nothing can be said about which

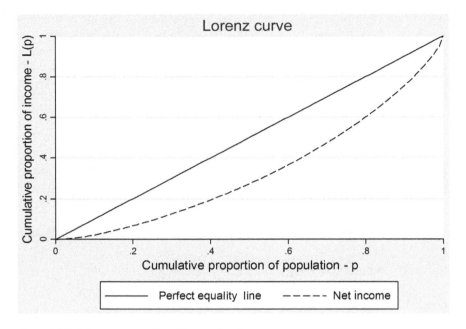

Figure 14.3 Lorenz curve and perfect equality line

Notes: author's elaboration using the Stata Package DASP (Araar and Duclos 2007)

income distribution has less inequality. Thus, Lorenz dominance is a partial ordering: Lorenz curves can be used to rank income distributions according to their inequality, provided that they do not intersect.

Inequality indices

We already described some of the simple measures used to summarize inequality in terms of a single number. Other commonly used indices include those based on quantile ratios, obtained as the ratio of two quantiles $Q(p)$ corresponding to the specific proportions of the population in the ordered list of incomes, for example, $Q(0.8)/Q(0.2)$. The ratio is one in the case of equality, and increases with inequality; however, it may produce ambiguous results when comparing distributions. A more informative measure takes into account the ratio of the shares of total income accrued by given proportions of the population at the bottom and top of the distribution: for example, the share of the total income accrued by 20% of the richest, divided by the share of the total income accrued by 20% of the poorest. The interpretation is the same as for the quantile ratio, but it provides more precise information on which of the two distributions features more inequality because it reproduces the Lorenz ranking. The limit of these kinds of measures is that they ignore all information on the distribution other than the quantiles selected.

Inequality indices can also be derived directly from the Lorenz curve. The ratio of shares is one of these. Another one is the Robin Hood index, which is defined as the largest difference between the Lorenz curve and the perfect equality line: it is equal to the proportion of total income that would have to be redistributed from those above the mean in order to achieve perfect equality (Jenkins and Van Kerm 2012). Anand (1997) has discussed indices based on the Lorenz diagram and also several other indices.

The Gini index

The most commonly used inequality index is the Gini coefficient, which can be derived from the Lorenz curve: it is equal to the ratio of the area enclosed by the Lorenz curve and the perfect equality line (concentration area) to the total area below the equality line (the area of maximum concentration).

The maximum concentration area corresponds to a distribution where a single individual owns the total income; therefore, the Gini index measures the distance of the area defined by any income distribution to the area of maximum concentration.

In practical terms, the area of maximum concentration is $1/2$, because it is a triangle with a base length of 1 and height length of 1. The concentration area is the difference between the maximum concentration area and the area below the Lorenz curve (see Figure 14.3). The area below the Lorenz curve is calculated as follows.[4]

Given $\left(y_1 \leq y_2 \leq \ldots \leq y_n \right)$ q_i is the cumulative proportion of income and p_i is the cumulative proportion of population as in the definition of the Lorenz curve, with $q_0 = p_0 = 0$ and $q_n = p_n = 1$.

The area under the Lorenz curve is the sum of the areas of a series of polygons (the first is a triangle while the others are rotated trapeziums) where q_i are the bases and $\left(p_i - p_{i-1} \right)$ are the heights.

As $q_0 = p_0 = 0$, the sum of all the areas is:

$$A = \sum_{i=1}^{n} A_i = \frac{1}{2} \sum_{i=1}^{n} \left[(q_i + q_{i-1}) \, (p_i - p_{i-1}) \right] \tag{2}$$

To calculate the concentration area (the numerator of the Gini index), now it is sufficient to subtract A from the maximum concentration area as follows:

$$\frac{1}{2} - \frac{1}{2} \sum_{i=1}^{n} \left[(q_i + q_{i-1}) \, (p_i - p_{i-1}) \right]$$

and the Gini index is therefore equal to:

$$G = \frac{\dfrac{1}{2} - \dfrac{1}{2} \sum_{i=1}^{n} \left[(q_i + q_{i-1}) \, (p_i - p_{i-1}) \right]}{2} = 1 - \sum_{i=1}^{n} \left[(q_i + q_{i-1}) \, (p_i - p_{i-1}) \right] \tag{3}$$

or, equivalently $G = 1 - 2A$, i.e. the Gini index is equal to one minus twice the area below the Lorenz curve.[5]

Other alternative formulations are possible (Yitzhaki 1998), for example, the Gini index is equal to the Relative Absolute Mean Difference:

$$G = \frac{1}{2n^2 \overline{y}} \sum_i^n \sum_j^n \left| y_i - y_j \right| \tag{4}$$

where $\overline{y} = \frac{1}{n} \sum_i^n y_i$ is the mean income.

The Gini index is zero when all incomes are equal (the concentration area is zero) and is equal to $(n\text{-}1)/n$ when all incomes are zero except for the last (maximum concentration). This limit approaches one for very large populations. The Gini index does not change by multiplying all incomes by a factor α; on the contrary, by adding/subtracting the same amount to/from all incomes, the Gini index would increase (decrease) accordingly. If the income is redistributed from richer individuals to poorer individuals, G decreases; the opposite happens if the income is redistributed from poorer to richer individuals. The properties of the Gini index make it belong to the class of relative inequality indexes (see below). The Gini index's main weakness is that it cannot differentiate different kinds of inequalities: Lorenz curves may intersect, reflecting different patterns of income distribution, nevertheless resulting in very similar Gini indexes. Moreover, it is more sensitive to inequalities in the middle part of the incomes range; for this reason, it is not "neutral" or value-free, because it embodies implicit judgments about the weight to be attached to inequality at different points on the income scale (Atkinson 1975).[6] However, in applied works, the characteristics of this index are very useful, hence the reason why it is so often used.

Generalized entropy indices

A family of inequality indices originating from different considerations is the Generalized Entropy (GE) class.

Theil (1967) has proposed an approach for inequality measurement using an analogy with the concept of entropy of a probability distribution from Information Theory.

Following this approach, Theil has proposed the following inequality index (see Cowell 2000, 2011):

$$T_1(Y) = \frac{1}{n} \sum_{i=1}^n \frac{y_i}{\mu} \log \frac{y_i}{\mu} \tag{5}$$

and also the index commonly known as Mean Logarithmic Deviation (MLD):

$$T_2(Y) = \sum_{i=i}^n \frac{1}{n} \log \frac{(1/n)}{(y_i/Y)} = \frac{1}{n} \sum_{i=1}^n \log \frac{\mu}{y_i} \tag{6}$$

where μ is the mean income and $Y = n\mu$ is the total income. $T_2(Y)$ is analogous to $T_1(Y)$ except that it reverses the role of income shares and population shares. Both Theil indices measure the divergence between income shares and population shares, but using different distance functions.

The two Theil measures are special cases of a more flexible class of inequality indices, the Generalized Entropy (EG) family of measures (Cowell and Kuga 1981; Cowell 2000):

$$E_\alpha(Y) = \frac{1}{\alpha^2 - \alpha} \sum_{i=1}^{n} \frac{1}{n}\left(\left(\frac{y_i}{\mu}\right)^\alpha - 1\right) \quad \alpha \neq 0,1 \tag{7}$$

Different α values correspond to differences in the sensitivity of the index to inequalities in different parts of income distribution. The smaller (and negative) the α, the more sensitive the index is to differences in income shares among the poorest incomes (lower tail); the greater (and positive) the α, the more sensitive the index is to differences in income shares among the rich (upper tail). The range of GE values is 0 to infinity, with 0 in the case of equal distribution.

The most-used indices in the class correspond to some particular values of α; for $\alpha = 1$ we obtain the Theil index $E_1(Y) = T_1(Y)$, and for $\alpha = 0$ we have the Mean Logarithmic Deviation $E_0(Y) = T_2(Y)$. For $\alpha = 2$ we have the Squared Coefficient of Variation $E_2(Y) = CV^2 / 2$. The importance of the GE class of inequality measures lies in its properties, which are described later in the chapter.

Social welfare function and the Atkinson inequality measures

A systematic approach to inequality measurement is to start with a Social Welfare Function (SWF) that encompasses specific ethical principles, and to derive an inequality index from it that reflects these same properties (Jenkins and Van Kerm 2012).

The starting problem is how to rank income distributions from a social welfare perspective. Actually, different stakeholders may have different views about what is better for a society, and this may lead to ranking two alternative "social states" differently. To obtain a unanimous consensus about the ranking, some common criteria on what is desirable for a society must be found.

Social welfare can be described by means of a SWF that aggregates information about the income distribution into a single number that provides an overall judgement on that distribution (Deaton 1997). Formally, the SWF is a function of the incomes y_i:

$$W = W(y_1, y_2, \dots, y_n) \tag{8}$$

with some basic characteristics. It only depends on individual incomes and satisfies the Pareto Principle: if an individual income increases, other things being equal, social welfare must increase or at least not decrease (formally, the first derivative is positive). Moreover, the social welfare is not affected if two individuals switch incomes and it is assumed to be additive in individual utilities, where utility for a person i is a function of their income only, $U(y_i)$. Social welfare is then the average of the individual utilities:

$$W = \frac{1}{n}\sum_{i}^{n}U(y_i)$$

(9)

Commonly, it is assumed that U is concave: the social marginal utility of income increases with income at a decreasing rate (the second derivative is negative). The degree of concavity of the SWF reflects the degree of "inequality aversion": social welfare is more sensitive to a shift in the income of a poorer individual than to the same shift affecting a richer individual, so the increase in social welfare is lower for additional income to richer individuals.

A linear SWF (no concavity) corresponds to inequality neutrality: social welfare is affected equally, irrespective of the position of individuals affected by a shift of income (the second derivative is zero).

Social welfare can be compared by means of welfare-based measures of inequality: they may provide for a complete ordering by reducing income distributions to a single number. The Equally Distributed Equivalent income ξ (EDE) is defined as the level of income that, if obtained by every individual, would enable a society to reach the same level of social welfare as actual incomes, so ξ satisfies $W(\xi) = W(Y)$ and $\xi \leq \mu$ (the mean income) due to social preference for equality (concavity of the SWF).

Thus an inequality index can be defined by the welfare loss due to inequality:

$$I(Y) = 1 - (\xi / \mu)$$

(10)

For this purpose, one needs to specify a particular functional form for the SWF.[7]

Atkinson (1970) has assumed a specific utility function with constant elasticity, i.e. equal proportional changes in each individual's income change total social welfare by the same proportion. The elasticity parameter ϵ, with $\epsilon > 0$ to ensure concavity, determines the exact specification of the SWF. If $\epsilon = 0$, the SWF collapses to the mean income: the higher the mean income, the higher the social welfare (inequality neutrality). As ϵ increases, increases in lower incomes weight relatively more in producing social welfare. Large values of ϵ (greater inequality aversion) correspond to a greater concern for inequality differences at the bottom of the distribution.

With these assumptions for the utility function, the expression for EDE is:

$$\xi = \left[\frac{1}{n}\sum_{i}^{n}y_i^{1-\epsilon}\right]^{\frac{1}{1-\epsilon}} \quad \epsilon \neq 1$$

(11)

$$\xi = \prod(y_i)^{\frac{1}{n}} \quad \epsilon = 1$$

Applying the equation (10), the expression of Atkinson's index is:

$$A_\epsilon(Y) = 1 - \left[\frac{1}{n}\sum_i^n\left(\frac{y_i}{\bar{y}}\right)^{1-\epsilon}\right]^{\frac{1}{1-\epsilon}} \quad \epsilon \neq 1$$

(12)

$$A_1(Y) = 1 - \left(\prod_i^n\left(\frac{y}{\bar{y}}\right)\right)^{1/n} \quad \epsilon = 1$$

where ϵ is the inequality aversion parameter. The index ranges between zero and one, assuming the value zero in the case of equal distribution.

By means of (10), an intuitive interpretation of the index is possible: if the index value is 0.20, the interpretation is that society is ready to release 20% of the total income to have an equal level of social welfare. Also, it makes it possible for us to directly derive a social evaluation function: for any income distribution, if we know the mean income and the value of A_ϵ, the level of welfare (measured by EDE) can be calculated and compared (Bellù and Liberati 2006a).

The Atkinson and the Generalized Entropy (GE) measures are closely related: for each value of ϵ there is a GE index E_α with $\alpha = 1-\epsilon$ that ranks a pair of distributions in the same way as A_ϵ.

Properties of inequality measures

One way to choose between inequality indices is to evaluate them in terms of their properties (axioms). They define the way in which inequality measures should behave. Three properties are particularly important[8]:

1 Principle of Population: requires the inequality index to be invariant to replications of the incomes in the original population.
2 Scale Invariance: requires the inequality index to be invariant to equiproportional changes of original incomes. This property ensures that the resulting measure evaluates the relative inequality in the distribution independently of the total amount of income.
3 Principle of Transfers: this is a fundamental property which requires the inequality measure to decrease when an income transfer occurs from richer to poorer individuals (Pigou–Dalton transfer) and to rise when an income transfer occurs from poorer to richer individuals.[9]

If an inequality index satisfies the three axioms at the same time, it belongs to the Relative Inequality Indices (RII) class. A property of the RII class is that they rank inequality in the same way as the Lorenz curve ordering: if the Lorenz curve of the distribution y dominates the Lorenz curve of a distribution $y\star$ (less inequality in y), all RIIs give the same ranking. If Lorenz dominance fails, there might be RIIs ranking the two distributions differently. The difference between the Lorenz criterion and RIIs is that the Lorenz curve gives a partial ordering while RIIs may give a complete ordering as they reduce income distributions to a single number (Bellù and Liberati 2006b).

All the measures above satisfy the Principle of Population. The variance is not Scale-Invariant while all other indices are. All the indices do satisfy the Principle of Transfer, except quantile ratios, Robin Hood, and RMD, which react to redistribution only for transfers across the mean. SDL has a peculiar type of sensitivity to income transfers: when income transfers occur in the lower part of an income distribution, SDL decreases proportionally more than other inequality indices. Regarding the Gini index, the size of the change after redistribution depends on the rank of the individuals involved, sample size, and total income. In particular, the Gini index is more sensitive to transfers occurring among individuals who have distant ranks.

Another useful property is decomposability: if the original income distribution is made of m groups, total inequality must be equal to the sum of the various group inequalities. Only the variance and GE indices are decomposable in a convenient way (see next section).

Explaining inequality: decomposition methods

Up to now we were concerned with the measurement of inequality as it has been traditionally intended in economics (i.e. income inequality). Inequality, however, can have several dimensions: non-income inequality includes inequality in skills, education, opportunities, health, and others. Relationships between inequality in income and non-income dimensions are of great interest. Decomposition methods aim at understanding either how income differences within particular population groups combine to obtain the overall level of inequality, or how the overall inequality is related to different sources of income.

Decomposition methods follow two different approaches: non-regression methods and methods based on multivariate regression.[10]

Non-regression methods

Partitioning the population into M distinct non-overlapping subgroups of individuals, defined by certain characteristics (such as age, education, occupation, etc.), decomposition disaggregates the overall inequality into two components, one for the contribution arising from inequality within each of the groups, and one for the contribution arising from inequality among the groups.

Usually this goal is accomplished via a decomposable inequality index. A prominent role is played by the GE inequality index: the total inequality can be disaggregated into the sum of inequality "Within" groups and inequality "Between" groups:

$$E_\alpha(Y) = E_\alpha^W(Y) + E_\alpha^B(Y) \tag{13}$$

The former is the weighted sum of inequalities within each subgroup:

$$E_\alpha^W(Y) = \sum_m^M \frac{N_m}{N} \left(\frac{\mu_m}{\mu}\right)^\alpha E_\alpha(Y_m)$$
(14)

where N_m is the number of individuals in the m-th group, μ_m is the mean of income in the m-th group, μ is the mean of income in the whole population, $E_\alpha(Y_m)$ is the GE index calculated in the m-th group. $E_\alpha^B(Y)$ is the "Between" inequality obtained by attributing to each person the mean income of their subgroup:

$$E_\alpha^B(Y) = \frac{1}{\alpha(\alpha-1)} \sum_m^M \frac{N_m}{N} \left[\left(\frac{\mu_m}{\mu}\right)^\alpha - 1\right]$$
(15)

Not all inequality indices are decomposable in this useful way: the Atkinson Index is decomposable but not additively decomposable (Blackorby, Donaldson and Auersperg 1981), and the Gini index requires a third term if the subgroup income ranges overlap.[11]

Another useful decomposition is the disaggregation by source. Usually, the income is the sum of incomes coming from different sources, for example labor income, capital income, and transfers. The decomposition by factor components identifies the contribution of each factor k to total inequality. The share of total inequality that factor k accounts for (Shorrocks 1982) is:

$$s_k = \frac{Cov(Y_k, Y)}{\sigma^2(Y)} = \rho(Y_k, Y) \times \frac{\mu_k}{\mu} \times \frac{CV(Y_k)}{CV(Y)}$$
(16)

where $\rho(Y_k, Y)$ is the correlation between the total incomes of individuals and the incomes from source k. The share s_k does not depend on the inequality index used; conversely, it depends on the correlation between the factor and total income, the share of the factor in total income, and the inequality (measured by CV) of the factor relative to the inequality of total income. Factors may produce less or more inequality in total income depending on $\rho(Y_k, Y)$ being negative or positive respectively (and so s_k). Social security transfers are usually expected to be inequality-reducing while labor and capital income tend to be inequality-increasing.

Regression-based methods

A different approach to explaining income distributions and its structure consists of using a regression framework (see Lemieux 2002 for a detailed discussion).

The core idea is to assume that the income is explained by a set of factors that vary systematically through a standard linear regression:

$$y_i = \beta_0 + \beta_1 X_{i1} + \ldots + \beta_k X_{ik} + \varepsilon_i = \beta X_i + \varepsilon_i$$
(17)

where $X_{i1}, \ldots, X_{ik}$ are observable characteristics (covariates) measured on a quantitative scale (for example age, years of experience at work, etc.) or categorical scale (such as level of education, professional occupation, etc.). The term ε_i is a stochastic component that accounts for some unobserved factors distributed randomly among individuals, and $\beta = (\beta_0, \beta_1, \ldots, \beta_k)$ is a set of parameters to be estimated. Variations in income may be explained by variations in age, level of education, etc., and each parameter measures the change in mean income corresponding to a unit change in a specific covariate, assuming the others are constant. Such a framework can be used to decompose the gap in the mean of incomes between two groups A and B. The gap is decomposed into the part that is due to group differences in the observed characteristics ("endowments"), on the one hand, and group differences in the effects ("returns") of these characteristics, on the other. In fact, the gap in the mean of incomes between group A and B:

$$\bar{y}_A - \bar{y}_B = \beta_A \bar{X}_A - \beta_B \bar{X}_B \tag{18}$$

can be rewritten equivalently as:

$$\bar{y}_A - \bar{y}_B = \beta_A (\bar{X}_A - \bar{X}_B) + (\beta_A - \beta_B) \bar{X}_B \tag{19}$$

where $\bar{X}_A$ and $\bar{X}_B$ are the means of the observed characteristic in group A and B, respectively, β_A are the returns for group A, and β_B are the returns for group B.

This is the "Oaxaca-Blinder" decomposition of the difference between the mean of two distributions (Oaxaca 1973; Blinder 1973), which has been used to study gender (or race) discrimination in wages.

However, this approach only considers differences in mean outcomes, and relies on linear regression. One alternative is to consider the quantile regression, where each income quantile is expressed as a combination of the observed characteristics, and to estimate the effect of covariates on the location and shape of the distribution. Applications of this approach to wage inequality can be found in Gosling, Machin and Meghir (2000) and in Machado and Mata (2005).

Other approaches model the conditional distribution itself, for example by assuming a parametric functional form for the income distribution and expressing its parameters as a regression function of observed characteristics, as in Biewen and Jenkins (2005).

Another approach (Di Nardo, Fortin and Lemieux 1996) decomposes the change in the PDF of income between two years (years 1 and 2) into the changes in the distribution of income for specific groups and changes in the relative sizes of these groups. Define $f_2(y) - f_1(y)$ as the difference in PDF between the two years. The PDF may be written as the weighted sum (integral) of the PDFs for each subgroup of individuals that is implicitly defined by a particular combination of observed characteristics:

$$f_m(y) = \int f_m(y \mid X) g_m(X) dX \tag{20}$$

where $f_m(y \mid X)$ is the conditional distribution of income in the m-th group with a specific combination $g_m(X)$ of the characteristics X. The aim is to decompose the overall change $f_2(y) - f_1(y)$ into differences due to changes in the conditional distributions and changes in group sizes as defined by $g_m(X)$.

The solution is to use a reweighting method. Defining a reweighting function:

$$\omega_{1,2}(X) = \frac{g_1(X)}{g_2(X)} = \frac{P(m=1 \mid X)}{P(m=2 \mid X)} \times \frac{P(m=2)}{P(m=1)} \tag{21}$$

where $P(m = i \mid X)$ is the probability that a randomly selected individual with characteristics X belongs to group i if individuals from both groups are pooled in a common population, and $P(m = i)$ is the probability that any randomly selected individual belongs to group i after pooling the groups. The four probabilities are relatively easy to estimate via probit regression and are used to simulate the effect of compositional changes using weighted kernel density estimation. The effects of subgroups' distributional changes are estimated from the difference that remains after taking into account the effect of composition differences (Jenkins and Van Kerm 2012).

Empirical implementation

The primary problem in measuring inequality is that of defining the variable y that we called "income". A number of preliminary considerations about the nature of y, and the way it is observed in practice, should be made. The practical definition of the variable y, and thus the picture of its distribution, is as good as the information on it.

There are, basically, two methods of collecting information: surveys and administrative sources. Neither method is without its' drawbacks. The main difficulty in surveys is that of non-response by those surveyed. A potentially significant bias may be introduced into the results if people that refuse to cooperate are among the rich (or the poor). The treatment of total non-response is usually accomplished by weighting raw data, and that of partial non-response by some imputation method, in order to mitigate the effect of non-response bias.

Administrative data are often a by-product of official obligations. It is usually possible to obtain a larger sample of the population and non-response bias is less important. However, information may not correspond exactly to the data requirements of the analyst: concepts, definitions, and subjects observed may be different from those significant for the analysis, the population considered for administrative purposes may cover the target population only partially, so some subgroups are over or under-represented, or even completely excluded (truncation).

There are other considerations to take into account in practical applications also. In processing data, we are concerned with their quality: misunderstanding, misrecording, or misreporting may lead to missing observations or errors in data, and this reflects on the bias of inequality estimates. Some estimation techniques and statistics are sensitive to extreme values (outliers), the presence of negative and zero values, and arbitrary truncation.

The effects of these problems might be reduced by using "robust" estimates. However, many inequality measures are sensitive to the presence of errors in data and may be affected by "data contamination", i.e. the practice of deleting negative or zero values, or the truncation of high income from the top for the sake of confidentiality (Cowell and Victoria-Feser 1996; Cowell 2000; Van Kerm 2007). Thus, the treatment of partial non-response, zeros, and extreme values requires particular attention.

Another point to consider concerns the availability of individual or household data: in the latter case, we need to adjust each household's income to allow for differences in needs between different types of household. The process involves dividing the income by an index (equivalence scale) that accounts for differences in household composition. There are a variety of alternative equivalence scales, and these adjustments may significantly affect the picture of inequality that emerges.

Finally, sampling error affects inequality estimates if data comes from sample surveys. An estimation of standard errors and development of the appropriate inference (confidence intervals, tests) are necessary.

Multidimensional approaches for inequalities in non-income factors

In the social sciences, the interest often focuses on discovering inequalities along multiple dimensions representing non-income factors, often related to gender, ethnicity, social classes, etc., and described through categorical variables, i.e. data collected by means of nominally or ordinally scaled categorical items.

We present two quantitative methods, Multiple Correspondence Analysis (MCA) and Latent Class Analysis (LCA). In social sciences, MCA is best known for its application by Bourdieu (1984), who used MCA to "illustrate his thesis that the determinants of taste, cultural discrimination, and choice lie in the possession of two forms of capital, economic and cultural, with sub-groupings defined by seniority in possession and related mode of acquisition" (Phillips 1995). Other applications of MCA and related methods are the study of the relationship between poverty, subjective well-being, and ethnicity (Neff 2007), the multidimensional concept of gender inequality, accounting for the different forms in which gender inequality appears (Ferrant 2014), and social risk and the concept of vulnerability (Busetta and Milito 2010), among others. The most common use of LCA is for discovering subgroups, or confirming hypothesized subgroups based on multivariate categorical data. Some applications are the identification of subjective social classes based on perceptions regarding social class position (Ping-Yin 2006), and the identification of poverty and social exclusion based on multiple dimensions of deprivation (Nolan and Whelan 2007).

Only a brief overview of the main concepts is offered here, and we indicate some references for technical and mathematical insights.

Simple and multiple correspondence analysis

Correspondence Analysis (CA) is an exploratory multivariate technique for the graphical and numerical analysis of tables of frequencies or counts, but it can be extended to almost any type of tabular data after suitable data transformation or recoding: presence/absence data, rankings and preferences, paired comparison data, multiresponse and multiway tables.

Simple CA is primarily applicable to a two-way contingency table, leading to a map that visualizes the association between two categorical variables. The rows or columns of a data matrix are assumed to be points in a high-dimensional Euclidean space; the method aims to redefine the dimensions of the space so that the principal dimensions capture the most variance possible, thus allowing for lower-dimensional descriptions of the data. Multiple correspondence analysis (MCA) tackles the more general problem of associations within a set of more than two categorical variables and may be viewed as an extension of simple CA.[12]

To illustrate the application of the concepts of CA, we will use an example reported on Greenacre and Blasius (2006: Chapter 2), dealing with questions on attitudes toward science. Respondents are asked to indicate, on a five-point scale ranging from "Agree strongly" to "Disagree strongly", how much they agree or disagree with each of these statements:

(a) We believe too often in science, and not enough in feelings and faith;
(b) Overall, modern science does more harm than good;
(c) Any change humans cause in nature, no matter how scientific, is likely to make things worse;
(d) Modern science will solve our environmental problems with little change to our way of life.

Table 14.1 reports the cross-classification of the responses to the two questions A (concerning belief in science) and B (concerning harm caused by science), both worded unfavorably toward science, so that disagreement indicates a favorable attitude toward science.

As a first step, the correspondence matrix **P** is calculated to represent the relative frequencies of each cell to the total number of observations (871): $p_{ij} = n_{ij} / n$. Corresponding to each element of P are a row sum $p_{i.} = n_{i.} / n$ and column sum $p_{.j} = n_{.j} / n$, denoted by r_i and c_j, respectively (called masses). Under the null hypothesis of independence, the expected values of the relative frequencies p_{ij} are the products $r_i c_j$ of the masses. The differences $\left(p_{ij} - r_i c_j\right)$ between observed and expected relative frequencies, divided by the square roots of $r_i c_j$, lead to a matrix **S** of standardized residuals s_{ij}. The sum of squared elements of the matrix of standardized residuals s_{ij}^2 is called the total inertia and quantifies the total variance in the cross-table. The standardized residuals in **S** are the elements of the Chi-square statistic X^2 divided by n to convert original

Table 14.1 Joint distribution of responses to questions on attitudes to science

Too much science, not enough feelings and faith (A)	Science does more harm (B)					
	Agree strongly	Agree	Neither agree nor disagree	Disagree	Disagree strongly	Total
Agree strongly	27	28	30	22	12	119
Agree	38	74	84	96	30	322
Neither agree nor disagree	3	48	63	73	17	204
Disagree	3	21	23	79	52	178
Disagree strongly	0	3	5	11	29	48
Total	71	174	205	281	140	871

Notes: author's elaboration using Stata. The example is described in Greenacre and Blasius (2006: 43) and in the Stata Multivariate Statistics Reference Manual (2015), command MCA (Remarks and Examples) that also gives access to the dataset.

frequencies to relative ones, so we have total inertia equal to x^2 / n. CA consists, essentially, of finding the Singular Value Decomposition of the matrix **S**: the eigenvalues of **S** are termed principal inertias, and their sum is equal to the total inertia; the eigenvectors define the dimensions of a new space where the clouds of points, representing the rows and columns, are projected, maximizing the original variance.

Figure 14.4 shows the usual CA map of the contingency table. This two-dimensional map is not an exact representation of data because it would require four dimensions to represent this 5 × 5 table perfectly. How satisfactory is the representation? Each orthogonal axis in CA accounts for a part of variance: the first axis explains 70.9% of total inertia, the second an additional 24.7%, so the two-dimensional map in Figure 14.4 accounts for 95.6% of the total "variance" in the table. The objective of CA is to represent the maximum possible variance in a map of few, usually two, dimensions. In this case there is only a small (4.4%) proportion of variance that is not represented.

The interpretation of the map consists of inspecting how the categories of question A lie relative to one another, and how the categories of question B are spread out relative to the categories of A. The first (horizontal) dimension reflects a clear subdivision of responses between those who trust/do not trust science, with the category "disagree strongly" of A and B on the left and the categories "agree strongly" on the right, while the intermediate categories are close together in between. The second (vertical) dimension reflects the "intensity" of agreement/disagreement, with a clear subdivision toward the extreme categories (strong agreement/disagreement). The proximity between the categories of A and B reflects the concordance of responses between the two statements.

When more than two variables are considered, MCA is performed by applying the CA algorithm to either an indicator matrix or a Burt table formed from these variables. An indicator matrix, denoted by **Z**, is a table where rows represent individuals and columns are dummy variables representing categories

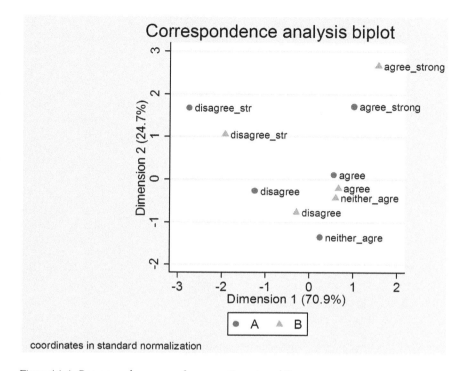

Figure 14.4 Correspondence map from questions A and B

Notes: author's elaboration using Stata. The example is described in Greenacre and Blasius (2006: 43) and in the Stata Multivariate Statistics Reference Manual (2015), command MCA (Remarks and Examples) that also gives access to the dataset.

of variables. The elements of Z are zeros apart from the ones in positions to indicate the categories of response of each respondent. Analyzing the indicator matrix makes it possible to directly represent individuals as points in a geometric space.

The Burt table is the symmetric matrix of all two-way cross-tabulations between categorical variables, and has an analogy to the covariance matrix of continuous variables. The Burt matrix is related quite simply to the indicator matrix, since $B = Z'Z$. Analyzing the Burt table is a more natural generalization of the simple correspondence analysis, and individuals or the means of groups of individuals can be added as supplementary points to the graphical display.

Figure 14.5 shows the correspondence map obtained by MCA on the Burt table for the four questions A, B, C, and D.

In this case, the first two axes account for 79% of the total inertia. We can see that the results from questions A, B, and C show the same pattern of responses, while question D follows a pattern of its own: because question D is formulated differently from A, B, and C, the plot shows its incompatibility with the others.

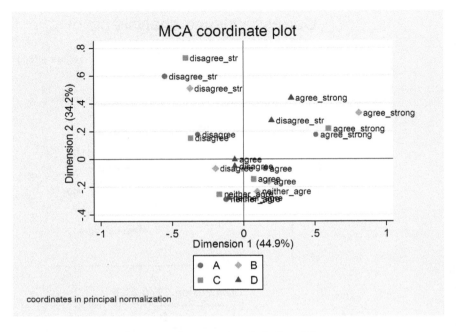

Figure 14.5 Correspondence map from questions A, B, C, and D

Notes: author's elaboration using Stata. The example is described in Greenacre and Blasius (2006: 43) and in the Stata Multivariate Statistics Reference Manual (2015), command MCA (Remarks and Examples) that gives also access to the dataset.

Latent class analysis

Latent Class Analysis (LCA) is a statistical method for finding subgroups of related cases (latent classes) from multivariate categorical data. That is, given a sample of cases (subjects, objects, respondents, etc.) measured on several variables (manifest variables), the aim is to know whether there are a small number of basic groups into which the cases fall. These subgroups form the categories of a categorical latent variable (latent because it is not directly observed). The results of an LCA can also be used to classify cases into their most likely latent class.

LCA supposes a simple probability parametric model and uses observed data to estimate parameter values for the model. The model parameters to be estimated are:

1   the prevalence of each C subpopulation or latent class;
2   the conditional response probabilities, for example the probability that a member of latent class 1 will answer "yes" to question 1.

To make things more concrete, consider the following example (taken from Vermunt and Magidson 2004) consisting of three dichotomous indicators Y_1, Y_2, and Y_3, which describe the responses to the following statements: "allow

Table 14.2 Patterns of response, frequencies, and posterior membership probabilities

Pattern of response $Y = (Y_1, Y_2, Y_3)$	Frequency	Posterior probabilities $P(X = 1 \mid Y = y)$	$P(X = 2 \mid Y = y)$
(1, 1, 1)	696	0.998	0.002
(1, 1, 2)	68	0.929	0.071
(1, 2, 1)	275	0.876	0.124
(1, 2, 2)	130	0.168	0.832
(2, 1, 1)	34	0.848	0.152
(2, 1, 2)	19	0.138	0.862
(2, 2, 1)	125	0.080	0.920
(2, 2, 2)	366	0.002	0.998

Notes: Adapted from Vermunt and Magidson (2004).

anti-religionist to speak" (1 = allowed, 2 = not allowed); "allow anti-religionist to teach" (1 = allowed, 2 = not allowed); "remove anti-religious books from library" (1= do not remove, 2 = remove). For each combination of responses (Y_1, Y_2, Y_3), the number of respondents is reported in the column labeled "Frequencies" in Table 14.2.

The goal is to identify subgroups with different degrees of tolerance toward anti-religionists.

The basic idea is that the probability $P(Y = y)$ of a response pattern $y = (y_1, y_2, y_3)$, is a weighted average of the C class specific probabilities $P(Y = y \mid X = x)$:

$$P(Y = y) = \sum_{x=1}^{C} P(X = x) P(Y = y \mid X = x) \tag{22}$$

Here, $P(X = x)$ denotes the proportion of persons belonging to the "latent class" x.

Also, the classical LC model assumes that the manifest variables (Y_1, Y_2, Y_3) are mutually independent within each latent class, so:

$$P(Y = y \mid X = x) = \prod_{l=1}^{L} P(Y_l = y_l \mid X = x) \tag{23}$$

Combining the two equations yields the following model for $P(Y = y)$:

$$P(Y = y) = \sum_{x=1}^{C} P(X = x) \prod_{l=1}^{L} P(Y_l = y_l \mid X = x) \tag{24}$$

Comparing the estimated conditional response probabilities $P(Y_l = y_l \mid X = x)$ between classes shows how they differ from one another, and this information can be used to name the classes. The result for a two-class model is shown in Table 14.3:

The two (latent) classes contain 62% and 38% of the individuals, respectively. The first class can be named "Tolerant" because people in this class have a

Table 14.3 Marginal and conditional estimated probabilities

Latent Class	Marginal probability P(X = x)	Conditional probabilities		
		$P(Y_1 = 1 \mid X = x)$	$P(Y_2 = 1 \mid X = x)$	$P(Y_3 = 1 \mid X = x)$
X = 1 – "Tolerant"	0.62	0.96	0.74	0.92
X = 2 – "Intolerant"	0.38	0.23	0.04	0.24

Notes: Adapted from Vermunt and Magidson (2004)

higher probability of selecting the "Tolerant" responses than people belonging to the second class (called "Intolerant"). In order to assign individuals to latent classes, the posterior probability of belonging to the latent class *x* can be obtained via Bayes' formula:

$$P(X = x \mid Y = y) = \frac{P(X = x) P(Y = y \mid X = x)}{P(Y = y)} \quad (25)$$

Each individual is assigned to the latent class with the highest posterior probability. The posterior probabilities reported in Table 14.2 show that people with at least two tolerant responses are classified in the "Tolerant" class.

Parameters are estimated by the maximum likelihood (ML) estimation method. ML estimates are the parameter values that most likely account for the observed responses (for the statistical properties of the model, estimation methods, and problems encountered, see Hagenaars and McCutcheon 2002).

Conclusions

The survey of the methods for the analysis of inequality presented here draws mainly from the methodological means developed for the analysis of economic inequality, which mainly focuses on income. They are typically designed for the study of the distribution of a single quantitative attribute between individuals.

They provide qualitatively different perspectives on "income" inequality. Depending on the specific application, it must be decided which analytical tool is better suited to answer each research question. The choice of one specific measure is not neutral: it implies assumptions that may affect results and the comparison between different distributions. Often a better strategy is to check the sensitivity of results and look at the varying perspectives of inequality using different measurement tools. Moreover, the quality of the inequality measurement is as good as the quality of data it relies upon. The treatment of non-response, zeros, negative values, and outliers demands particular attention, especially when using micro-data. On the other hand, if one relies on the inequality measures reported in secondary data sets,[13] it is necessary to check the correspondence and appropriateness of definitions and concepts to the intended ones.

Other methods are necessary for investigating inequalities in non-income factors, particularly from a multidimensional perspective; the focus is mainly on inequalities among groups that differentiate along many dimensions or some unobservable construct. We introduce two quantitative multivariate methods that can be applied when the observed variables are categorical, but other approaches may be applied as well.

Some issues would have deserved a more detailed discussion, for example data quality problems, inference, and general problems encountered in practical application, as well as regression-based decomposition methods, which are useful for explaining inequality and its relation to non-income factors.

Notes

1 A good discussion of these measures can be found in Sen (1973) and Cowell (2000, 2011).
2 Other simple measures include the range, defined as the ratio of the difference between the maximum and the minimum income to the mean income, and the interquantile difference, defined as the difference between the cut points of two quantiles representing the two extremes of the income distribution. The limitation of these measures is that they ignore information of the distribution other than the two points selected.
3 When household incomes are considered, a weight should be attached to each of them to account for the different household size.
4 This description of the calculation of the Gini Index follows Bellù and Liberati (2005).
5 In the continuum, the expression of the Gini index is: $G = 1-2 </EN>$.
6 A generalization of the Gini coefficient was introduced by Yitzhaki (1983). The new index accommodates differing aversions to inequality and is obtained as a derivation of a social welfare function.
7 For this reason, these indices should be cross-checked with those deriving from the use of other SWF.
8 Other properties are: the inequality index depends only on the income values used to construct it (Symmetry); and the inequality index is invariant to additions or subtractions of the same amount to original incomes (Translation invariance).
9 The stronger version of the principle of transfers also requires that the change in inequality due to an income transfer depends only on the distance between individual ranks, no matter their location in the income distribution (Bellù and Liberati, 2006b).
10 This section closely follows the discussion in Jenkins and Van Kerm (2012).
11 For different decomposition methods of the Gini index, see Aarar (2006).
12 See Everitt and Dunn (2001) for an introduction to CA and MCA, and Greenacre and Blasius (2006) for a more in-depth discussion and mathematical and geometrical insights.
13 The most-used are the WIID dataset, developed by the World Bank, and the LIS dataset (Luxemburg Income Study).

References

Aarar, Abdelkrim (2006) 'On the Decomposition of the Gini Coefficient: An Exact Approach, With an Illustration Using Cameroonian Data', CERPEE Working Paper 06–02.
Anand, Sudhir (1997) 'The Measurement of Income Inequality', in S. Subramanian (ed.) *Measurement of Inequality and Poverty*, Oxford: Oxford University Press.

Aarar, Abdelkrim and Jean-Yves Duclos (2007) 'DASP: Distributive Analysis Stata Package', PEP, World Bank, UNDP and Université Laval.

Atkinson, Anthony (1970) 'On the Measurement of Inequality', *Journal of Economic Theory*, Vol. 2: 244–63.

Atkinson, Anthony (1975) *The Economics of Inequality*, Oxford: Clarendon Press.

Bellù, Lorenzo G. and Paolo Liberati (2005) 'Inequality Analysis: The Gini Index', *Easypol*, Module 040, FAO.

Bellù, Lorenzo G. and Paolo Liberati (2006a) 'Policy Impacts on Inequality Welfare Based Measures of Inequality: The Atkinson Index', *Easypol*, Module 050, FAO.

Bellù, Lorenzo G. and Paolo Liberati (2006b) 'Policy Impacts on Inequality. Inequality and Axioms for its Measurement', *Easypol*, Module 054, FAO.

Biewen, Martin and Stephen P. Jenkins (2005) 'Accounting for Differences in Poverty Between the USA, Britain and Germany', *Empirical Economics*, Vol. 30: 331–58.

Blackorby, Charles, David Donaldson and Maria Auersperg (1981) 'A New Procedure for the Measurement of Inequality Within and Among Subgroups', *Canadian Journal of Economics*, Vol. 14: 665–85.

Blinder, Alan (1973) 'Wage Discrimination: Reduced Forms and Structural Estimation', *Journal of Human Resources*, Vol. 8: 436–55.

Bourdieu, Pierre (1984) *Distinction: A Social Critique of the Judgement of Taste*, London: Routledge & Kegan Paul.

Busetta, Annalisa and Anna Maria Milito (2010) 'Socio-Demographic Vulnerability: The Condition of Italian Young People', *Social indicators Research*, Vol. 97: 375–96, DOI:10.1007/s11205-009-9507-9

Cowell, Frank A. (2000) 'Measurement of Inequality', in A. B. Atkinson and F. Bourguignon (eds.) *Handbook of Income Distribution*, Vol. 1, London: Elsevier, 87–166.

Cowell Frank A. (2011) *Measuring Inequality*, LSE Perspective in Economic Analysis, Oxford: Oxford University Press.

Cowell, Frank A. and Kiyoshi Kuga (1981) 'Inequality Measurement: An Axiomatic Approach', *European Economic Review*, Vol. 15, No. 3: 287–305.

Cowell, Frank A. and Maria-Pia Victoria-Feser (1996) 'Robustness Properties of Inequality Measures', *Econometrica*, Vol. 64, No. 1: 77–101.

Deaton, Angus (1997) *The Analysis of Household Surveys*, Baltimore, MD and London: The Johns Hopkins University Press.

DiNardo, John, Nicole M. Fortin and Thomas Lemieux (1996) 'Labor Market Institutions and the Distribution of Wages, 1973–1992: A Semiparametric Approach', *Econometrica*, Vol. 64: 1001–44.

Everitt, Brian S. and Graham Dunn (2001) *Applied Multivariate Data Analysis*, London: Arnold.

Ferrant, Gaëlle (2014) 'The Multidimensional Gender Inequalities Index (MGII): A Descriptive Analysis of Gender Inequalities Using MCA', *Social Indicators Research*, Vol. 115: 653–90, DOI:10.1007/s11205-012-0233-3.

Gosling, Amanda, Stephen Machin and Costas Meghir (2000) 'The Changing Distribution of Male Wages in the U.K.', *Review of Economic Studies*, Vol. 67: 635–66.

Greenacre, Michael and Jörg Blasius (2006) *Multiple Correspondence Analysis and Related Methods*, London: Chapman & Hall/CRC.

Hagenaars, Jacques and Allan L. McCutcheon (2002) *Applied Latent Class Analysis*, Cambridge: Cambridge University Press.

Jenkins, Stephen P. and Philippe Van Kerm (2012) 'The Measurement of Economic Inequality', in Brian Nolan, Weimer Salverda and Timothy Smeeding (eds.) *Oxford Handbook on Economic Inequality*, Oxford: Oxford University Press, 40–67.

Lemieux, Thomas (2002) 'Decomposing Changes in Wage Distribution: A Unified Approach', *Canadian Journal of Economics*, Vol. 35: 646–88.

Machado, José A. F. and José Mata (2005) 'Counterfactual Decomposition of Changes in Wage Distributions Using Quantile Regression', *Journal of Applied Econometrics*, Vol. 20: 445–65.

Neff, Daniel F. (2007) 'Subjective Well-Being, Poverty and Ethnicity in South Africa: Insights From an Exploratory Analysis', *Social Indicators Research*, Vol. 80: 313–41.

Nolan, Brian and Christopher T. Whelan (2007) 'On the Multidimensionality of Poverty and Social Exclusion', in S. Jenkins and J. Micklewright (eds.) *Inequality and Poverty Re-Examined*, Oxford: Oxford University Press.

Oaxaca, Ronald (1973) 'Male-Female Wage Differentials in Urban Labor Markets', *International Economic Review*, Vol. 14: 693–709.

Phillips, Dianne (1995) 'Correspondence Analysis', Social Research Update, No. 7, Department of Sociology, University of Surrey.

Ping-Yin, Kuan (2006) 'Class Identification in Taiwan: A Latent Class Analysis', *Taiwanese Journal of Sociology*, Vol. 37: 169–206.

Sen, Amartya (1973) *On Economic Inequality*, Oxford: Calarendon Press.

Shorrocks, Anthony F. (1982) 'Inequality Decomposition by Factor Components', *Econometrica*, Vol. 50: 193–211.

Theil, Henri (1967) *Economics and Information Theory*, Amsterdam: North-Holland.

Van Kerm, Philippe (2007) 'Extreme Incomes and the Estimation of Poverty and Inequality Indicators From EU-SILC', CEPS/INSTEAD, Differdange, Luxembourg, IRISS Working Paper 2007–01.

Vermunt, Jeroen K. and Jay Magidson (2004) 'Latent Class Analysis', in M. S. Lewis-Beck, A. Bryman and T. F. Liao (eds.) *The Sage Encyclopedia of Social Sciences Research Methods*, Thousand Oaks, CA: Sage Publications, 549–53.

Yitzhaki, Shlomo (1983) 'On the Extension of the Gini Index', *International Economic Review*, Vol. 24: 617–28.

Yitzhaki, Shlomo (1998) 'More Than a Dozen Alternative Ways of Spelling Gini', in D. J. Slottje (ed.) *Research on Economic Inequality*, Vol. 8, Stamford, CT: JAI Press, 13–30.

15 Qualitative approaches to inequality

Christian Schneickert

Introduction

In recent years, a variety of qualitative methods has been developed and qualitative research designs are increasingly institutionalized in the social sciences (Flick 2009). Some scholars even speak of a "qualitative revolution" in the social sciences (Denzin and Lincoln 2008). Hence, qualitative research designs comprise a large number of different methods, starting with the five major analytical frameworks, narrative research, phenomenology, grounded theory, ethnography, and case study (Lichtmann 2011; Creswell 2013; Hesse-Biber 2006), ranging to critical approaches (e.g. feminist and queer studies or critical race theory, for an overview see Marshall and Rossman 2011), up to visual and media analysis, sociolinguistic and discourse analytical approaches such as Critical Discourse Analysis (Wodak and Meyer 2009; Fairclough 2013) or the Discourse Historical Approach (Wodak 2001; Forchtner 2011; Forchtner and Tominc 2012). Recent contributions established a link between inequality research inspired by Bourdieusian field theory and discourse analysis (e.g. Maesse 2015; Forchtner and Schneickert 2016). However, the relevance of qualitative methods and of the quantitative-qualitative divide differs between research traditions in different countries, disciplines, and fields of interest (e.g. cf. Angermüller 2005 on the specific role of qualitative methods in France). That is, within as well as over and above these analytic frames multiple forms of data collection and accordingly types of qualitative data and techniques of data analysis were established. This led to an extremely diversified universe of qualitative methods (for an overview cf. Seale et al. 2004).

Methods of data collection include, amongst others, interviews, oral history, biographical research, ethnographic methods, unobtrusive methods, or participant observation (Hesse-Biber 2006; Marshall and Rossman 2011), creating multiple types of qualitative data, including talk, text, sounds, images, and virtual data, ranging from official documents, to media files, journalistic articles, narrative interviews, group discussions and focus groups, biographic interviews, expert interviews, or guided interviews (Marvasti 2004; Flick 2014). Depending on the material and the interest of research, social scientists may choose from a range of elaborated techniques of data analysis, from coding, semantic analysis, discourse analysis, narrative analysis, grounded theory, or content analysis (e.g. cf. Marvasti 2004; Bernard and Ryan 2010; Denzin and Lincoln 2011). Although multimedia and visual contents are gaining in importance, the most common form of qualitative data material is still text, whether documents or transcribed interviews.

However, regarding research on socio-economic inequality, quantitative research is still prevalent. Inequality by definition is a structural or "objective" relation between individuals or groups and it seems plausible to first have a look at these structures on the large-scale macro-level. Social scientists can analyze such relations using structural data (e.g. the distribution of social, cultural, and economic resources; see the contribution of Pinuccia Calia in this volume). Moreover, these basic social structures of society may correspond with values, attitudes, and lifestyles, which can adequately be analyzed using quantitative data. However, what quantitative research misses are the subjective aspects of inequality that are equally important to the understanding of how inequality works. For people affected by inequality these subjective experiences may even be more important than any macro-indicators like the Gini coefficient – as useful as such indicators are for quantitative researchers or policymakers.

Quantitative research predominantly relies on the analysis of large-scale structural or survey data, operating on a quite decontextual level of analysis. Furthermore, only limited access to information on the process of data generation is available most of the time. On the contrary, in qualitative research reflexivity plays a fundamental role, especially regarding the various contexts in which empirical data is collected and the interactions between interviewers and interviewees (cf. e.g. Ganga and Scott 2006; Broom, Hand and Tovey 2009; Dwyer and Buckle 2009).

Qualitative research not only brings subjectivity back into the analysis as a research object, but it also puts the social position of the scientists into the spotlight. While quantitative research distances itself from the individual case, focusing on large numbers to gain the ability of long-range generalizations, qualitative research does exactly the opposite. It focuses on individual cases in a specific context and this is why reflexivity and reliability are so important here. In this sense, qualitative research focuses on subjectivity, is person-oriented, holistic, in-depth, inductive, contextual, and not neutral (Padgett 2008). Sometimes qualitative research therefore appears to have a strong normative impetus and this is especially obvious tackling politically contested issues like inequality. However, one should be aware that quantitative research is not neutral either, and it would be desirable for all research in the social sciences to be more reflexive and transparent about the researchers' social position and their political and normative claims (Denzin and Giardina 2008).

Although qualitative research often focuses on integral areas of inequality research, it is not the primary focus of qualitative approaches. Many such studies deepen their focus on very specific contexts and individual cases and it is sometimes hard to reconnect these findings with a broader framework of inequality research. However, in recent years one finds an increasing number of studies approaching inequality, e.g. as class relations, distinction, status seeking, etc. Moreover, the perception of inequality by individuals, groups, classes, or milieus deserves more attention. Perception and evaluation of inequality might be especially interesting regarding the elites (Hertz and Imber 1995). Overall, qualitative research contributes to different aspects of class analysis from the subjective experience of actors.

In the following, I briefly outline the potential of qualitative research designs for the study of inequality. Therefore, I will first focus on recent qualitative contributions to class analysis. In a second step, I discuss promising approaches to the analysis of dimensions of inequality outlined in this volume: gender, migration, race, caste, education, and poverty. I conclude with some remarks on the future of qualitative research in inequality research. Regarding the vast number of qualitative studies published in recent years it is not possible to provide an exhaustive discussion of all the noteworthy studies. Instead, I focus on the main themes related to the general analysis of inequality in the social sciences.

Capitalism and qualitative class analysis

Many studies from the last 25 years have shown the capacity of qualitative accounts to analyze the class structure of society. Class analysis beyond orthodox Marxism focused on the intersection of different dimensions of inequality, especially gender and race (e.g. Reay 1998). Yet, qualitative research contributed to themes of class and status identity, class cultures, and class consciousness in everyday life as well (e.g. Travers 1999; Payne and Grew 2005). Such studies are particularly valuable since it is a specific feature of modern, liberal democracies to disclaim their class character. Therefore, the analysis of the emotional and psychological consequences of class requires special attentiveness (Reay 2005). In this context, the main focus of qualitative research lies in the (negative) consequences of a class society for the individual. Therefore, the experiences of lower classes are heavily focused. For example Reay (2005) analyzed the "injuries of class" of school children. First, group discussions were conducted to focus on concrete interactions between children. The findings from this text analysis were later cross-validated by participant observations in the classroom.

In general, fields of interest regard the experience of the lack of resources to participate adequately in social life, the experience of poverty, material deprivation, the feeling of cultural inferiority, and lack of recognition as well as other forms of symbolic violence. Qualitative research contributes by focusing on the subjective perspective of these structures of inequality, such as coping strategies and agency to deal with the lack of economic, social, and cultural resources. Ethnographic approaches, biographic interviews, and focus groups are widespread in these areas. One of the most famous social science studies with a qualitative design is "The Weight of the World" (Bourdieu et al. 1999). The research team collected in-depth qualitative data in French banlieus over three years, using innovative interview techniques as well as recruiting interviewers right from the neighborhood. This approach was based on the insight that people from lower class neighborhoods do not recognize science and scientists as autonomous or neutral observers but as part of state authorities. Due to its cautious and respectful approach – "Do not deplore, do not laugh, do not hate – understand" (Bourdieu 1999) – it is still one of the most remarkable social sciences studies on lower classes. In the following, a similar study was conducted on the German lower classes (Schultheis and Schulz 2005) and it inspired many other qualitative studies on the lower strata of society. Another research focus was set up by the enlightening work of Newman (1999) on the working poor in Harlem, focusing on the intersection of lower and lower middle classes as well as on class and race.

In class societies, middle classes are by definition those layers of society struggling simultaneously for upward mobility and against downward mobility. This arbitrary position in the social strata leads to permanent insecurity increasing status competition. Thus, qualitative research focuses on the fear and struggle against downward mobility, including various forms of status anxiety, and it can focus on strategies of upward mobility, e.g. increased competition on education, cultural participation and lifestyles, in the job market, etc. (e.g. Lareau 2011). Another theme tackles the specific identity, values, and morality of working and middle classes in the context of globalization but also at the intersection of class and race (e.g. Lamont 2000). In the context of globalization, the transnationalization of middle classes is decisive for the inclusion of migrants (e.g. Weiß 2006).

In contrast to the analysis of lower and middle classes, qualitative investigations of the highest ranks in society are rare (Hertz and Imber 1995), mostly focusing on professional elites like the noteworthy work of Lamont (1992) drawing on interviews with US and French professional classes and their habitus for distinguishing themselves from others. Some scholars focus on the perceptions of poverty and inequality by the elites in different countries (Reis and Moore 2005). This is particularly relevant, since elites are usually considered capable of shaping the social structures of society in a significant way.

Sklair (2001) built up his path-breaking work on the "Transnational Capitalist Class" on qualitative interviews with CEOs from globalized companies, focusing on their view of capitalist globalization. Hartmann (2000) is another of the few researchers focusing on elites who conducted qualitative interviews with top CEOs, reconstructing class-specific habitus and cultural capital as main mechanisms of closure in the top ranks of society. However, there is a growing interest in the necessity of studying elites qualitatively.

Dimensions of inequality

Regarding dimensions of inequality – such as outlined in this volume: gender, migration, race, caste, education, or poverty – one finds a large number of qualitative studies, which I cannot discuss in detail here. Overall, these works often do a great job providing in-depth information from the micro-level, reconstructing subjective experiences. However, such studies are often focused on very specific aspects.

Since knowledge is one of the central features of modern society, the analysis of inequality in education is closely linked to the analysis of the class structure, as it was mentioned above. Classes may be distinguished not only by cultural capital but also according to their attitude and expectations regarding education, as an integral part of the specific class habitus (Schneickert 2013). Research on educational inequalities probably represents the most institutionalized area of qualitative research on inequality. Although a large number of qualitative studies on specialized fields of interest exist, one finds only a few systematic overviews particularly in recent years (e.g. Luttrell 2010; Lichtmann 2011). Social sciences have already analyzed some of the major mechanisms of reproducing inequalities within the education system. However, all phases of schooling include very complex and subjective decision-making processes. Parents, teachers, and students show a diverse range of strategies, expectations, and aims in education (for a seminal overview cf. Delamont 2012), that need to be analyzed qualitatively.

Gender inequalities constitute another major research focus in the social sciences conducting qualitative research (Järviluoma 2003). Two main themes seem to be most important for qualitative studies: First, the intersection between gender and class (e.g. Hebson 2009) as well as other dimensions of inequality (e.g. Bhopal 2010; cf. Olesen 2011 for an overview), including the construction and diversification of gender identities (Preves 2000). In these contexts the analysis does not usually focus primarily on the manifest content of the interviews (such as material working conditions, etc.). Rather the hermeneutic text interpretation seeks to unravel the latent constructs of how class shapes the thinking and feeling of concrete actors. Second, the sphere of work, diversity politics, gender mainstreaming, and the compatibility of family and work life. Both themes are addressed by postcolonial theory to some degree and accordingly the issue of reflexivity is central here (e.g. Thurlow, Mills and Mills 2006; Ward 2016).

Qualitative research on migration seconds this special focus on reflexivity (e.g. Ganga and Scott 2006). Transnational networks of migrants are often considered to challenge some basic assumptions of social sciences such as the relevance of the nation state (e.g. Weiß 2005). Weiß (2005) reconstructed the strategies of highly skilled transnational migrants coping with the devaluation of their capital stocks using one to four hours qualitative in-depth-interviews. Qualitative research in this area is especially useful to investigate experiences of ethnic discrimination, racism, and xenophobia – mainly but not only regarding inclusion in the labor markets – which is often hidden and not accessible for quantitative research (Iosifides 2011). Moreover, qualitative studies on migrants are particularly interesting to analyze the changes in the class structure of societies in the context of globalization (Weiß 2006).

This leads to qualitative research on class and race in particular. Many such studies focus on the agency of people of color facing racism and discrimination in various social contexts but also on identity construction, (black) counter-cultures, or conflicts about socio-cultural values (e.g. Lamont 1999). Discourse analytical approaches linking different kinds of racism, xenophobia, or anti-Semitism are rare but promising (e.g. Reisigl and Wodak 2005). Critical Race Theory has become particularly important in this area, e.g. for studies on race in the education system but also regarding the critique of the alleged universal values and neutrality of science in a predominantly white academic field (e.g. Parker and Lynn 2002; Lopez and Parker 2003).

Similar to the studies on lower classes, qualitative research on lower castes not only pursues analytic goals but rather can give a voice to those who do not usually appear in public or academic discourses, e.g. Dalit women (Rege 2006; Irudayam 2011). On the other hand, qualitative studies focusing on higher castes equally contribute to the understanding of persisting caste structures, e.g. in elite recruitment (Jodhka 2015) or the construction of caste identity in everyday life (Bairy 2010). Addressing inequality is always highly sensitive, but regarding the multiple political, religious, and cultural connotations involved, talking about caste is particularly delicate. Therefore, taping interviews is often regarded problematic. Thus, cautious ethnographic fieldwork seems to work very well (e.g. Natrajan 2011). However, qualitative in-depth studies are still needed to understand the diversity of reality shaped by caste structures, and not only in India.

A traditional field of qualitative social research linked to inequality is research on poverty. Recent studies focus on working poverty, class-specific socialization, welfare programs, family formation, or neighborhood effects (e.g. Newman and Massengill 2006). For example Newman and Massengill (2006) highlight the important contributions of qualitative research in large-scale mixed-method designs regarding the link between abuse, family formation, and poverty (see "The Three City Study": www.jhu.edu/threecitystudy) or of cultural expectations on family roles and marriage (see the "Fragile Families Project": www.fragilefamilies.princeton.edu). In the Three City Study ethnographic data was collected by researchers visiting families one or two times a month over a period of up to 18 months. Moreover, families were accompanied while visiting welfare offices, doctors, stores, workplaces, etc.

Qualitative longitudinal studies may help to understand phases of transition and individual coping strategies; e.g. regarding agency in long-term precarious situations such as unemployment or low income. This links to class-specific strategies of maintaining or aspiring to certain levels of living standard (Millar 2007).

Since poverty is often the subject of heated public debate, the decontextual perspective of large-scale quantitative studies may be as problematic as being too involved in single cases. Mixed-method designs to approach poverty seem to be the solution, but are still rare (e.g. Hargreaves et al. 2007).

Mixed-method designs: the example of habitus analysis

In this context, I would like to emphasize a mixed-method approach to habitus analysis that is not well known in international research on inequality but is promising for research on classes and inequality on an international comparative as well as global level. The so-called "habitus hermeneutics" were developed in the tradition of Bourdieusian class analysis by scholars of the German sociologist Michael Vester and his research team in Hanover (Vester et al. 2001; Lange-Vester 2012; Bremer and Teiwes-Kügler 2013; Lange-Vester and Teiwes-Kügler 2013). It was then further developed within the context of an international research project on inequality and classifications by the research team of Boike Rehbein at Humboldt-University in Berlin (Rehbein et al. 2015). Habitus hermeneutics is the initial and qualitative part of a comprehensive mixed-method-design of habitus analysis (Baumann, Kleinod and Schneickert 2015). It is possible to conduct such an analysis with different forms of qualitative data, but it usually starts with biographic interviews or group discussions. The material is then analyzed in systematic sequence analysis, extracting so-called "elementary categories of the habitus". The elementary categories – expressed by "antagonistic adjectives" (Bourdieu 1984: 468f) – are reconstructed inductively. Together, these categories build the individual "syndrome" of a person (Adorno et al. 1950). These configurations of dispositions are the basis to construct types comprising of similar habitus, ultimately leading to the construction of social milieus. In the Berlin project, departing from in-depth biographic interviews (N=61) with people from all ten SINUS-Milieus (www.sinus-institut.de) of the German population, 27 elementary categories were extracted and used as indicators in a representative population survey. Using Geometric Data Analysis (Le Roux and Rouanet 2004; Greenacre and Blasius 2006) on this data, seven major habitus types were derived for the German population in 2013. By bridging the gap between micro- and macro-analysis as well as between qualitative and quantitative methods, it is a seminal approach for future mixed-methods designs in inequality research.

Conclusion

Research on inequality is still predominantly quantitative-oriented, analyzing large-scale datasets of structural and survey data, e.g. regarding income distribution, life chances according to class, race, and gender, discrimination in the labor market, impact of state welfare regimes, etc. However, a remarkable amount of qualitative studies on various aspects of structures of inequality were published in the last 25 years, contributing invaluably to the understanding of inequality on the subjective level. Qualitative studies have focused on different aspects of class analysis in general as well as to the analysis of dimensions of inequality in particular. Moreover, it seems as if qualitative research not only contributes analytically but also serves the political function of giving people a voice who do not usually appear in public or academic discourses (Ribbens and Edwards 1997).

However, progress in methodology not only requires further specializing methods in one area, but even more importantly acknowledging the specific boundaries and limits of each approach (Onwuegbuzie and Leech 2005). This kind of reflexivity is important for methodology in the social sciences and particularly in those fields of research that are heavily contested in political debates. In these contexts, social scientists require all sources of empirical data available and qualitative as well as quantitative approaches are "equally indispensable to a science of the social world that cannot be reduced either to a social phenomenology or to a social physics" (Bourdieu 1990: 25). Therefore, while more systematic qualitative in-depth research on inequality is most necessary, particularly on the international comparative level, the future of such empirical research lies in mixed-method-designs.

References

Adorno, Theodor W., Else Frenkel-Brunswik, Daniel J. Levinson and R. Nevitt Sanford (1950) *The Authoritarian Personality*, New York: Harper & Row.

Angermüller, Johannes (2005) '"Qualitative" Methods of Social Research in France: Reconstructing the Actor, Deconstructing the Subject', *Forum Qualitative Sozialforschung/Forum: Qualitative Social Research*, Vol. 6, No. 3, Art. 19.

Bairy, T. S. Ramesh (2010) *Being Brahmin, Being Modern: Exploring the Lives of Caste Today*, New Delhi and New York: Routledge.

Baumann, Benjamin, Michael Kleinod and Christian Schneickert (2015) 'Habitustypen', in Boike Rehbein et al. (eds.) *Reproduktion sozialer Ungleichheit in Deutschland*, Konstanz and München: UVK, 81–109.

Bernard, H. Russell and Gery Wayne Ryan (2010) *Analyzing Qualitative Data: Systematic Approaches*, Los Angeles, CA: Sage.

Bhopal, Kalwant (2010) 'Gender, Identity and Experience: Researching Marginalized Groups', *Women's Studies International Forum*, Vol. 33, No. 3: 188–95.

Bourdieu, Pierre ([1980] 1990) *The Logic of Practice*, Stanford, CA and Cambridge: University Press and Polity Press.

Bourdieu, Pierre (1984) *Distinction: A Social Critique of the Judgement of Taste*, London: Routledge.

Bourdieu, Pierre et al. (eds.) (1999) *The Weight of the World: Social Suffering in Contemporary Society*, Oxford: Polity Press.

Bremer, Helmut and Christel Teiwes-Kügler (2013) 'Habitusanalyse als Habitus-Hermeneutik', *ZQF-Zeitschrift für Qualitative Forschung*, Vol. 14, No. 2: 199–219.

Broom, Alex, Kelly Hand and Philip Tovey (2009) 'The Role of Gender, Environment and Individual Biography in Shaping Qualitative Interview Data', *International Journal of Social Research Methodology*, Vol. 12, No. 1: 51–65.

Creswell, John W. (2013) *Qualitative Inquiry and Research Design: Choosing Among Five Approaches*, Los Angeles, CA: Sage.

Delamont, Sara (2012) *Handbook of Qualitative Research in Education*, Cheltenham: Edward Elgar.

Denzin, Norman K. and Michael D. Giardina (2008) *Qualitative Inquiry and the Politics of Evidence*, Walnut Creek, CA: Left Coast Press.

Denzin, Norman K. and Yvonna S. Lincoln (2008) *The Landscape of Qualitative Research*, Sage.

Denzin, Norman K. and Yvonna S. Lincoln (2011) *The SAGE Handbook of Qualitative Research: Handbook of Qualitative Research*, Thousand Oaks, CA: Sage.

Dwyer, Sonya Corbin and Jennifer L. Buckle (2009) 'The Space Between: On Being an Insider-Outsider in Qualitative Research', *International Journal of Qualitative Methods*, Vol. 8, No. 1: 54–63.

Fairclough, Norman (2013) *Critical Discourse Analysis: The Critical Study of Language*, London and New York: Routledge.

Flick, Uwe (2009) *An Introduction to Qualitative Research*, Los Angeles, CA: Sage.

Flick, Uwe (2014) *The SAGE Handbook of Qualitative Data Analysis*, Los Angeles, CA: Sage.

Forchtner, Bernhard (2011) 'Critique, the Discourse – Historical Approach, and the Frankfurt School', *Critical Discourse Studies*, Vol. 8, No. 1: 1–14.

Forchtner, Bernhard and Christian Schneickert (2016) 'Collective Learning in Social Fields: Bourdieu, Habermas and Critical Discourse Studies', *Discourse & Society*, Vol. 27, No. 3: 293–307.

Forchtner, Bernhard and Ana Tominc (2012) 'Critique and Argumentation: On the Relation Between the Discourse-Historical Approach and Pragma-Dialectics', *Journal of Language and Politics*, Vol. 11, No. 1: 31–50.

Ganga, Deianira and Sam Scott (2006) 'Cultural "Insiders" and the Issue of Positionality in Qualitative Migration Research: Moving "Across" and Moving "Along" Researcher-Participant Divides', *Forum Qualitative Sozialforschung/Forum Qualitative Social Research*, Vol. 7, Art. 7.

Greenacre, Michael and Jörg Blasius (2006) *Multiple Correspondence Analysis and Related Methods*, Boca Raton, FL: Chapman & Hall.

Hargreaves, James R., Linda A. Morison, John S. S. Gear, Mzamani B. Makhubele, John D. H. Porter, Joanna Busza, Charlotte Watts, Julia C. Kim and Paul M. Pronyk (2007) '"Hearing the Voices of the Poor": Assigning Poverty Lines on the Basis of Local Perceptions of Poverty. A Quantitative Analysis of Qualitative Data From Participatory Wealth Ranking in Rural South Africa', *World Development*, Vol. 35, No. 2: 212–29.

Hartmann, Michael (2000) 'Class-Specific Habitus and the Social Reproduction of the Business Elite in Germany and France', *The Sociological Review*, Vol. 48: 241–61.

Hebson, Gail (2009) 'Renewing Class Analysis in Studies of the Workplace: A Comparison of Working-Class and Middle-Class Women's Aspirations and Identities', *Sociology*, Vol. 43, No. 1: 27–44.

Hertz, Rosanna and Jonathan B. Imber (1995) *Studying Elites Using Qualitative Methods*, Thousand Oaks, CA: Sage.

Hesse-Biber, Sharlene Nagy (2006) *The Practice of Qualitative Research*, Thousand Oaks, CA: Sage.

Iosifides, Theodoros (2011) *Qualitative Methods in Migration Studies: A Critical Realist Perspective*, Farnham, Surrey/Burlington, VT: Ashgate.

Irudayam, Aloysius (2011) *Dalit Women Speak Out: Caste, Class and Gender Violence in India*, New Delhi: Cambridge University Press.

Järviluoma, Helmi, Pirkko Moisala and Anni Vilkko (2003) *Gender and Qualitative Methods*, Sage.

Jodhka, Surinder S. (2015) *Caste in Contemporary India*, New Delhi: Routledge.

Lamont, Michèle (1992) *Money, Morals, and Manners: The Culture of the French and American Upper middle Class*, Chicago: University of Chicago Press.

Lamont, Michèle (1999) *The Cultural Territories of Race: Black and White Boundaries*, Chicago: University of Chicago Press.

Lamont, Michèle (2000) *The Dignity of Working Men. Morality and the Boundaries of Race, Class, and Immigration*, New York and Cambridge, MA: Harvard University Press.

Lange-Vester, Andrea (2012) 'Teachers and Habitus: The Contribution of Teachers' Action to the Reproduction of Social Inequality in School Education', *Revista de la Asociación de Sociología de la Educación*, Vol. 5, No. 3: 455–76.

Lange-Vester, Andrea and Christel Teiwes-Kügler (2013) 'Das Konzept der Habitushermeneutik in der Milieuforschung', in Alexander Lenger, Christian Schneickert and Florian

Schumacher (eds.) *Pierre Bourdieus Konzeption des Habitus: Grundlagen, Zugänge, Forschungs-perspektiven.* Wiesbaden: VS Verlag für Sozialwissenschaften, 149–74.

Lareau, Annette (2011) *Unequal Childhoods: Class, Race, and Family Life: Second Edition With an Update a Decade Later,* Berkeley, Los Angeles, CA and London: University of California Press.

Le Roux, Brigitte and Henry Rouanet (2004) *Geometric Data Analysis: From Correspondence Analysis to Structured Data Analysis,* Dordrecht: Kluwer Academic Publishers.

Lichtman, Marilyn (2011) *Understanding and Evaluating Qualitative Educational Research,* Los Angeles, CA: Sage.

Lopez, Gerardo R. and Laurence Parker (2003) *Interrogating Racism in Qualitative Research Methodology,* Counterpoints, New York: P. Lang.

Luttrell, Wendy (2010) *Qualitative Educational Research: Readings in Reflexive Methodology and Transformative Practice,* New York: Routledge.

Maesse, Jens (2015) 'Economic Experts: A Discursive Political Economy of Economics', *Journal of Multicultural Discourses,* Vol. 10, No. 3: 279–305.

Marshall, Catherine and Gretchen B. Rossman (2011) *Designing Qualitative Research,* Thousand Oaks, CA, London and New Delhi: Sage.

Marvasti, Amir B. (2004) *Qualitative Research in Sociology: An Introduction,* London and Thousand Oaks, CA: Sage.

Millar, Jane (2007) 'The Dynamics of Poverty and Employment: The Contribution of Qualitative Longitudinal Research to Understanding Transitions, Adaptations and Trajectories', *Social Policy and Society,* Vol. 6, No. 4: 533–44.

Natrajan, Balmurli (2011) *The Culturalization of Caste in India. Identity and Inequality in a Multicultural Age,* London: Routledge.

Newman, Katherine S. (1999) *No Shame in My Game: The Working Poor in the Inner City,* New York: Vintage.

Newman, Katherine S. and Rebekah Peeples Massengill (2006) 'The Texture of Hardship: Qualitative Sociology of Poverty, 1995–2005', *Annual Review of Sociology,* Vol. 32: 423–46.

Olesen, Virginia (2011) 'Feminist Qualitative Research in the Millennium's First Decade', in Norman K. Denzin and Yvonna S. Lincoln (eds.) *The Sage Handbook of Qualitative Research,* Thousand Oaks, CA: Sage, 129–46.

Onwuegbuzie, Anthony J. and Nancy L. Leech (2005) 'On Becoming a Pragmatic Researcher: The Importance of Combining Quantitative and Qualitative Research Methodologies', *International Journal of Social Research Methodology,* Vol. 8, No. 5: 375–87.

Padgett, Deborah K. (2008) *Qualitative Methods in Social Work Research,* Thousand Oaks, CA, London, New Delhi and Singapore: Sage.

Parker, Laurence and Marvin Lynn (2002) 'What's Race Got to Do With It? Critical Race Theory's Conflicts With and Connections to Qualitative Research Methodology and Epistemology', *Qualitative Inquiry,* Vol. 8, No. 1: 7–22.

Payne, Geoff and Clare Grew (2005) 'Unpacking "Class Ambivalence": Some Conceptual and Methodological Issues in Accessing Class Cultures', *Sociology,* Vol. 39, No. 5: 893–910.

Preves, Sharon Elaine (2000) 'Negotiating the Constraints of Gender Binarism: Intersexuals' Challenge to Gender Categorization', *Current Sociology,* Vol. 48, No. 3: 27–50.

Reay, Diane (1998) 'Rethinking Social Class: Qualitative Perspectives on Class and Gender', *Sociology,* Vol. 32, No. 2: 259–75.

Reay, Diane (2005) 'Beyond Consciousness? The Psychic Landscape of Social Class', *Sociology,* Vol. 39, No. 5: 911–28.

Rege, Sharmila (2006) *Writing Caste, Writing Gender: Reading Dalit Women's Testimonies,* New Delhi: Zubaan.

Rehbein, Boike et al. (eds.) (2015) *Reproduktion sozialer Ungleichheit in Deutschland,* Konstanz/München: UVK.

Reis, Elisa P. and Mick Moore (2005) *Elite Perceptions of Poverty and Inequality*, Chicago: Zed Books.

Reisigl, Martin and Ruth Wodak (2005) *Discourse and Discrimination: Rhetorics of Racism and Antisemitism*, London and New York: Routledge.

Ribbens, Jan and Rosalind Edwards (1997) *Feminist Dilemmas in Qualitative Research: Public Knowledge and Private Lives*, London: Sage.

Schneickert, Christian (2013) *Studentische Hilfskräfte und MitarbeiterInnen: Soziale Herkunft, Geschlecht und Strategien auf dem wissenschaftlichen Feld*, Konstanz: UVK.

Schultheis, Franz und Kristina Schulz (2005) *Gesellschaft mit begrenzter Haftung: Zumutungen und Leiden im deutschen Alltag*, Konstanz: UVK.

Seale, Clive, Giampietro Gobo, Jaber F. Gubrium and David Silverman (2004) *Qualitative Research Practice*, London: Sage.

Sklair, Leslie (2001) *The Transnational Capitalist Class*, Oxford: Blackwell.

Thurlow, Amy, Albert J. Mills and Jean Helms Mills (2006) 'Feminist Qualitative Research and Workplace Diversity', in A Konrad, P Pushkala and J Pringle (eds.) *Handbook of Workplace Diversity*, London: Sage: 217–36.

Travers, Max (1999) 'Qualitative Sociology and Social Class', *Sociological Research Online*, Vol. 4, No. 1.

Vester, Michael, Peter von Oertzen, Heiko Geiling, Thomas Hermann and Dagmar Müller (2001) *Soziale Milieus im gesellschaftlichen Strukturwandel: Zwischen Integration und Ausgrenzung*, Frankfurt am Main: Suhrkamp.

Ward, Michael R. M. (2016) *Gender Identity and Research Relationships*, Emerald Group Publishing.

Weiß, Anja (2005) 'The Transnationalization of Social Inequality: Conceptualising Social Positions on a World Scale', in Ulrike Schuerckens (ed.) *Current Sociology: Thematic Issue "Transnational Migrations and Social Transformations"*, Vol. 53, 707–28.

Weiß, Anja (2006) 'Comparative Research on Highly Skilled Migrants. Can Qualitative Interviews Be Used in Order to Reconstruct a Class Position?', *Forum Qualitative Social Research*, Vol. 7, No. 3, Art. 2.

Wodak, Ruth (2001) 'The Discourse-Historical Approach', in Ruth Wodak and Michael Meyer (eds.) *Methods of Critical Discourse Analysis*, London: Sage, 63–94.

Wodak, Ruth and Michael Meyer (2009) *Methods for Critical Discourse Analysis*, London: Sage.

Index